STUDIES IN ISLAMIC MYSTICISM

R

STUDIES IN ISLAMIC MYSTICISM

REYNOLD ALLEYNE
NICHOLSON

CURZON
PRESS

4 by
td.
os
Church Road
Richmond
Surrey TW9 2QA

ISBN 0 7007 0278 4

First published in 1921
by Cambridge University Press

British Library Cataloguing-in-Publication Data
A CIP record for this title is available
from the British Library

Printed in England by
BPC Ltd.

PREFACE

As was explained in the preface to my *Studies in Islamic Poetry*, the following essays conclude a series of five, which fall into two groups and are therefore published in separate volumes. While mysticism, save for a few casual references, found no place in the studies on the *Lubábu 'l-Albáb* of 'Awfí and the *Luzúmiyyát* of Abu 'l-'Alá al-Ma'arrí, in these now brought together it has taken entire possession of the field. Ibnu 'l-Fáriḍ, indeed, is an exquisite poet; and the picture of Abú Sa'íd ibn Abi 'l-Khayr, drawn by pious faith and coloured with legendary romance, may be looked upon as a work of art in its way. But on the whole the literary interest of the present volume is subordinate to the religious and philosophical. I have tried to make the reader acquainted with three Ṣúfís famous in the East and worthy of being known in Europe. Most of what has hitherto been written concerning Abú Sa'íd begins and ends with the quatrains passing as his, though (for the chief part, at any rate) they were neither composed nor recited by him. As to Jílí, the masterly sketch in Dr Muḥammad Iqbál's *Development of Metaphysics in Persia* stands almost alone. Ibnu 'l-Fáriḍ had the misfortune to be translated by Von Hammer, and the first intelligent or intelligible version of his great *Tá'iyya* appeared in Italy four years ago. It will be seen that the subjects chosen illustrate different aspects of Ṣúfism and exhibit racial contrasts, of which perhaps the importance has not yet been sufficiently recognised. Abú Sa'íd, the free-thinking free-living dervish, is a Persian through and through, while Ibnu 'l-Fáriḍ in the form of his poetry as well as in the individuality of his spiritual enthusiasm displays the narrower and tenser genius of the Semite. Nearly a third of this volume is concerned with a type of Ṣúfism, which—

as represented by Ibnu 'l-'Arabí and Jílí—possesses great interest for students of medieval thought and may even claim a certain significance in relation to modern philosophical and theological problems. Mysticism is such a vital element in Islam that without some understanding of its ideas and of the forms which they assume we should seek in vain to penetrate below the surface of Mohammedan religious life. The forms may be fantastic and the ideas difficult to grasp; nevertheless we shall do well to follow them, for in their company East and West often meet and feel themselves akin.

I regret that I have not been able to make full use of several books and articles published during the final stages of the war or soon afterwards, which only came into my hands when these studies were already in the press. Tor Andrae's *Die person Muhammeds in lehre und glauben seiner gemeinde* (Upsala, 1917) contains by far the best survey that has yet appeared of the sources, historical evolution and general characteristics of the Mohammedan Logos doctrine. This, as I have said, is the real subject of the *Insánu 'l-Kámil*. Its roots lie, of course, in Hellenism. Andrae shows how the notion of the *θεῖος ἄνθρωπος* passed over into Islam through the Shí'ites and became embodied in the Imám, regarded as the living representative of God and as a semi-divine personality on whom the world depends for its existence. Many Shí'ites were in close touch with Ṣúfism, and there can be no doubt that, as Ibn Khaldún observed, the Shí'ite Imám is the prototype of the Ṣúfistic Quṭb. It was inevitable that the attributes of the Imám and Quṭb should be transferred to the Prophet, so that even amongst orthodox Moslems the belief in his pre-existence rapidly gained ground. Particularly instructive to students of the *Insánu 'l-Kámil* is Andrae's account of the Logos doctrine of Ibnu 'l-'Arabí, whose influence is manifest in every page that Jílí wrote. In this connexion another book by another Swedish scholar—H. S. Nyberg's *Kleinere Schriften des Ibn al-'Arabī* (Leiden, 1919)—provides new and valuable material. The introduction, to which I have now and then referred in the footnotes, not only elucidates the mystical philosophy of the *Insánu 'l-Kámil* but enables us to trace in detail the indebtedness of Jílí to his great predecessor. In the 16th and 17th centuries the *Insánu 'l-Kámil* exerted a powerful influence upon Indonesian Ṣúfism, which has been studied by the Dutch Orientalists D. A. Rinkes, B. J. O. Schrieke, and H. Kraemer. I should like to call attention to the account given by the last-named scholar in *Een Javaansche primbon uit de zestiende eeuw* (Leiden, 1921), p. 40 foll. and p. 83 foll.

Some months after my work had gone to the press, I received from Prof. C. A. Nallino an off-print of his article *Il poema mistico arabo d'Ibn al-Fāriḍ in una recente traduzione italiana*[1], from which I learned that a prose translation by Sac. Ignazio Di Matteo of Ibnu 'l-Fáriḍ's most celebrated ode, the *Tá'iyyatu 'l-Kubrá*, had been published in 1917 at Rome. As this book was reproduced in autograph for private circulation, it would have been inaccessible to me, if the author had not kindly presented me with a copy. He replied to Nallino in a paper entitled *Sulla mia interpretazione del poema mistico d'Ibn al-Fāriḍ* (*RDSO.*, 1920, vol. VIII. 479–500), which was immediately followed by a second article from Nallino, *Ancora su Ibn al-Fāriḍ e sulla mistica musulmana* (*ibid.* vol. VIII. 501–562). Having myself attempted to translate the *Tá'iyya*, I am impressed with the merit of Di Matteo's version rather than inclined to dwell on its faults. He has given us, for the first time, a careful and tolerably correct rendering of the original; and that is no slight achievement. The articles by Nallino, which include a critical examination of numerous passages in the poem, are the most important contribution that any European Orientalist has so far made to the study of Ibnu 'l-Fáriḍ. In an essay consisting largely of translations, I could but indicate (pp. 193–5 *infra*) my views on the main question which he has discussed in his friendly controversy with Di Matteo. To him, as to me, it seems clear that the view put forward by Di Matteo is erroneous. Neither the form nor the substance of the *Tá'iyya* suggests that it was inspired by Ibnu 'l-'Arabí, though some traces of his influence may perhaps be found in

[1] Published in *Rivista degli studi orientali* (1919), vol. VIII. 1–106.

it[1]. It differs in kind from poems indubitably so inspired, such as the *'Ayniyya* of Jílí. Above all, it is a mystic's autobiography, a poet's description of his inner life, and the terms which it employs belong to the psychological vocabulary of Ṣúfism, with few exceptions. I have no quarrel with those who call Ibnu 'l-Fáriḍ a pantheist; but his pantheism (unlike that of his commentators) is essentially a state of feeling, not a system of thought. The poem, however, requires explanation, and I do not think it can be interpreted without reference to the corresponding philosophical doctrine. In other words, if we are to elicit any definite meaning from the symbols which shadow forth a consciousness of mystical union, we must somehow connect them with metaphysical propositions. But although mysticism is not an allegory, still less is it a theology or philosophy. Hence the sayings of "God-intoxicated" men will not serve as a sure criterion of their attitude towards religion. Moslems themselves, as a rule, want better evidence of heresy than this.

I desire to express my gratitude to Prof. C. A. Nallino and Sac. Ignazio Di Matteo for their gifts of books and for the courtesy which accompanied them; to Mr A. G. Ellis for the loan of his copy of the *Insánu 'l-Kámil*; and to the authorities of the India Office Library for placing at my disposal the manuscripts mentioned on p. 77 *infra*. Especial thanks are due to Mr Rhuvon Guest, who most generously sent me his unpublished translation of the *Tá'iyya* of Ibnu 'l-Fáriḍ and allowed me to use it for the purpose of correcting and improving my own, before the latter was in print. Mr Guest's version, while keeping very close to the original, is thoughtful and judicious, and I found it of great service in dealing with passages which to me seemed obscure. If I have sometimes preferred my interpretation to his, he has at least as often

[1] There is no trustworthy basis (cf. p. 164 *infra*) for the statement that Ibnu 'l-Fáriḍ was acquainted with Ibnu 'l-'Arabí. The latter is said to have asked the poet's permission to write a commentary on his *Tá'iyya*, and to have received the reply that the *Futúḥátu 'l-Makkiyya* was a commentary on it (Maqqarí, Leiden ed., I. 570, 16–18); this, however, is the kind of story that could scarcely fail to be invented. The *Futúḥát* was completed in A.H. 629, only three years before the death of Ibnu 'l-Fáriḍ.

convinced me that his was more likely to be the right one. Besides thanking the scholars who have helped me in the second part of these studies, I wish to acknowledge the appreciative criticism which the first volume has received. Both Nöldeke and Goldziher have declared their agreement with the view there taken of the character of Ma'arrí. The remarks of my old teacher, Prof. Nöldeke, are so interesting that I cannot refrain from quoting them:

In der Gesammtauffassung des Dichters und Denkers muss ich Ihnen durchweg beistimmen. Zunächst darin, dass M. kein Muslim mehr war, sondern als einzigen, allerdings festen Punct aus der religiösen Ueberlieferung das Vorhandensein eines allmächtigen Gottes behielt, der in seiner Willkür so ziemlich dem koranischen glich. Dabei halte ich es immerhin für möglich, dass M. hie und da auch sonst an Einzelheiten der Lehre Muhammeds festhielt, je nach verschiedenen Zeiten und Stimmungen. Dass die Widersprüche innerhalb der Sammlung nicht alle auf absichtliche Täuschung herauskommen, möchte ich damit betonen. Welche Weltanschauung und welche Dogmatik ist ohne innere Widersprüche? Das christliche Dogma habe ich hier vor Allem im Auge; ich meine die Dogmatik aller christlichen Confessionen. ...Was man auch an M. aussetzen mag, man muss vor seiner Selbständigkeit doch die grösste Achtung haben. Wie eigen berühren uns nr. 117–119, worin die Fürsten als Diener und Besoldete des Volkes erscheinen, bei einem Orientalen! (Friedrich der Grosse dachte wenigstens *theoretisch* auch so.) So fern uns oder mir (da ich mich doch als strenger Rationalist ihm verwandt fühle) seine übertriebene Askese liegt, die z. B. nicht berücksichtigt, dass "Die grossen Fische fressen stets die kleinen," dass die Singvögel grösstenteils von Insecten leben und dazu, dass wir Menschen von den Tieren direct oder indirect aufgefressen würden, wenn wir sie nicht vielfach töteten, so muss man doch auch in der Hinsicht vor ihm Achtung haben. Wenn er den Wein verabscheut, so muss man bedenken, dass dieser damals wie jetzt (namentlich bei den Persern) ganz besonders dazu diente, rasch sinnlos betrunken zu werden (cfr. Gen. xliii. 34, וישכרו). Der Standpunct war also vernünftiger als der der americanischen Gesetzgebung, die das Kind mit dem Bade ausschüttet. Wie verständig ist M. auch darin, das er nicht an dem fast zum Dogma der islamischen Ueberlieferung gewordenen Satze festhielt, dass die Menschen in früheren Zeiten besser gewesen wären als die Zeitgenossen (nr. 162, 4 als zweifelhaft, 146, 3 bestimmt ausgesprochen)! Vermutlich wollte er damit besonders den Vorzug der "Genossen des Propheten" treffen.

Prof. Nöldeke laid me under a further obligation by reading the text of the pieces selected from the *Luzúmiyyát* and proposing a number of emendations. These are given below, together with some which I owe to the kindness of Prof. Bevan. Misprints are included, and the English version has been corrected in a few places where, as Prof. Bevan pointed out, the original was mistranslated or not fully understood.

P. 66, No. 20, first line. *Read*

"Ah, let us go, whom nature joined of old in friendship fast."

P. 79, No. 52, eighth line. *Read*

"With blackness of stony wastes, parched desolate highlands."

P. 101, note 4. "The dark raiment" (شية العظلم) refers to Death. "Er (Abú Muslim) hatte der Dynastie treu gedient: darauf bekleidete die ihn mit der Farbe der Finsterniss" (N.).

P. 109, No. 124. Although I have deliberately rendered الكلامُ كُلومٌ by "words are wounds," that rendering gives too wide an application to the Arabic phrase. As the context shows, الكلام has here its technical meaning and refers to the dialectic of the *mutakallimún* (scholastic theologians).

P. 116, No. 144, lines 5–6. *Read*

"Be just and live on earth what can?
And none is more unjust than Man."

In the original, فوقها stands for فوق الارض (B.).

P. 121, No. 163, third line. *Read*

"Thou deem'st thy being here calamity."

P. 123, No. 171, third line. *Read*

"If nonsense be all the coin we exchange, then better."

P. 132, No. 192, last line. *Read*

"To succour, and shall surpass in excellence Ḥájib's bow."

Note 2 should be deleted. For "Ḥájib's bow" see *Naqá'iḍ*, 462 (B.).

P. 141, seventh line from foot. By an oversight, "Jáḥiẓ" has been written instead of "Abú ʿAbdallah al-Khwárizmí."

P. 145, note 1. The animal called by the Arabs الفهد and by the Persians يوز is not the lynx but, as Prof. Nöldeke reminds me, the hunting-leopard (*cynaelurus*), commonly known in Europe as the cheetah.

P. 157, note 2, last line. *Read* قَبْلَهُ *for* فَبْلَهُ.

P. 165, note 2, first line. *Read* قبيحَ *for* فبيحَ.

P. 167, No. 240, first verse. *Read*

"Say to wine, which is a foe to (men's) understandings, ever drawing against them the swords of a warrior."

Nöldeke writes: "240, 1 ist سيوفَ doch wohl richtig, da نضا schwerlich als Intransitiv gebraucht werden kann. نُهًى wird als Fem. gebraucht, Ibn Qotaiba, '*Uyūn*, 277, 2, wie es ja regelrechter Plural von نُهْيَةٌ ist (Baiḍāwī zu Sūra xx, 56, 128); und so passt das لها gut."

P. 178, No. 264, first verse. *For* "my nose" *read* "noses."

P. 191, No. 301, second verse. *Read* "howbeit akin to them are stones that were kicked."

P. 192, No. 303, second verse. *Read*

"But pardon me, O my God! At Mecca shall I throw off
Amongst pilgrims newly come the weeds of a widowed frame."

Prof. Bevan justly observes that سَليب in conjunction with ثياب can scarcely have any other meaning than "a woman who is wearing the black garments of mourning." Moreover, although طَرَحَ, when followed by على, can be used of "throwing on (a garment)," it properly means "to throw off." I suggest that سليب denotes here the poet's body, which—as bereaved of sight, strength, and all its pleasures—he compares to a woman clad in mourning, while ثياب refers to the garments which would be laid aside on assuming the *iḥrám*.

P. 204, No. 326, lines 3–4. The general sense is given correctly, but I should have noticed that the words بالحمد والاخلاص allude to two short *Súras* of the Koran, *viz.* *Súra* I (cf. the Commentary of Bayḍáwí, ed. Fleischer, p. 3, l. 6) and *Súra* CXII. These are contrasted with the two long *Súras* mentioned in note 1.

P. 216, No. 30, *v.* 8. *For* للخلقُ *read* الخلقُ.

P. 220, No. 40, *v.* 16. *For* يُعرِّى *read* يُعدِّى (B.).

P. 228, No. 69, *v.* 3. *For* خليلَها *read* حليلَها (B.).

P. 229, No. 72, *v.* 8. خاملٌ (B.) is better than خامدٌ.

P. 237, No. 107, *v.* 5. *Read* على غَضَبٍ, "im Zorne" (N.).

P. 240, No. 115, *v.* 3. *For* فَبْلُ *read* قَبْلُ.

P. 246, No. 143, *v.* 2. *For* أَقْبَحُ *read* لَأَقْبَحُ (N.).

P. 248, No. 149, *v.* 4. *For* الفَتْحُ *read* الفَتْخُ.

Ibid. *For* والمُرعُ *read* والمُرَعُ. Cf. Wellhausen, *Scholien zum Diwan Hudail*, 277, 5 (*ZDMG.*, XXXIX, 479) and *Lisán*, X, 211, 4 fr. foot and foll. "Die Bedeutung scheint 'Wachtel' zu sein" (N.).

P. 251, No. 163, *v.* 2. *For* ويَعُدُّ *read* وتَعُدُّ (B.).

P. 251, No. 167, *v.* 1. *For* بخلاض *read* بخلاص.

P. 253, No. 174, *v.* 6. *For* سفيًّا *read* سقيًّا.

P. 255, No. 181, *v.* 3. *For* حلّى *read* جلّى, "ihre Geheimnisse mit Wissen aufdeckt = klar erkennt. جلى und سرّ bilden ja natürliche Gegensätze" (N.).

P. 262, No. 210, *v.* 4. *For* مَنْصَبُ *read* مَنْصِبُ (B.).

P. 265, No. 225, *v.* 2. *For* باذْن *read* بإذْن.

P. 266, No. 229, *v.* 6. *For* متواقفين *read* متوافقين.

P. 268, No. 238, *v.* 1. *For* كُتُبُ *read* كُتْبُ.

P. 269, No. 240, *v.* 1. *For* سُيوفُ *read* سُيوفَ (N.).

P. 274, No. 262, *v.* 2. *For* الخَذَمُ *read* الخِذَمُ.

P. 274, No. 264, *v.* 1. *For* الأُنْفَ *read* الآنُفَ (N.).

P. 277, No. 274, *v.* 7. There is, of course, a word-play here, as ظليم can also mean "the male ostrich" and نعامة "the female ostrich." Nöldeke suggests that the sense may be, "Fear the prayer of an oppressed man on behalf of his wife."

P. 279, No. 284, *v.* 1. *Read* تُقِلُّ *for* تَقِلُّ.

P. 282, No. 302, *v.* 4. *Read* قِراها *for* قَراها (the rhyme-word).

P. 286, No. 318, *v.* 1. If يَجْزِيَ be retained, its subject is the individual implied by the preceding words. The reading تَجْزِيَ gives an easier and more natural sense.

Even the minutiae in this list will be carefully noted, I hope, by students of the *Luzúmiyyát*. Success in mastering the difficulties of Arabic poetry depends on the conviction that no detail is small enough to be neglected.

REYNOLD A. NICHOLSON.

March, 1921.

CONTENTS

CHAPTER I

ABÚ SA'ÍD IBN ABI 'L-KHAYR

ABÚ SA'ÍD and Omar Khayyam are associated in the history of Persian literature by the circumstance that each of them is the reputed author of a famous collection of *rubá'iyyát* in which his individuality has almost disappeared. That these collections are wholly, or even mainly, the work of Abú Sa'íd and Omar no one who examines the evidence is likely to assert: they should rather be regarded as anthologies—of which the nucleus, perhaps, was formed by the two authors in question—containing poems of a particular type composed at various periods by many different hands. It is possible, no doubt, that Omar's view of life and his general cast of thought are more or less reflected in the quatrains attributed to him, but we can learn from them nothing definite and distinctive. The same considerations apply with equal force to the mystical *rubá'ís* passing under the name of Abú Sa'íd. In his case, however, we possess excellent and copious biographical materials which make us intimately acquainted with him and throw a welcome light on many aspects of contemporary Persian mysticism.

The oldest of these documents is a short treatise on his life and sayings, which is preserved in a manuscript of the British Museum (Or. 249). It bears neither title nor indication of authorship, but Zhukovski in his edition of the text (Petrograd, 1899) identifies it with the *Ḥálát ú Sukhunán-i Shaykh Abú Sa'íd ibn Abi 'l-Khayr*, a work composed about a century after Abú Sa'íd's death by one of his descendants whose name is unknown. He was a cousin of Muḥammad ibnu 'l-Munawwar, the great-great-grandson of Abú Sa'íd.

Using the *Ḥálát ú Sukhunán* as a foundation, Muḥammad ibnu 'l-Munawwar compiled a much larger biography of his ancestor which he entitled *Asráru 'l-tawḥíd fí maqámáti 'l-Shaykh Abí Sa'íd* (ed. by Zhukovski, Petrograd, 1899) and dedicated to the Ghúrid prince, Ghiyáthu'ddín Muḥammad ibn Sám (*ob.* A.D. 1203). The author, like Abú Sa'íd himself, was a native of Mayhana or Mihna in Khurásán. From his earliest youth it had been a labour of love for him to gather the sayings of the Saint and to verify the records and traditions which were handed down in his family and were still fresh in the minds of his fellow-townsmen. The task was undertaken not a moment too soon. In A.D. 1154 the Turcoman tribe of the Ghuzz swept over the borders of Khurásán and carried fire and sword through that flourishing province. Everywhere the population was massacred; the author tells us that 115 descendants of Abú Sa'íd, young and old, were tortured to death in Mayhana alone, and that no memorial of him was left except his tomb. Religion, he says, fell into utter ruin; the search after Truth ceased, unbelief became rampant; of Islam only the name, and of Ṣúfism only the form survived. Impelled by divine grace, he complied with the request of some novices that he should write an account of the spiritual experiences and memorable sayings of Shaykh Abú Sa'íd, for the encouragement of those who desired to enter upon the Path (*ṭaríqa*) and for the guidance of those who were travelling on the road of the Truth (*ḥaqíqa*)[1]. Abú Sa'íd died in A.D. 1049, and the *Asráru 'l-tawḥíd* was probably completed not less than 120 or more than 150 years later. As Zhukovski points out, it is almost the first example in Persian of a separate work having for its subject the life of an individual mystic. The portrait of Abú Sa'íd amidst the circle of Ṣúfís and dervishes in which he lived is drawn with extraordinary richness of detail, and gains in vividness as well as in value from the fact that a great part of the story is told by himself. Although the Mohammedan system of oral tradition by which these autobiographical passages have been preserved forbids us to suppose that we have before us an exact transcript of Abú Sa'íd's words as they were spoken to the original reporter, there is no reason to doubt that in most cases the substance of them is given correctly. His own veracity is not incontestable, but this question, which leads at once into the darkest abysses of psychology, I must leave in suspense.

[1] *Asrár*, 4, 16—6, 5.

The *Ḥálát ú Sukhunán* and the *Asráru 'l-tawḥíd* render the more recent biographies of Abú Sa'íd all but superfluous[1]. A certain amount of new material is found in the Supplement to Farídu'ddín 'Aṭṭár's *Tadhkiratu 'l-Awliyá* (vol. II of my edition, pp. 322–337) and Jámí's *Nafaḥátu 'l-Uns* (ed. by Nassau Lees, No. 366)[2].

For the sake of clearness, I have divided the following study into three sections, of which the first deals with the life of Abú Sa'íd, the second with his mystical sayings and doctrines, and the third with miracles and other matter belonging to his legend.

I.

Abú Sa'íd Faḍlu'llah was born at Mayhana, the chief town of the Kháwarán district of Khurásán, on the 1st of Muḥarram, A.H. 357 (December 7th, A.D. 967). His father Abu 'l-Khayr, known in Mayhana as Bábú Bu 'l-Khayr, was a druggist, "a pious and religious man, well acquainted with the sacred law of Islam (*sharí'a*) and with the Path of Ṣúfism (*ṭaríqa*)[3]." He and other Ṣúfís were in the habit of meeting every night in the house of one of their number. Whenever a strange Ṣúfí arrived in the town, they would invite him to join them, and after partaking of food and finishing their prayers and devotions they used to listen to music and singing (*samá'*). One night, when Bábú Bu 'l-Khayr was going to meet his friends, his wife begged him to take Abú Sa'íd with him in order that the dervishes might look on him with favour; so Bu 'l-Khayr let the lad accompany him. As soon as it was time for the music to begin, the singer (*qawwál*) chanted this quatrain:

God gives the dervish love—and love is woe;
By dying near and dear to Him they grow.
The generous youth will freely yield his life,
The man of God cares naught for worldly show.

[1] In referring to these two works I shall use the abbreviations H = *Ḥálát* and A = *Asrár*. Since A includes almost the whole of H, I have usually given references to the former only.

[2] The oldest notice of Abú Sa'íd occurs in the *Kashf al-Maḥjúb* of his contemporary, Hujwírí, who mentions him frequently in the course of that work. See especially pp. 164–6 of the translation.

[3] A 13, 4.

On hearing this song the dervishes fell into ecstasy and kept up the dance till daybreak. The *qawwál* sang the quatrain so often that Abú Sa'íd got it by heart. When he returned home, he asked his father the meaning of the verses that had thrown the dervishes into such transports of joy. "Hush!" said his father, "you cannot understand what they mean: what does it matter to you?" Afterwards, when Abú Sa'íd had attained to a high spiritual degree, he used sometimes to say of his father, who was then dead, "I want Bábú Bu 'l-Khayr to-day, to tell him that he himself did not know the meaning of what he heard on that night[1]."

Abú Sa'íd was taught the first rudiments of Moslem education—to read the Koran—by Abú Muḥammad 'Ayyárí, an eminent divine, who is buried at Nasá[2]. He learned grammar from Abú Sa'íd 'Ayyárí and the principles of Islam from Abu 'l-Qásim Bishr-i Yásín, both of Mayhana. The latter seems to have been a remarkable man.

I have already referred to the mystical quatrains which Abú Sa'íd was fond of quoting in his discourses and which are commonly thought to be his own. Against this hypothesis we have his definite statement that these quatrains were composed by other Ṣúfís and that Bishr-i Yásín was the author of most of them[3]. From Bishr, too, Abú Sa'íd learned the doctrine of disinterested love, which is the basis of Ṣúfism.

[1] A 13, 9.

[2] H 8, 10. A 14, 16.

[3] H 54, 3. The following is a translation of the text as it stands in Zhukovski's edition: "Whenever I have addressed poetry to any one, that which falls from my lips is the composition of venerable Ṣúfís (*'azízán*), and most of it is by Shaykh Abu 'l-Qásim Bishr." I am not sure that instead of the first clause (ما هر كرا شعر بگفته ايم) we ought not to read ما هرگز شعر نگفته ايم. The statement will then run: "I have never composed poetry. That which falls from my lips, etc." In another passage (A 263, 10) it is stated on the authority of the writer's grandfather (Abú Sa'íd's grandson) that of all the poetry attributed to Abú Sa'íd only one verse and one *rubá'í*, which are cited, were his own composition, the remainder being quoted from his spiritual directors. The credibility of this is not affected by the explanation that he was too absorbed in ecstasy to think about versifying. In addition to the single *rubá'í*, of which Abú Sa'íd is expressly named as the author, H and A contain twenty-six which he is said to have quoted on different occasions. Of the latter, two occur in Ethé's collection (Nos. 35 and 68).

One day Abu 'l-Qásim Bishr-i Yásín (may God sanctify his honoured spirit!) said to me: "O Abú Sa'íd, endeavour to remove self-interest (*ṭama'*) from thy dealings with God. So long as that exists, sincerity (*ikhláṣ*) cannot be attained. Devotions inspired by self-interest are work done for wages, but devotions inspired by sincerity are work done to serve God. Learn by heart the Tradition of the Prophet—*God said to me on the night of my Ascension, O Mohammed! as for those who would draw nigh to Me, their best means of drawing nigh is by performance of the obligations which I have laid upon them. My servant continually seeks to win My favour by works of supererogation until I love him; and when I love him, I am to him an ear and an eye and a hand and a helper: through Me he hears, and through Me he sees, and through Me he takes.*" Bishr explained that to perform obligations means "to serve God," while to do works of supererogation means "to love God"; then he recited these lines:

Perfect love proceeds from the lover who hopes naught for himself;
What is there to desire in that which has a price?
Certainly the Giver is better for you than the gift:
How should you want the gift, when you possess the very Philosopher's Stone[1]?

On another occasion Bishr taught his young pupil how to practise "recollection" (*dhikr*). "Do you wish," he asked him, "to talk with God?" "Yes, of course I do," said Abú Sa'íd. Bishr told him that whenever he was alone he must recite the following quatrain, no more and no less:

Without Thee, O Beloved, I cannot rest;
Thy goodness towards me I cannot reckon.
Tho' every hair on my body becomes a tongue,
A thousandth part of the thanks due to Thee I cannot tell.

Abú Sa'íd was constantly repeating these words. "By the blessing which they brought," he says, "the Way to God was opened to me in my childhood." Bishr died in A.H. 380 (A.D. 990). Whenever Abú Sa'íd went to the graveyard of Mayhana his first visit was always paid to the tomb of the venerated teacher who had given him his first lesson in Ṣúfism[2].

[1] A 16, 9. [2] A 16, 20.

If we can believe Abú Sa'íd when he declares that in his youth he knew by heart 30,000 verses of pre-Islamic poetry, his knowledge of profane literature must have been extensive[1]. After completing this branch of education, he set out for Merv with the purpose of studying theology under Abú 'Abdallah al-Ḥuṣrí, a pupil of the famous Sháfi'ite doctor, Ibn Surayj. He read with al-Ḥuṣrí for five years, and with Abú Bakr al-Qaffál for five more[2]. From Merv he moved to Sarakhs, where he attended the lectures of Abú 'Alí Záhir[3] on Koranic exegesis (in the morning), on systematic theology (at noon), and on the Traditions of the Prophet (in the afternoon)[4].

Abú Sa'íd's birth and death are the only events of his life to which a precise date is attached. We know that he studied at Merv for ten years, and if we assume that his *Wanderjahre* began at the usual time, he was probably between 25 and 28 when he first came to Sarakhs. Here his conversion to Ṣúfism took place. He has described it himself in the following narrative, which I will now translate without abridgement. I have relegated to the foot of the page, and distinguished by means of square brackets, certain passages that interrupt the narrative and did not form part of it originally.

Abú Sa'íd said as follows[5]:

'At the time when I was a student, I lived at Sarakhs and read with Abú 'Alí, the doctor of divinity. One day, as I was going into the city, I saw Luqmán of Sarakhs seated on an ash-heap near the gate, sewing a patch on his gaberdine[a]. I went up to him and

[a] [This Luqmán was one of the "intelligent madmen" (*'uqalá'u 'l-majánín*)[6]. At first he practised many austerities and was scrupulous in his devotions. Then of a sudden he experienced a revelation (*kashf*) that deprived him of his reason. Abú Sa'íd said: "In the beginning Luqmán was a man learned

---

[1] H 8, 20. A 17, 16. [2] H 9, 1. A 17, 18; 22, 6.

[3] Died A.H. 389 (A.D. 999). See Subkí, *Ṭabaqátu 'l-Sháfi'iyya al-Kubrá*, Cairo, A.H. 1324, II. 223. Yáqút, *Mu'jamu 'l-Buldán*, IV. 72, 12.

[4] A 22, 14.

[5] H 10, 14—12, 7. A 23, 6—26, 10. There is not much to choose between the two versions. I have generally preferred the latter, which adds some interesting details, although it is not quite so tersely and simply written.

[6] Concerning this numerous class of Mohammedan mystics see Paul Loosen, *Die weisen Narren des Naisābūrī* (Strassburg, 1912).

stood looking at him, while he continued to sew[b]. As soon as he had sewn the patch on, he said, "O Abú Sa'íd! I have sewn thee on this gaberdine along with the patch." Then he rose and took my hand, leading me to the convent (*khánaqáh*) of the Ṣúfís in Sarakhs, and shouted for Shaykh Abu 'l-Faḍl Ḥasan, who was within. When Abu 'l-Faḍl appeared, Luqmán placed my hand in his, saying, "O Abu 'l-Faḍl, watch over this young man, for he is one of you[c]." The Shaykh took my hand and led me into the convent. I sat down in the portico and the Shaykh picked up a volume and began to peruse it. As is the way of scholars, I could not help wondering what the book was. The Shaykh perceived my thought. "Abú Sa'íd!" he said, "all the hundred and twenty-four thousand prophets were sent to preach one word. They bade the people say 'Allah' and devote themselves to Him. Those who heard this word with the ear alone, let it go out by the other ear; but those who heard it with their souls imprinted it on their souls and repeated it until it penetrated their hearts and souls, and their whole being became this word. They were made independent of the pronunciation of the word, they were released from the sound and the letters. Having understood the spiritual meaning of this word, they became so absorbed in it that they were no more conscious of their own non-existence[1]." This saying took hold of me

in the law and pious, but afterwards he ceased to perform the duties of religion. When he was asked how this change had come to pass, he replied: 'The more I served God, the more service was required of me. In my despair I cried, "O God! kings set free a slave when he grows old. Thou art the Almighty King. Set me free, for I have grown old in Thy service." I heard a voice that said, "Luqmán! I set thee free."' " The sign of his freedom was that his reason was taken away from him. Abú Sa'íd used often to say that Luqmán was one whom God had emancipated from his commandments.]

[b] [Abú Sa'íd was standing in such a position that his shadow fell on Luqmán's gaberdine.]

[c] [Shaykh Abu 'l-Faḍl was exceedingly venerable. When, after the death of Abu 'l-Faḍl, Abú Sa'íd became an adept in mysticism, he was asked what was the cause of his having attained to such a degree of perfection. He answered, "The cause was a look that Shaykh Abu 'l-Faḍl gave me. I was a student of theology under Shaykh Abú 'Alí. One day, when I was walking on the bank of a stream, Shaykh Abu 'l-Faḍl approached from the opposite direction and looked at me out of the corner of his eye. From that day to this, all my spiritual possessions are the result of that look."]

---

[1] This rendering of Abu 'l-Faḍl's admonition agrees with H 11, 5 foll., where the text is given most fully.

and did not allow me to sleep that night. In the morning, when I had finished my prayers and devotions, I went to the Shaykh before sunrise and asked permission to attend Abú 'Alí's lecture on Koranic exegesis. He began his lecture with the verse, *Say Allah! then leave them to amuse themselves in their folly*[1]. At the moment of hearing this word a door in my breast was opened, and I was rapt from myself. The Imám Abú 'Alí observed the change in me and asked, "Where were you last night?" I said, "With Abu 'l-Faḍl Ḥasan." He ordered me to rise and go back to Abu 'l-Faḍl, saying, "It is unlawful for you to come from that subject (Ṣúfism) to this discourse." I returned to the Shaykh, distraught and bewildered, for I had entirely lost myself in this word. When Abu 'l-Faḍl saw me, he said: "Abú Sa'íd!

mastak shuda'í hamí nadání pas u písh[2].

Thou art drunk, poor youth! Thou know'st not head from tail."

"O Shaykh!" I said, "what is thy command?" He said, "Come in and sit down and devote thyself wholly to this word, for this word hath much work to do with thee." After I had stayed with him for a long time, duly performing all that was required by this word, he said to me one day, "O Abú Sa'íd! the doors of the letters of this word[3] have been opened to thee. Now the hosts (of spiritual grace) will rush into thy breast, and thou wilt experience diverse kinds of self-culture (*adab*)." Then he exclaimed, "Thou hast been transported, transported, transported! Go and seek a place of solitude, and turn aside from men as thou hast turned aside from thyself, and behave with patience and resignation to God's will." I abandoned my studies and came home to Mayhana and retired into the niche of the chapel in my own house. There I sat for seven years, saying continually, "Allah! Allah! Allah!" Whenever drowsiness or inattention arising from the weakness of human nature came over me, a soldier with a fiery spear—the most terrible and alarming figure that can possibly be imagined—appeared in front of the niche[4] and shouted at me, saying, "O Abú Sa'íd, say Allah!" The dread of that apparition used to keep me

[1] Kor. 6, 91.

[2] Though printed as prose in both texts, this line appears to belong to a *rubá'í*, since it is written in one of the metres peculiar to that form of verse.

[3] According to H: "the doors of the spiritual gifts (فتوح) of this word."

[4] H has merely: "a terrible figure appeared in front of the niche."

burning and trembling for whole days and nights, so that I did not again fall asleep or become inattentive; and at last every atom of me began to cry aloud, "Allah! Allah! Allah!"

Countless records of mystical conversion bear witness to the central fact in this description—the awakening of the soul in response to some unsuspected stimulus, by which, as Arnold says,

> A bolt is shot back somewhere in the breast,

opening a way for the flood of transcendental consciousness to burst through. The accompanying ecstasy is a normal feature, and so is the abandonment of past occupations, habits, ambitions, and the fixing of every faculty upon that supreme reality which is henceforth the single object of desire. All these phenomena, however sudden they may seem, are the climax of an interior conflict that perhaps only makes itself known at the moment when it is already decided. Probably in Abú Sa'íd's case the process was at least to some extent a conscious one. He had been long and earnestly engaged in the study of theology.

I possessed many books and papers, but though I used to turn them over and read them one after the other, I was never finding any peace. I prayed to God, saying, "O Lord, nothing is revealed to my heart by all this study and learning: it causes me to lose Thee, O God! Let me be able to do without it by giving me something in which I shall find Thee again[1]."

Here Abú Sa'íd acknowledges that he sought spiritual peace, and that all his efforts to win it from intellectual proofs ended in failure. The history of that struggle is unwritten, but not until the powers of intellect were fully tried and shown to be of no avail, could mightier forces drawn from a deeper source come overwhelmingly into action. As regards the perpetual iteration of the name Allah, I need hardly remind my readers that this is a method everywhere practised by Moslem mystics for bringing about *faná*, *i.e.* the passing-away from self, or in Pascal's phrase, "oubli du monde et de tout hormis Dieu."

[1] A 50, 12.

We have seen that the first act of Abú Sa'íd after his conversion was to enquire of Shaykh Abu 'l-Faḍl what he must do next. That is to say, he had implicitly accepted Abu 'l-Faḍl as his spiritual director, in accordance with the rule that "if any one by means of asceticism and self-mortification shall have risen to an exalted degree of mystical experience, *without having a Pír to whose authority and example he submits himself*, the Ṣúfís do not regard him as belonging to their community[1]." In this way a continuous tradition of mystical doctrine is secured, beginning with the Prophet and carried down through a series of dead Pírs to the living director who forms the last link of the chain until he too dies and is succeeded by one of his pupils.

Abú Sa'íd's lineage as a Ṣúfí is given in the following table:

Mohammed, the Prophet
|
'Alí (*ob.* A.D. 661)
|
Ḥasan of Baṣra (*ob.* A.D. 728)
|
Ḥabíb 'Ajamí (*ob.* A.D. 737)
|
Dáwud Ṭá'í (*ob.* A.D. 781)
|
Ma'rúf Karkhí (*ob.* A.D. 815)
|
Sarí Saqaṭí (*ob.* A.D. 867)
|
Junayd of Baghdád (*ob.* A.D. 909)
|
Murta'ish of Baghdád (*ob.* A.D. 939)
|
Abú Naṣr al-Sarráj of Ṭús (*ob.* A.D. 988)
|
Abu 'l-Faḍl Ḥasan of Sarakhs
|
Abú Sa'íd ibn Abi 'l-Khayr

[1] A 55, 15.

The appearance of Mohammed and his son-in-law at the head of a list of this kind fits in with the fiction—which was necessary for the existence of Ṣúfism within Islam—that the Ṣúfís are the legitimate heirs and true interpreters of the esoteric teaching of the Prophet. Ḥasan of Baṣra, Ḥabíb 'Ajamí, and Dáwud Ṭá'í were ascetics and quietists rather than mystics. Even if we take the ninth century as a starting-point, it must not be supposed that any fixed body of doctrine was handed down. Such a thing is foreign to the nature of Ṣúfism, which essentially is not a system based on authority and tradition, but a free movement assuming infinitely various forms in obedience to the inner light of the individual soul. Before the time of Abú Sa'íd, certain eminent theosophists—Junayd, for instance—had founded schools which owed their origin to controversies over particular questions of mystical theory and practice, while at a later period Ṣúfism branched off into great organisations comparable to the Christian monastic orders. Everywhere we find divergent tendencies asserting themselves and freely developing a vigorous life.

There is no difficulty in believing that Abú Sa'íd, after passing through the spiritual crisis which has been described, returned to Mayhana and spent some time in solitary meditation, though doubts are suggested by the statement, which occurs in the two oldest biographies, that his seclusion (*khalwat*) lasted for seven years. According to the *Ḥálát ú Sukhunán*, at the end of this period—Shaykh Abu 'l-Faḍl having died in the meanwhile—he journeyed to Ámul in order to visit Shaykh Abu 'l-'Abbás Qaṣṣáb[1]. The *Asrár*, however, mentions a second period during which he practised the most severe austerities, first at Sarakhs under the care of Shaykh Abu 'l-Faḍl and then, for seven years[2], in the deserts and mountains of Mayhana, until at the age of 40 he attained to perfect saintship. These numbers can only be regarded as evidence of a desire to make him exemplify a theoretically symmetrical scheme of the mystic's progress towards perfection, but it is none the less probable that for many years

[1] H 12, 7. [2] A 41, 3.

after his conversion Abú Sa'íd was painfully treading the *via purgativa*, which Ṣúfís call "the Path" (*ṭaríqa*). His biographers give an interesting account of his self-mortification (*mujáhada*). The details are derived either from his public discourses or from the testimony of eye-witnesses[1].

The author of the *Asrár* relates that after seven years of solitary retirement Abú Sa'íd came back to Shaykh Abu 'l-Faḍl, who gave him a cell opposite his own, in order that he might keep him always under observation, and prescribed such moral and ascetic discipline as was necessary[2]. When some time had passed, he was transferred to the cell of Abu 'l-Faḍl himself and subjected to still closer supervision (*muráqabat-i aḥwál*). We are not told how long he remained in the convent at Sarakhs. At last Abu 'l-Faḍl bade him return to Mayhana and take care of his mother. Here he lived in a cell, apparently in his father's house, though he also frequented several cloisters in the neighbourhood, especially one known as "The Old Cloister" (*Ribáṭ-i Kuhan*) on the Merv road[3]. Among the ascetic exercises in which he was now constantly engaged the following are recorded[4]:

He showed excessive zeal in his religious ablutions, emptying a number of water-jugs for every single *wuḍú'*.

He was always washing the door and walls of his cell.

He never leaned against any door or wall, or rested his body on wood or on a cushion, or reclined on a couch.

All the time he wore only one shirt, which gradually increased in weight because, whenever it was torn, he would sew a patch on it. At last it weighed 20 maunds.

He never quarrelled with any one nor spoke to any one, except when necessity forced him to do so.

He ate no food by day, and broke his fast with nothing more than a piece of bread.

He did not sleep by day or night but shut himself in his cell, where he had made an excavation in the wall, just high and broad enough to stand in, which could be closed by means

[1] H 18, 17. About 200 of Abú Sa'íd's discourses were in circulation when the *Ḥálát ú Sukhunán* was written (H 55, 21).

[2] A 26, 10; 27, 2. [3] A 27, 17; 30, 7. [4] A 27, 18.

of a door. He used to stand here and close the door and occupy himself with recollection (*dhikr*), stuffing his ears with cotton-wool in order that no disturbing sound might reach him, and that his attention might remain concentrated. At the same time he never ceased to watch over his inmost self (*murá-qabat-i sirr*), in order that no thought except of God might cross his mind[1].

After a while he became unable to bear the society or even the sight of men. He wandered alone in desert and mountainous places and would often disappear for a month or more. His father used to go in search of him and find out where he was from labourers or travellers who had seen him. To please his father, he would come home, but ere long he would feel the presence of human creatures to be unendurable and would again flee to mountains and wildernesses, where he was sometimes seen roaming with a venerable old man clad in white raiment. Many years afterwards, when Abú Sa'íd had risen to eminence, he declared to those who questioned him that this old man was the prophet Khaḍir[2].

Although he was carefully watched, Abú Sa'íd contrived to escape from his father's house night after night. On one occasion his father (who felt a natural anxiety as to the object of these nocturnal excursions) followed him, unperceived, at a little distance.

My son (he relates) walked on until he reached the Old Cloister (*Ribáṭ-i Kuhan*). He entered it and shut the gate behind him, while I went up on the roof. I saw him go into a chapel, which was in the *ribáṭ*, and close the door. Looking through the chapel window, I waited to see what would happen. There was a stick lying on the floor, and it had a rope fastened to it. He took up the stick and tied the end of the rope to his foot. Then, laying the stick across the top of a pit that was at the corner of the chapel, he slung himself into the pit head downwards, and began to recite the Koran. He remained in that posture until daybreak, when, having recited the whole Koran, he raised himself from the pit, replaced the stick where he had found it, opened the door, came out of the chapel, and commenced to perform his ablution in the middle

[1] A 28, 8. [2] A 28, 15.

of the *ribáṭ*. I descended from the roof, hastened home, and slept until he came in[1].

The following passage illustrates another side of Abú Sa'íd's asceticism. He said,

One day I said to myself, "Knowledge, works, meditation—I have them all; now I want to become absent from them (*ghaybatí az ín*)." On consideration I saw that the only way to attain this was by acting as a servant to the dervishes, for *when God wishes to benefit a man, He shows to him the path of self-abasement*. Accordingly I made it my business to wait upon them, and I used to clean their cells and privies and lavatories. I persevered in this work for a long time, until it became a habit. Then I resolved to beg for the dervishes, which seemed to me the hardest thing I could lay upon myself. At first, when people saw me begging, they would give me a piece of gold, but soon it was only copper, and by degrees it came down to a single raisin or nut. In the end even this was refused. One day I was with a number of dervishes, and there was nothing to be got for them. For their sake I parted with the turban I had on my head, then I sold one after the other my slippers, the lining of my *jubba*, the cloth of which it was made, and the cotton quilting[2].

During the period of ascetic discipline which he underwent at Mayhana, Abú Sa'íd sometimes visited Sarakhs for the purpose of receiving spiritual guidance from Shaykh Abu 'l-Faḍl. His biographer says that he travelled on his bare feet, but if we may trust 'Abdu 'l-Ṣamad, one of his disciples, he usually flew through the air; it is added that this phenomenon was witnessed only by persons of mystical insight[3]. According to the *Asrár*, he returned to Abu 'l-Faḍl for another year's training and was then sent by him to Abú 'Abd al-Raḥmán al-Sulamí, who invested him with the patched frock (*khirqa*) that proclaims the wearer to be a recognised member of the brotherhood of Ṣúfís[4]. Al-Sulamí of Níshápúr (*ob.* A.D. 1021), a pupil of Abu 'l-Qásim al-Naṣrábádí, was a celebrated mystic. He is the author of the *Ṭabaqátu 'l-Ṣúfiyya*—biographies of the early Ṣúfí Shaykhs—and other important works.

On Abú Sa'íd's return, Shaykh Abu 'l-Faḍl said to him,

[1] A 32, 4. [2] A 34, 5. [3] A 35, 4. [4] A 35, 15.

"Now all is finished. You must go to Mayhana and call the people to God and admonish them and show them the way to the Truth." He came back to Mayhana, as his Director enjoined, but instead of contenting himself with Abu 'l-Faḍl's assurance that all was now finished, he increased his austerities and was more assiduous than ever in his devotions. In the following discourse he refers to the veneration which the people began to manifest towards him at this time[1].

When I was a novice, I bound myself to do eighteen things: I fasted continually; I abstained from unlawful food; I practised recollection (*dhikr*) uninterruptedly; I kept awake at night; I never reclined on the ground; I never slept but in a sitting posture; I sat facing the Ka'ba; I never leaned against anything; I never looked at a handsome youth or at women whom it would have been unlawful for me to see unveiled; I did not beg; I was content and resigned to God's will; I always sat in the mosque and did not go into the market, because the Prophet said that the market is the filthiest of places and the mosque the cleanest. In all my acts I was a follower of the Prophet. Every four-and-twenty hours I completed a recitation of the Koran. In my seeing I was blind, in my hearing deaf, in my speaking dumb. For a whole year I conversed with no one. People called me a lunatic, and I allowed them to give me that name, relying on the Tradition that a man's faith is not made perfect until he is supposed to be mad. I performed everything that I had read or heard of as having been done or commanded by the Prophet. Having read that when he was wounded in the foot in the battle of Uḥud, he stood on his toes in order to perform his devotions—for he could not set the sole of his foot upon the ground—I resolved to imitate him, and standing on tiptoe I performed a prayer of 400 genuflexions. I modelled my actions, outward and inward, upon the Sunna of the Prophet, so that habit at last became nature. Whatever I had heard or found in books concerning the acts of worship performed by the angels, I performed the same. I had heard and seen in writing that some angels worship God on their heads. Therefore I placed my head on the ground and bade the blessed mother of Abú Ṭáhir tie my toe with a cord and fasten the cord to a peg and then

[1] A 36, 8.

shut the door behind her. Being left alone, I said, "O Lord! I do not want myself: let me escape from myself!" and I began a recitation of the whole Koran. When I came to the verse, *God shall suffice thee against them, for He heareth and knoweth all*[1], blood poured from my eyes and I was no longer conscious of myself. Then things changed. Ascetic experiences passed over me of a kind that can be described in words[2], and God strengthened and aided me therein, but I fancied that all these acts were done by me. The grace of God became manifest and showed me that this was not so, and that these were the acts of divine favour and grace. I repented of my belief and realised that it was mere self-conceit. Now if you say that you will not tread this path because it is self-conceit, I reply that your refusal to tread it is self-conceit. Until you have undergone all this, its self-conceit will not be revealed to you. Self-conceit appears only when you fulfil the Law, for self-conceit lies in religion, and religion is of the Law. To abstain from religious acts is infidelity, and to perform such acts self-consciously is dualism. If "thou" exists and "He" exists, "two" exists; and that is dualism. You must put your "self" away altogether.

I had a cell in which I sat, and sitting there I was enamoured of passing-away from myself. A light flashed upon me, which utterly destroyed the darkness of my being. God Almighty revealed to me that I was neither that nor this: that this was His grace even as that was His gift. So it came to pass that I said:

When I mine eyes have opened, all Thy beauty I behold;
When I tell Thee my secret, all my body is ensouled.
Methinks, unlawful 'tis for me to talk with other men,
But when with Thee I am talking, ah! the tale is never told.

Then the people began to regard me with great approval. Disciples gathered round me and were converted to Ṣúfism. My neighbours too showed their respect for me by ceasing to drink wine. This proceeded so far that a melon-skin which I had thrown away was bought for twenty pieces of gold. One day when I was riding on horseback, my horse dropped dung. Eager to gain a blessing, the people came and picked up the dung and smeared their heads and faces with it. After a time it was revealed to me that I was not the real object of their veneration. A voice cried from the corner of the mosque, *Is not thy Lord enough for thee*[3]?

[1] Kor. 2, 131. [2] Reading عبارت. [3] Kor. 41, 53.

A light gleamed in my breast, and most veils were removed. The people who had honoured me now rejected me, and even went before the cadi to bear witness that I was an infidel. The inhabitants of every place that I entered declared that their crops would not grow on account of my wickedness. Once, whilst I was seated in the mosque, the women went up on to the roof and bespattered me with filth; and still I heard a voice saying, *Is not thy Lord enough for thee?* The congregation desisted from their prayers, saying, "We will not pray together so long as this madman is in the mosque." Meanwhile I was reciting these verses:

I was a lion—the fierce pard was ware
Of my pursuit. I conquered everywhere.
But since I drew Thy love close to my heart,
Lame foxes drive me from my forest-lair.

This joyous transport was followed by a painful contraction (*qabḍ*). I opened the Koran, and my eye fell on the verse, *We will prove you with evil and with good, to try you; and unto Us shall ye return*[1], as though God said to me, "All this which I put in thy way is a trial. If it is good, it is a trial, and if it is evil, it is a trial. Do not stoop to good or to evil, but dwell with Me!" Once more my "self" vanished, and His grace was all in all[2].

After the death of his father and mother—which the biographer leaves undated, only observing, in the spirit of a true Ṣúfí, that these events removed the obstacle of filial affection from his path—Abú Sa'íd is said to have roamed for seven years in the deserts between Mayhana and Báward (Abíward) and between Merv and Sarakhs[3]. He then returned to Mayhana. By this time Shaykh Abu 'l-Faḍl, to whom he had hitherto confided all his perplexities, was dead. Feeling that he required a spiritual Director, Abú Sa'íd set out for Ámul in Ṭabaristán, whither many Ṣúfís were flocking in consequence of the fame of Shaykh Abu 'l-'Abbás Qaṣṣáb. He was accompanied by Aḥmad Najjár and Muḥammad Faḍl, his disciple and lifelong friend, who is buried at Sarakhs. They journeyed to Báward and thence along the Gaz valley (*Darra-i Gaz*) to Nasá[4]. At Sháh Mayhana[5], a village in this

[1] Kor. 21, 36. [2] H 19, 6. A 37, 8. [3] A 40, 19. [4] A 43, 9.
[5] According to the *Asrár*, 44, 9, the inhabitants of Báward called the

valley, having performed their ablutions and prayers on the rocky bank of a stream, they were approaching the tomb of Abú 'Alí حوجى (?), which it was their purpose to visit, when they saw a lad driving an ox and ploughing, and on the edge of the field an old man sowing millet-seed. The old man seemed to have lost his wits, for he was always looking towards the tomb and uttering loud cries.

"We were deeply moved," said Abú Sa'íd, "by his behaviour. He came to meet us and salaamed and said, 'Can you lift a burden from my breast?' 'If God will,' I replied. 'I have been thinking,' he said, 'if God, when He created the world, had created no creatures in it; and if He had filled it full of millet from East to West and from earth to heaven; and if then He had created one bird and bidden it eat one grain of this millet every thousand years; and if, after that, He had created a man and had kindled in his heart this mystic longing and had told him that he would never win to his goal until this bird left not a single millet-seed in the whole world, and that he would continue until then in this burning pain of love—I have been thinking, it would still be a thing soon ended!' The words of the old peasant (said Abú Sa'íd) made all the mystery plain to me[1]."

Nasá, which the travellers skirted but did not enter, was known amongst Ṣúfís by the name of "Little Syria" (*Shám-i kúchak*), because it boasted as many tombs of saints as Syria of prophets. The author of the *Asrár* says that in his time the cemetery overlooking the town contained 400 sepulchres of great Shaykhs and holy men[2]. The prevailing belief that the sanctity of the place protected it from devastation he declares to have been verified by what he himself witnessed

village Shámína (شامينه) or Sháhína (شاهينه), but changed its name to Sháh Mayhana (شاه ميهنه) on the suggestion of Abú Sa'íd. This story appears to indicate that ميهنه was pronounced Míhna, and that the pronunciation Mayhana (which I have adopted in deference to Yáqút) is not the original one. In this case مِهْنه and ميهْنه, the two names of the town, may be compared with such parallel forms as مِهمان, ميهمان, مِنو, مينو, etc. Sam'ání gives ميهَنى (Míhaní) as the pronunciation of the *nisba*.

[1] A 44, 12.

[2] A 46, 7.

during the massacres and ravages of more than thirty years.

Every calamity that threatened Nasá has been averted by the favour and kindness of God and by the blessings of the tombs of departed Shaykhs and by the prayers of the living. Even now (he continues), when religion in Khurásán is almost extinct and scarcely any vestige of Ṣúfism is left, there are still in Nasá many excellent Shaykhs and Ṣúfís, richly endowed with inward experiences, as well as numerous hidden saints who exert a powerful and beneficent influence[1].

In the upper part of the town, adjoining the cemetery, stood a convent for Ṣúfís, the Khánaqáh-i Saráwí. It had recently been founded by the famous mystic, Abú 'Alí Daqqáq of Níshápúr (*ob.* A.D. 1015). The legend concerning its foundation was that Abú 'Alí had a dream in which the Prophet ordered him to build a house for Ṣúfís, and not only pointed out the site but also drew a line showing its dimensions. Next morning, when Abú 'Alí went to the place indicated, he and all those who were with him saw a line distinctly marked on the ground; and upon this line the outer wall of the convent was raised[2]. When Abú Sa'íd arrived at Yaysama[3], a village in the neighbourhood of Nasá, he went to visit the tomb of Aḥmad 'Alí Nasawí[4]. Meanwhile Shaykh Aḥmad Naṣr[5], who was then in charge of the convent at Nasá, put out his head from his cell and said to the Ṣúfís seated in the portico, "The royal falcon of the mystic Way (*sháhbáz-i ṭaríqa*) is passing! Whoever wants to catch him must go to Yaysama[6]."

While passing through the village, Abú Sa'íd and his

[1] A 46, 11. [2] A 45, 14.

[3] In the *Nafaḥátu 'l-Uns* (ed. by Nassau Lees), p. 327, 2, where this passage is quoted, the name of the village is written بسمه (Basma).

[4] A pupil of Abú 'Uthmán Ḥírí. It is stated in the *Asrár*, 48, 1, that his name is given by Abú 'Abd al-Raḥmán al-Sulamí in the *Ṭabaqátu 'l-Ṣúfiyya* as Muḥammad 'Ulayyán al-Nasawí, but that in Nasá he is generally known by the name of Aḥmad 'Alí. According to the British Museum MS. of the *Ṭabaqát*, f. 96 *a*, his name is Muḥammad b. 'Alí and he is generally known as Muḥammad b. 'Ulayyán.

[5] Cf. *Nafaḥátu 'l-Uns*, No. 357. [6] A 47, 10.

friends noticed a butcher who wore a fur gaberdine (*púštín*) and was seated in his shop, with pieces of meat hanging in front of him. He came forward to greet the strangers, and bade an apprentice follow them and see where they lodged. They found quarters in a mosque beside the river, and when they had performed their ablutions and prayers the butcher appeared, bringing some viands of which they partook.

"After we had done," said Abú Sa'íd, "he asked whether any of us could answer a question. My friends pointed to me. He then said, 'What is the duty of a slave and what is the duty of a labourer for hire?' I replied in terms of the religious law. He asked, 'Is there nothing else?' I remained silent. With a stern look he exclaimed, 'Do not live with one whom thou hast divorced!' meaning that since I had discarded exoteric knowledge (*'ilm-i ẓáhir*), I must not have any further dealings with it. Then he added, 'Until thou art free, thou wilt never be a slave[1], and until thou art an honest and sincere labourer, thou wilt never receive the wages of everlasting bliss.'"[2]

To digress a little, as the leisurely style of Oriental biography permits, it will be remembered that on his conversion to Ṣúfism Abú Sa'íd immediately abandoned the study of theology and jurisprudence in which he had spent so much of his youth. He collected all the volumes that he had read, together with his own note-books, buried them, and erected over them a mound of stone and earth (*dúkání*). On this mound he planted a twig of myrtle, which took root and put forth leaves, and in the course of time became a large tree. The people of Mayhana used to pluck boughs from it, hoping thereby to win a blessing for their new-born children, or in order to lay them on their dead before interment. The author of the *Asrár*, who had often seen it and admired its beautiful foliage, says that it was destroyed, with other relics of the saint, during the invasion of Khurásán by the Ghuzz[3]. When Abú Sa'íd buried his books, it was suggested that he might have done better to give them to some one who would

[1] *I.e.*, thou wilt never serve God truly until thou art free from 'self.'
[2] A 49, 4.
[3] A 50, 1.

profit by reading them. "I wished," he said, "that my heart should be entirely void of the consciousness of having conferred an obligation and of the recollection of having bestowed a gift[1]." Once he was heard wailing in his cell the whole night long. Next morning he explained that he had been visited with a violent toothache as a punishment for having dipped into a tome which he took away from a student[2].

Here are two more of his sayings on the same topic: "Books! ye are excellent guides, but it is absurd to trouble about a guide after the goal has been reached." "The first step in this affair (Ṣúfism) is the breaking of ink-pots[3] and the tearing-up of books and the forgetting of all kinds of (intellectual) knowledge[4]."

We left Abú Sa'íd on his way to Ámul. He is said to have resided there for one year[5] in the convent of which Shaykh Abu 'l-'Abbás Qaṣṣáb was the head. The Shaykh gave him a cell in the assembly-room (*jamá'at-khána*), facing the oratory[6] reserved for himself, where he had sat for forty-one years in the midst of his disciples[7]. It was the custom of Shaykh Abu 'l-'Abbás, when he saw a dervish performing supererogatory prayers at night, to say to him, "Sleep, my son! All the devotions of your Director are performed for your sake, for they are of no use to him and he does not need them himself"; but he never said this to Abú Sa'íd, who used to pray all night and fast all day. During the night Abú Sa'íd kept his eyes continually fixed upon his navel, and his mind upon the spiritual "states" (*aḥwál*) and acts of the Shaykh. One day the Shaykh had some blood let from his arm. At night the bandage slipped off, uncovering the vein, so that his garment was stained with blood. As he came out of the oratory, Abú Sa'íd, who was always on the watch to serve him, ran up to

[1] A 51, 18. [2] A 52, 7.

[3] Reading كسر for كبس. [4] A 51, 14.

[5] Two and a half years, according to another tradition which has less authority (A 52, 17).

[6] *Záwiya-gáh*. It seems to have been a place surrounded by a railing or lattice, since it is compared in the text to a penfold (*ḥaẓíra*).

[7] A 53, 1.

him, washed and bandaged his arm, and taking from him the soiled garment offered his own, which the Shaykh put on, while Abú Sa'íd clad himself in a *khashan*[1] that he had. Then he washed and cleaned the Shaykh's garment, hung it on the rope (*ḥabl*) to dry, rubbed and folded it, and brought it to the Shaykh. "It is thine," said the Shaykh, "put it on!" "Nay," cried Abú Sa'íd, "let the Shaykh put it on me with his own blessed hand!"

This was the second gaberdine (*khirqa*) with which Abú Sa'íd was invested, for he had already received one from Abú 'Abd al-Raḥmán al-Sulamí of Níshápúr[2].

Here the author of the *Asrár* introduces a disquisition on the meaning of such investiture[3], with the object of refuting those who hold that a Ṣúfí ought not to accept a *khirqa* from more than one Pír. In the first place, he describes the endowments in virtue of which the Pír is privileged to invest a disciple with the *khirqa*. The Pír should be worthy of imitation, *i.e.*, he should have a perfect knowledge, both theoretical and practical, of the three stages of the mystical life—the Law, the Path, and the Truth; he should also be entirely purged of fleshly attributes (*ṣifát-i bashariyya*), so that nothing of his lower "self" (*nafs*) remains in him. When such a Pír has become thoroughly acquainted with a disciple's acts and thoughts and has proved them by the test of experience and, through spiritual insight, knows that he is qualified to advance beyond the position of a famulus (*maqám-i khidmat*)—whether his being thus qualified is due to the training which he has received from this Pír or to the guidance and direction of another Pír possessing a like authority—then he lays his hand on the disciple's head and invests him with the *khirqa*. By the act of investiture he announces his conviction that the disciple is fit to associate with the Ṣúfís, and if he is a person of credit and renown amongst them, his declaration carries the same weight as, in matters of law, the testimony of an

[1] *Khashan* is properly the name of a grass from which coarse garments are made.

[2] See p. 14 *supra*.

[3] A 54, 6—59, 5. Cf. the fourth chapter of Hujwírí's *Kashf al-Maḥjúb*, pp. 45–47, in my translation.

honest witness and the sentence of an incorruptible judge. Accordingly, whenever an unknown dervish comes into a convent or wishes to join a company of Ṣúfís, they ask him, "Who was the Pír that taught thee[1]?" and "From whose hand didst thou receive the *khirqa*?" Ṣúfís recognise no relationship but these two, which they regard as all-important. They do not allow any one to associate with them, unless he can show to their satisfaction that he is lineally connected in both these ways with a fully accredited Pír.

Having insisted that the whole Path of Ṣúfism turns upon the Pír (*madár-i ṭaríqa bar pír ast*[2]), the author of the *Asrár* comes to the question in dispute—"Is it right to receive investiture from the hands of more than one[3]?" He answers, in effect, "Yes, it is right, provided that the second investiture is not accompanied with the intention of annulling the first[4]." His argument is a universal principle, which can be stated in a few words. Ultimately and essentially all things are one. Difference and duality are phenomena which disappear when unity is reached. The sayings of the great mystics differ in expression, but their meaning is the same. There are many religions, but only one God; diverse ways, but only one goal. Hence those who raise an objection against the double investiture proclaim themselves to be still on the plane of dualism, which the Pírs have transcended. In reality, all Ṣúfís, all Pírs, and all *khirqas* are one. Amidst these sublime truths it is rather a shock to meet with the remark that the novice who receives two *khirqas* resembles a man who calls two witnesses to attest his competence[5].

On his departure from Ámul, Abú Sa'íd was directed by

[1] *Pír-i ṣuḥbat*, *i.e.*, the Pír to whom one stands in the relation of disciple (*ṣáḥib*). The *pír-i ṣuḥbat* of Abú Sa'íd was Abu 'l-Faḍl Ḥasan of Sarakhs (A 26, 10). Abú Sa'íd used to call him 'Pír,' while he spoke of Abu 'l-'Abbás Qaṣṣáb simply as 'the Shaykh' (A 43, 18). The second question implies that a Pír might confer the *khirqa* upon a novice whom he had not personally trained.

[2] A 56, 1.

[3] The *khirqa* with which the novice is invested by a Pír is named "the *khirqa* of origin" (*khirqa-i aṣl*) or "the *khirqa* of blessing" (*khirqa-i tabarruk*). A 57, 7, where دیگر آنرا should be read in place of دیگرانرا.

[4] A 59, 1.

[5] A 57, 12.

Shaykh Abu 'l-'Abbás Qaṣṣáb to return once more to Mayhana[1]. This event approximately coincides with the beginning of a new period in his spiritual history. The long discipline of the Path, broken by fleeting visions and ecstasies, brought him at last into the full and steady splendour of illumination. The veil, which had hitherto been lifted only to fall again, was now burst asunder. Henceforth no barrier (*ḥijáb*) in the shape of "self"—that insidious obstacle which it is the whole business of the *via purgativa* to remove—could even temporarily shut off his consciousness of the Unseen. While conversing with Abú 'Alí Daqqáq, Abú Sa'íd asked him whether this experience was ever permanent. "No," said Abú 'Alí. Abú Sa'íd bowed his head, then he repeated the question and received the same answer, whereupon he bowed his head as before. On being asked for the third time, Abú 'Alí replied, "If it ever is permanent, it is extremely rare." Abú Sa'íd clapped his hands joyfully and exclaimed several times, "This"—referring to his own case—"is one of these rarities[2]." Continuous though his illumination may have been, it was not of uniform intensity, but was subject to the fluctuations which are described in the technical language of Ṣúfism as contraction (*qabḍ*) and expansion (*basṭ*)[3]. Often, when he fell into the former state, he would go about asking questions of every one, in the hope of hearing some words that might relieve his oppression[4]. When *qabḍ* was violent, he would visit the tomb of Shaykh Abu 'l-Faḍl Ḥasan at Sarakhs. His eldest son, Abú Ṭáhir, relates that one day Abú Sa'íd, while preaching, began to weep, and the whole congregation wept with him. Giving orders that his horse should be saddled, he immediately set out for Sarakhs, accompanied by all who were present. As soon as they entered the desert, his feeling of "contraction" was dispelled. He began to speak freely, while those around him shouted with joy. On arriving at Sarakhs he turned aside from the highroad in the direction

[1] A 59, 16. [2] A 62, 9.

[3] Concerning these terms see my translation of the *Kashf al-Maḥjúb*, pp. 374–376.

[4] A 62, 18.

of the tomb of Shaykh Abu 'l-Faḍl Ḥasan and bade the *qawwál* sing this verse:

Here is the mansion of delight, the home of bounty and of grace!
All eyes towards the Ka'ba turn, but ours to the Beloved's face.

During the *qawwál's* chant Abú Sa'íd and the dervishes with bare heads and feet circumambulated the tomb, shrieking ecstatically. When quiet was restored, he said, "Mark the date of this day, for you will never see a day like this again." Afterwards he used to tell any of his disciples who thought of making the pilgrimage to Mecca that they must visit the tomb of Shaykh Abu 'l-Faḍl Ḥasan and perform seven circumambulations there[1].

It is stated on the authority of Abú Sa'íd's grandson, Shaykhu 'l-Islám Abú Sa'íd, who was the grandfather of Muḥammad ibnu 'l-Munawwar, the compiler of the *Asrár*, that Abú Sa'íd attained to perfect illumination at the age of forty[2]. That statement may be approximately correct, though we cannot help regarding as suspicious its combination with the theory founded on a passage in the Koran[3], that no one under forty years of age ever attained to the rank of prophecy or saintship, excepting only Yaḥyá ibn Zakariyyá (John the Baptist) and Jesus. At this point the biographer concludes the first chapter of his work, describing Abú Sa'íd's conversion and novitiate, and enters on the mature period of his mystical life—the period of illumination and contemplation.

In the foregoing pages we have been mainly concerned with his progress as an ascetic. We are now to see him as Theosophist and Saint. It must be added, however, that in this higher stage he did not discontinue his austerities. He took pains to conceal them, and all our information about them is derived from allusions in his public speeches or from the exhortations which he addressed to novices. According to his disciples, after becoming an adept there was no rule or practice of the Prophet that he left unperformed[4].

From this time (*circa* A.H. 400 = A.D. 1009) until his death, which occurred in A.H. 440 = A.D. 1049, the materials avail-

[1] A 64, 6. [2] A 61, 1. [3] Kor. 46, 14. [4] A 65, 9.

able for Abú Sa'íd's biography, consisting for the most part of miscellaneous anecdotes, are of such a kind that it is impossible to give a connected account of events in their chronological order. Concerning his movements we know nothing of importance beyond the following facts:

(*a*) He left Mayhana and journeyed to Níshápúr, where he stayed for a considerable time.

(*b*) Shortly before quitting Níshápúr he paid a visit to Abu 'l-Ḥasan Kharaqání at Kharaqán[1].

(*c*) Finally, he returned from Níshápúr to Mayhana.

The anecdotes in the second chapter of the *Asrár* form three groups in correspondence with this local division:

1. Níshápúr (pp. 68–174).
2. Kharaqán (pp. 175–190).
3. Mayhana (pp. 191–247).

Various circumstances indicate that his residence in Níshápúr was a long one, probably extending over several years, but we find no precise statement[2], and the evidence that can be obtained from his reported meetings with famous contemporaries is insufficient, in my opinion, to serve as a basis for investigation. His visit to Kharaqán supplies a *terminus ad quem*, for Abu 'l-Ḥasan Kharaqání is known to have died in A.H. 425 = A.D. 1033–4. Unless the stories of his friendship with Qushayrí are inventions, he can hardly have settled in Níshápúr before A.H. 415 = A.D. 1024, since Qushayrí (born A.H. 376 = A.D. 986) is described at the date of Abú Sa'íd's arrival as a celebrated teacher with numerous pupils.

For the reasons mentioned above, we must now content ourselves with the barest outline of a narrative and seek compensation in episodes, incidents, and details which often reveal the personality and character of Abú Sa'íd in a sur-

[1] A village near Bisṭám. According to Sam'ání and Yáqút, the correct pronunciation is Kharaqán. Khurqán, the spelling preferred by Mr Le Strange (*Eastern Caliphate*, pp. 23 and 366), has less authority.

[2] The words "He was one year in Níshápúr" (A 94, 4) refer, as the context makes plain, only to the first year of his stay in that city. Possibly the period of his residence there was not continuous. It is worth notice that, according to H 72, 17, he usually spent the winter at Mayhana and the summer at Níshápúr.

prising manner and at the same time let us see how the monastic life was lived and by what methods it was organised.

When Abú Sa'íd set out for Níshápúr, he did not travel alone, but was attended by the disciples whom he had already gathered round him at Mayhana, while many new converts joined the party at Ṭús. Here he preached to crowded assemblies and moved his audience to tears. On one of these occasions an infant fell from the gallery (*bám*), which was thronged with women. Abú Sa'íd exclaimed, "Save it!" A hand appeared in the air and caught the child and placed it unhurt on the floor. The spectators raised a great cry and scenes of ecstasy ensued. "I swear," says Sayyid Abú 'Alí, who relates the story, "that I saw this with my own eyes. If I did not see it, may both my eyes become blind[1]!" At Ṭús Abú Sa'íd is said to have passed by a number of children standing together in the street of the Christians (*kúy-i tarsáyán*) and to have pointed out one of them to his companions, saying, "If you wish to look at the prime minister of the world, there he is!" The boy, whose future eminence was thus miraculously foretold, and who, forty years afterwards, repeated those prophetic words to a great-grandson of Abú Sa'íd, was the illustrious statesman Niẓámu 'l-Mulk (born A.D. 1018)[2].

On entering Níshápúr Abú Sa'íd was met by an influential patron of the Ṣúfís, Khwája Maḥmúd-i Muríd, who installed him and his disciples in the monastery (*khánaqáh*) of Abú 'Alí Ṭarasúsí in the street of the carpet-beaters (?)[3], which seems to have been his headquarters as long as he remained in Níshápúr[4]. His preaching and, above all, the extraordinary powers of telepathy which he displayed in public made many converts and brought in large sums of money[5]. Ḥasan-i

[1] A 69, 14.

[2] A 70, 8. Cf. A 115, 16. According to another version (A 233, 5 foll.), the prophecy was made after Abú Sa'íd's return from Níshápúr to Mayhana, where he was visited by Niẓámu 'l-Mulk, who was then a young student.

[3] A 73, 4. The MSS. give the name of the street as کوی عدنی کوبان or عدنی کویان (A 73, 14; 119, 15). Cf. عدنی باف (A 463, 9).

[4] This convent was destroyed by the Ghuzz who sacked Níshápúr in A.H. 548 = A.D. 1154 (A 195, 11).

[5] A 84, 10.

Mu'addib—afterwards his principal famulus and major-domo —relates his own experience as follows:

When people were proclaiming everywhere in Níshápúr that a Ṣúfí Pír had arrived from Mayhana and was preaching sermons in the street of the carpet-beaters and was reading men's secret thoughts, I said to myself—for I hated the Ṣúfís—"How can a Ṣúfí preach, when he knows nothing about theology? How can he read men's thoughts, when God has not given knowledge of the Unseen to any prophet or to any other person?" One day I went to the hall where he preached, with the intention of putting him to the proof, and sat down in front of his chair. I was handsomely dressed and had a turban of fine Ṭabarí stuff wound on my head. While the Shaykh was speaking, I regarded him with feelings of hostility and disbelief. Having finished his sermon, he asked for clothes on behalf of a dervish. Every one offered something. Then he asked for a turban. I thought of giving mine, but again I reflected that it had been brought to me from Ámul as a present and that it was worth ten Níshápúrí dínárs, so I resolved not to give it. The Shaykh made a second appeal, and the same thought occurred to me, but I rejected it once more. An old man who was seated beside me asked, "O Shaykh! does God plead with His creatures?" He answered, "Yes, but He does not plead more than twice for the sake of a Ṭabarí turban. He has already spoken twice to the man sitting beside you and has told him to give to this dervish the turban which he is wearing, but he refuses to do so, because it is worth ten pieces of gold and was brought to him from Ámul as a present." On hearing these words, I rose, trembling, and went forward to the Shaykh and kissed his foot and offered my turban and my whole suit of clothes to the dervish. Every feeling of dislike and incredulity was gone. I became a Moslem anew, bestowed on the Shaykh all the money and wealth I possessed, and devoted myself to his service[1].

While Abú Sa'íd was enthusiastically welcomed by the Ṣúfís of Níshápúr, he met with formidable opposition from the parties adverse to them[2], namely, the Karrámís[3], whose

[1] A 75, 12.

[2] He compares his reception to that of a dog who on entering a parish where he is unknown is set upon and mauled by all the dogs belonging to it (A 265, 12).

[3] The Karrámís interpreted the Koran in the most literal sense. See Macdonald, *Muslim Theology*, p. 170 foll.

chief was Abú Bakr Isḥáq, and the *Aṣḥáb-i ra'y* (liberal theologians) and Shí'ites led by Qáḍí Ṣá'id. The leaders of those parties drew up a written charge against him, to the following effect:

A certain man has come hither from Mayhana and pretends to be a Ṣúfí. He preaches sermons in the course of which he recites poetry but does not quote the Traditions of the Prophet. He holds sumptuous feasts and music is played by his orders, whilst the young men dance and eat sweetmeats[1] and roasted fowls and all kinds of fruit. He declares that he is an ascetic, but this is neither asceticism nor Ṣúfism. Multitudes have joined him and are being led astray. Unless measures be taken to repair it, the mischief will soon become universal.

The authorities at the court of Ghazna, to whom the document was sent, returned it with the following answer written on the back: "Let the leaders of the Sháfi'ites and Ḥanafites sit in council and inquire into his case and duly inflict upon him whatever penalty the religious law demands." This answer was received on a Thursday. The enemies of Abú Sa'íd rejoiced and immediately held a meeting and determined that on Saturday he and all the Ṣúfís should be gibbeted in the market-place. His friends were anxious and alarmed by rumours of what was impending, but none dared tell him, since he desired to have nothing communicated to him, and in fact always knew by miraculous intuition all that was going on.

When we had performed the afternoon prayers (says Ḥasan-i Mu'addib), the Shaykh called me and asked, "How many are the Súfís?" I replied, "A hundred and twenty—eighty travellers (*musáfir*) and forty residents (*muqím*)." "To-morrow," said he, "what will you give them for dinner?" "Whatever the Shaykh bids," I replied. "You must place before each one," said he, "a lamb's head and provide plenty of crushed sugar to sprinkle on the lamb's brains, and let each one have a pound of khalífatí sweets, and see that there is no lack of aloes-wood for burning and rose-water for spraying over them, and get well-laundered linen robes.

[1] *Lawzína* and *gawzína*. For the former see Dozy. The latter is said to be a sweetmeat made of walnut kernels.

Lay the table in the congregational mosque, in order that those who slander me behind my back may behold with their own eyes the viands that God sends from the unseen world to his elect." Now, at the moment when the Shaykh gave me these directions, there was not a single loaf in the store-room of the convent, and in the whole city I did not know any one of whom I could venture to beg a piece of silver, because these rumours had shaken the faith of all our friends; nor had I courage to ask the Shaykh how I should procure the things which he required. It was near sunset. I left him and stood in the street of the carpet-beaters, utterly at a loss what to do, until the sun had almost set and the merchants were closing their shops and going home. When the hour of evening prayer arrived and it was now dark, a young man running to his house—for he was late—saw me as I stood there, and cried, "O Ḥasan! what are you doing?" I told him that the Shaykh had given me certain orders, that I had no money, and that I would stay there till morning, if necessary, since I durst not return. Throwing back his sleeve, he bade me put my hand in. I did so and drew forth a handful of gold, with which I returned in high spirits to the convent. On making my purchases, I found that the sum was exactly right—not a dirhem too much or too little. Early next morning I got the linen robes and laid the table in the congregational mosque, as the Shaykh had directed. He came thither with all his disciples, while many spectators occupied the galleries above. Now, when Qáḍí Ṣá'id and Ustád Abú Bakr Karrámí were informed that the Shaykh had prepared a feast for the Ṣúfís in the mosque, Qáḍí Ṣá'id exclaimed, "Let them make merry to-day and eat roast lamb's head, for to-morrow their own heads will be devoured by crows"; and Abú Bakr said, "Let them grease their bellies to-day, for to-morrow they will grease the scaffold." These threats were conveyed to the Ṣúfís and made a painful impression. As soon as they finished the meal and washed their hands, the Shaykh said to me, "Ḥasan! take the Ṣúfís' prayer-rugs to the chancel (*maqṣúra*) after Qáḍí Ṣá'id (who was the official preacher), for to-day we will perform our prayers under his leadership." Accordingly, I carried twenty prayer-rugs into the chancel and laid them in two rows; there was no room for any more. Qáḍí Ṣá'id mounted the pulpit and delivered a hostile address; then he came down and performed the service of prayer.

As soon as he pronounced the final salutation (*salám*), the Shaykh rose and departed, without waiting for the customary devotions (*sunna*). Qáḍí Ṣá'id faced towards him, whereupon the Shaykh looked at him askance. The Qáḍí at once bowed his head. When the Shaykh and his disciples returned to the convent, he said, "Ḥasan! go to the Kirmání market-place. There is a confectioner there who has fine cakes made of white sesame and pistachio kernels. Buy ten maunds' worth. A little further on you will find a man who sells raisins. Buy ten maunds' worth and clean them. Tie up the cakes and raisins in two white cloths (*du izár-i fúṭa-i káfúrí*) and put them on your head and take them to Ustád Abú Bakr Isḥáq and tell him that he must break his fast with them to-night." I followed the Shaykh's instructions in every particular. When I gave his message to Abú Bakr Isḥáq, the colour went out of his face and he sat in amazement, biting his fingers. After a few minutes he bade me be seated and having summoned Bu 'l-Qásimak, his chamberlain, despatched him to Qáḍí Ṣá'id. "Tell him," said he, "that I withdraw from our arrangement, which was that to-morrow we should bring this Shaykh and the Ṣúfís to trial and severely punish them. If he asks why, let him know that last night I resolved to fast. To-day, while riding on my ass to the congregational mosque, I passed through the Kirmání market-place and saw some fine cakes in a confectioner's shop. It occurred to me that on returning from prayers I would send to purchase them and break my fast with them to-night. Further on, I saw some raisins which I thought would be very nice with the cakes, and I resolved to buy some. When I came home, I had forgotten all about the matter and I had not spoken of it to any one. Now Shaykh Abú Sa'íd sends me the same cakes and raisins which I noticed this morning and desired to buy, and bids me break my fast with them! I have no course but to abandon proceedings against a man who is so perfectly acquainted with the thoughts of his fellow-creatures." The chamberlain went to Qáḍí Ṣá'id and returned with the following message: "I was on the point of sending to you in reference to this affair. To-day the Shaykh was present when I conducted public worship. No sooner had I pronounced the salutation than he went off without performing the *sunnat*. I turned towards him, intending to ask how his neglect of devotions on a Friday was characteristic of ascetics and Ṣúfís and to make this the foundation of a bitter attack upon him. He looked askance at me. I almost fainted with fear. He seemed to be a hawk and I a sparrow which he was about to destroy. I struggled to speak but could not utter a word. To-day he has shown to me his power and majesty. I have no quarrel with him. If the Sultan has issued an edict against him you were responsible. You were the principal and I was only a subordinate." When the chamberlain had delivered this message, Abú Bakr Isḥáq turned to me and said: "Go and tell your Shaykh that Abú Bakr Isḥáq Karrámí with 20,000 followers, and Qáḍí Ṣá'id with 30,000, and the Sultan with 100,000 men and 750 war elephants, made ready for battle and tried to subdue him, and that he has defeated all their armies with ten maunds of cake and raisins and has routed right wing, left wing, and centre. He is free to hold his religion, as we are free to hold ours. *Ye have your religion and I have my religion*[1]."

I came back to the Shaykh (said Ḥasan-i Mu'addib) and told him all that had passed. He turned to his disciples and said, "Since yesterday ye have been trembling for fear that the scaffold would be soaked with your blood. Nay, that is the lot of such as Ḥusayn-i Manṣúr Ḥalláj, the most eminent mystic of his time in East and West. Scaffolds drip with the blood of heroes, not of cowards." Then he bade the *qawwál* sing these lines:

> With shield and quiver meet thine enemy!
> Vaunt not thyself but make thy vaunt of Me.
> Let Fate be cool as water, hot as fire,
> Do thou live happy, whichsoe'er it be!

The *qawwál* sang and all the disciples began to shout and fling their gaberdines away.

After that day no one in Níshápúr ventured to speak a word in disparagement of the Ṣúfís[2].

The story may not be entirely fictitious. It shows, at any rate, that Moslems ascribe a miraculous character to telepathic powers, nor does it exaggerate the awe inspired by a holy man who displays them effectively. Most of Abú Sa'íd's recorded miracles are of this kind. That Mohammedan saints have often been thought-readers seems to me beyond question,

[1] Kor. 109, 6.

[2] A 84, 10—91, 17.

whatever doubts one may feel as to a great part of the evidence preserved in their legends. Whether Abú Sa'íd was actually threatened with legal prosecution or not, we can well believe that the orthodox parties were scandalised by his luxurious manner of living and by the unlicensed practices in which he and his disciples indulged. He made no attempt to rebut the charges brought against him, and from numerous anecdotes related by those who held him in veneration it is clear that if the document said to have been sent to Ghazna be genuine, his accusers set down nothing but what was notoriously true. They gained sympathy, if not active support, from many Ṣúfís who perceived the danger of antinomianism and desired above all things to secure the position of Ṣúfism within Islam. Of this party the chief representative in Níshápúr was Abu 'l-Qásim Qushayrí, well known as the author of *al-Risálatu 'l-Qushayriyya fí 'ilmi 'l-taṣawwuf*, which he composed in A.H. 437 = A.D. 1045–6 with the avowed object of demonstrating that the history and traditions of Ṣúfism are bound up with strict observance of the Mohammedan religious law.

The biographer gives an interesting but probably untruthful account of Abú Sa'íd's public and private relations with Qushayrí, who is depicted as having been induced by personal experience of his miraculous intuition to repent of the hostile feelings with which he regarded the new-comer. During the first year of Abú Sa'íd's stay in Níshápúr, his prayer-meetings were attended by seventy disciples of Qushayrí, and finally he himself agreed to accompany them. While Abú Sa'íd was preaching, Qushayrí reflected: "This man is inferior to me in learning and we are equal in devotion: whence did he get this power of reading men's thoughts?" Abú Sa'íd at once paused in his discourse and fixing his eye on Qushayrí reminded him of a certain ritual irregularity of which he had been guilty in private on the preceding day. Qushayrí was dumbfounded. Abú Sa'íd, as soon as he left the pulpit, approached him and they embraced each other[1]. Their harmony, however, was not yet complete, for they

[1] A 94, 3.

differed in the great controversy, which had long been raging, whether audition (*samá'*) was permissible; in other words, "Did the religious law sanction the use of music, singing, and dancing as a means of stimulating ecstasy[1]?" One day Qushayrí, while passing Abú Sa'íd's convent, looked in and saw him taking part with his disciples in an ecstatic dance. He thought to himself that, according to the Law, no one who dances like this is accepted as a witness worthy of credit. Next day he met Abú Sa'íd on his way to a feast. After they had exchanged salutations, Abú Sa'íd said to him, "When have you seen me seated amongst the witnesses?" Qushayrí understood that this was the answer to his unspoken thought[2]. He now dismissed from his mind all unfriendly feelings, and the two became so intimate that not a day passed without one of them visiting the other[3], while on Qushayrí's invitation Abú Sa'íd conducted a service once a week in the former's convent[4].

These anecdotes and others of the same tendency may be viewed, not as records of what happened, but rather as illustrations of the fact that in balancing the rival claims of religious law and mystical truth Qushayrí and Abú Sa'íd were inclined by temperament to take opposite sides. In every case, needless to say, the legalist is worsted by the theosophist, whose inner light is his supreme and infallible authority. The following stories, in which Qushayrí plays his usual rôle, would not have been worth translating unless they had incidentally sketched for us the ways and manners of the dervishes whom Abú Sa'íd ruled over.

One day Shaykh Abú Sa'íd with Abu 'l-Qásim Qushayrí and a large number of Ṣúfí disciples were going through the market-place of Níshápúr. A certain dervish let his eye fall on some boiled turnips set out for sale at the door of a shop and felt a craving for them. The Shaykh knew it by clairvoyance (*firása*). He pulled in

[1] See, for example, my abstract of the contents of the *Kitáb al-Luma'*, 69 foll., and Hujwírí, *Kashf al-Maḥjúb*, 393 foll. It is certain that Qushayrí did not condemn *samá'* outright. He seems to have held the view, which was favoured by many Ṣúfís that *samá'* is bad for novices, but good for adepts. Cf. Richard Hartmann, *Al-Ḳuschairîs Darstellung des Ṣûfîtums*, 134 foll.

[2] A 95, 15. [3] A 97, 10. [4] A 106, 8.

the reins of his horse and said to Ḥasan, "Go to that man's shop and buy all the turnips and beetroot that he has and bring them along." Meanwhile he and Qushayrí and the disciples entered a neighbouring mosque. When Ḥasan returned with the turnips and beetroot, the dinner-call was given and the dervishes began to eat. The Shaykh joined them, but Qushayrí refrained and secretly disapproved, because the mosque was in the middle of the market-place and was open in front. He said to himself, "They are eating in the street!" The Shaykh, as was his custom, took no notice. Two or three days afterwards he and Qushayrí with their disciples were present at a splendid feast. The table was covered with viands of all sorts. Qushayrí wished very much to partake of a certain dish, but he could not reach it and was ashamed to ask for it. He felt extremely annoyed. The Shaykh turned to him and said, "Doctor, when food is offered, you refuse it, and when you want it, it is not offered." Qushayrí silently begged God to forgive him for what he had done[1].

One day Qushayrí unfrocked a dervish and severely censured him and ordered him to leave the city. The reason was that the dervish admired Ismá'ílak-i Daqqáq, one of Qushayrí's disciples, and had requested a certain friend to make a feast and invite the singers (*qawwálán*) and bring Ismá'ílak with him. "Let me enjoy his company this evening (he pleaded) and shout in ecstasy at the sight of his beauty, for I am on fire with love for him." The friend consented and gave a feast which was followed by music and singing (*samá'*). On hearing of this, Qushayrí stripped the dervish of his gaberdine and banished him from Níshápúr. When the news came to the convent of Shaykh Abú Sa'íd, the dervishes were indignant, but they said nothing about it to the Shaykh, knowing that he was acquainted by clairvoyance with all that passed. The Shaykh called Ḥasan-i Mu'addib and bade him make ready a fine banquet and invite the reverend Doctor (Qushayrí) and all the Ṣúfís in the town. "You must get plenty of roast lamb," he said, "and sweetmeats, and light a great many candles." At nightfall, when the company assembled, the Shaykh and the Doctor took their seats together on a couch, and the Ṣúfís sat in front of it in three rows, a hundred men in each row. Khwája Abú Ṭáhir, the Shaykh's eldest son, who was exceedingly handsome, presided

[1] A 102, 10.

over the table. As soon as the time came for dessert, Ḥasan placed a large bowl of *lawzína* before the Shaykh and the Doctor. After they had helped themselves, the Shaykh said to Abú Ṭáhir, "Take this bowl and go to yonder dervish, Bú 'Alí Turshízí, and put half of this *lawzína* in his mouth and eat the other half yourself." Abú Ṭáhir went to the dervish, and kneeling respectfully before him, took a portion of the sweetmeat, and after swallowing a mouthful put the other half in the dervish's mouth. The dervish raised a loud cry and rent his garment and ran forth from the convent, shouting "Labbayk!" The Shaykh said, "Abú Ṭáhir! I charge you to wait upon that dervish. Take his staff and ewer and follow him and be assiduous in serving him until he reaches the Ka'ba." When the dervish saw Abú Ṭáhir coming after him, he stopped and asked him where he was going. Abú Ṭáhir said, "My father has sent me to wait upon you," and told him the whole story. Bú 'Alí returned to the Shaykh and exclaimed, "For God's sake, bid Abú Ṭáhir leave me!" The Shaykh did so, whereupon the dervish bowed and departed. Turning to Qushayrí, the Shaykh said, "What need is there to censure and unfrock and disgrace a dervish whom half a mouthful of *lawzína* can drive from the city and cast away into the Ḥijáz? For four years he has been devoted to my Abú Ṭáhir, and except on your account I should never have divulged his secret." Qushayrí rose and prayed God to forgive him and said, "I have done wrong. Every day I must learn from you a new lesson in Ṣúfism." All the Ṣúfís rejoiced and there were manifestations of ecstasy[1].

Abú Sa'íd's invariable success in conciliating his opponents is perhaps the greatest miracle that his biographers record, but their belief in it will hardly be shared by us. His mode of life in Níshápúr, as depicted by his own friends and followers, must have shocked Ṣúfís of the old school who had been taught to model themselves upon the saintly heroes of Moslem asceticism. What were they to think of a man whose visitors found him lolling on cushions, like a lord, and having his feet massaged by one of his dervishes[2]? A man who prayed every night that God would give his disciples something nice to eat[3], and spent all the money he received on costly entertainments?

[1] A 103, 14. [2] A 109, 17; 179, 12. [3] A 294, 11.

Could their objections be removed by exhibitions of thought-reading or by appeals to the divine right of the saint—

> Thou art thus because thy lot is thus and thus,
> I am so because my lot is so and so[1]—

or by exhortations to regard the inward nature and disposition rather than the outward act[2]? From the following anecdote it appears that such arguments did not always suffice.

When Abú Sa'íd was at Níshápúr, a merchant brought him a present of a large bundle of aloes-wood and a thousand Níshápúrí dínárs. The Shaykh called Ḥasan-i Mu'addib and bade him prepare a feast; and in accordance with his custom he handed over the thousand dínárs to him for that purpose. Then he ordered that an oven should be placed in the hall and that the whole bundle of aloes-wood should be put in it and burned, saying, "I do this that my neighbours may enjoy its perfume with me." He also ordered a great number of candles to be lighted, though it was still day. Now, there was at that time in Níshápúr a very powerful inspector of police, who held rationalistic views[3] and detested the Ṣúfís. This man came into the monastery and said to the Shaykh, "What are you doing? What an unheard-of extravagance, to light candles in the daytime and burn a whole bundle of aloes-wood at once! It is against the law[4]." The Shaykh replied, "I did not know that it is against the law. Go and blow out these candles." The inspector went and puffed at them, but the flame flared over his face and hair and dress, and most of his body was scorched. "Did not you know," said the Shaykh, "that

> Whoever tries to blow a candle out
> That God hath lighted, his moustache gets burnt?"

The inspector fell at the Shaykh's feet and became a convert[5].

While the relations which Abú Sa'íd established with the jurists and theologians of Níshápúr cannot have been friendly, it is likely enough that he convinced his adversaries of the wisdom or necessity of leaving him alone. In order to under-

[1] A 117, 16. [2] A 110, 3. [3] صاحب رأى.

[4] Extravagance (*isráf*) is forbidden in the Koran, 6, 142; 7, 29, etc.

[5] A 134, 9. In another version of this story (A 157, 11) the offender is smitten with paralysis.

stand their attitude, we must remember the divinity that hedges the Oriental saint not merely in the eyes of mystics but amongst all classes of society. He wields an illimitable and mysterious power derived from Allah, whose chosen instrument he is. As his favour confers blessing, so his displeasure is fraught with calamity. Countless tales are told of vengeance inflicted on those who have annoyed or insulted him, or shown any want of respect in his presence. Even if his enemies are willing to run the risk, they must still reckon with the widely spread feeling that it is impious to criticise the actions of holy men, which are inspired and guided by Allah Himself.

Naturally, Abú Sa'íd required large sums of money for maintaining the convent with, perhaps, two or three hundred disciples, on such a liberal scale of living as he kept up. A certain amount was contributed by novices who, on their conversion, put into the common stock all the worldly goods they possessed, but the chief part of the revenues came in the shape of gifts from lay brethren or wealthy patrons or persons who desired the Shaykh to exert his spiritual influence on their behalf. No doubt, much food and money was offered and accepted; much also was collected by Ḥasan-i Mu'addib, who seems to have been an expert in this business. When voluntary contributions failed, the Shaykh's credit with the tradesmen of Níshápúr enabled him to supply the needs of his flock. Here are some anecdotes which describe how he triumphed over financial difficulties.

The 'Amíd of Khurásán relates as follows:

The cause of my devotion to Shaykh Abú Sa'íd and his disciples was this. When I first came to Níshápúr, my name was Ḥájib Muḥammad and I had no servant to attend upon me. Every morning I used to pass the gate of the Shaykh's convent and look in, and whenever I saw the Shaykh, that day brought me a blessing, so that I soon began to regard the sight of him as a happy omen. One night I thought that on the morrow I would go and pay my respects to him and take him a present. I took a thousand silver dirhems of the money which had been recently coined—thirty dirhems to the dínár—and wrapped them in a piece of paper, intending to visit the Shaykh next day and lay them before him. I was alone in the house at the time when I formed this plan, nor did I speak of it to any one. Afterwards it occurred to me that a thousand dirhems are a great sum, and five hundred will be ample; so I divided the money into two equal parts, which I placed in two packets. Next morning, after prayers, I went to visit the Shaykh, taking one packet with me and leaving the other behind my pillow. As soon as we had exchanged greetings, I gave the five hundred dirhems to Ḥasan-i Mu'addib, who with the utmost courtesy approached the Shaykh and whispered in his ear—"Ḥájib Muḥammad has brought some pieces of money (*shikasta-í*)." The Shaykh said, "God bless him! but he has not brought the full amount: he has left half of it behind his pillow. Ḥasan owes a thousand dirhems. Let him give Ḥasan the whole sum in order that Ḥasan may satisfy his creditors and be freed from anxiety." On hearing these words, I was dumbfounded and immediately sent a servant to bring the remainder of the money for Ḥasan. Then I said to the Shaykh, "Accept me." He took my hand and said, "It is finished. Go in peace[1]."

During Shaykh Abú Sa'íd's stay in Níshápúr Ḥasan-i Mu'addib, his steward, had contracted many debts in order to provide the dervishes with food. For a long time he received no gift of money and his creditors were dunning him. One day they came in a body to the convent gate. The Shaykh told Ḥasan to let them in. On being admitted, they bowed respectfully to the Shaykh and sat down. Meanwhile a boy passed the gate, crying "Sweet cakes (*náṭif*)!" "Go and fetch him," said the Shaykh. When he was brought in, the Shaykh bade Ḥasan seize the cakes and serve them out to the Ṣúfís. The boy demanded his money, but the Shaykh only said, "It will come." After waiting an hour, the boy said again, "I want my money" and got the same reply. At the end of another hour, having been put off for the third time, he sobbed, "My master will beat me," and burst into tears. Just then some one entered the convent and placed a purse of gold before the Shaykh, saying, "So-and-so has sent it and begs that you will pray for him." The Shaykh ordered Ḥasan to pay the creditors and the cake-boy. It was exactly the sum required, neither more nor less. The Shaykh said, "It came in consequence of the tears of this lad[2]."

[1] A 113, 1. [2] A 123, 19.

There was in Níshápúr a rich broker, Bú 'Amr by name, who was such an enthusiastic admirer (*muḥibbi*) of Shaykh Abú Sa'íd that he entreated Ḥasan-i Mu'addib to apply to him for anything that the Shaykh might want, and not to be afraid of asking too much. One day (said Ḥasan) the Shaykh had already sent me to him seven times with divers requisitions which he satisfied in full. At sunset the Shaykh told me to go to him once more and procure some rosewater, aloes-wood, and camphor. I felt ashamed to return to him; however, I went. He was closing his shop. When he saw me, he cried, "Ḥasan! what is it? You come late." I expressed to him the shame which I felt for having called upon him so frequently in one day and I made him acquainted with the Shaykh's instructions. He opened the shop-door and gave me all that I needed; then he said, "Since you are ashamed to apply to me for these trifles, to-morrow I will give you a thousand dínárs on the security of the caravanseray and the bath-house, in order that you may use that sum for ordinary expenses and come to me for matters of greater importance." I rejoiced, thinking that now I was quit of this ignoble begging. When I brought the rose-water, aloes-wood, and camphor to the Shaykh, he regarded me with disapproval and said, "Ḥasan! go and purge thy heart of all desire for worldly vanities, that I may let thee associate with the Ṣúfís." I went to the convent gate and stood with bare head and feet and repented and asked God to forgive me and wept bitterly and rubbed my face on the ground; but the Shaykh did not speak to me that night. Next day when he preached in the hall, he paid no attention to Bú 'Amr, although he was accustomed to look at him every day in the course of his sermon. As soon as he had finished, Bú 'Amr came to me and said, "Ḥasan! what ails the Shaykh? He has not looked at me to-day." I said that I did not know, and then I told him what had passed between the Shaykh and me. Bú 'Amr went up to the Shaykh's chair and kissed it, saying, "O prince of the age, my life depends on thy look. To-day thou hast not looked at me. Tell me what I have done, that I may ask God's forgiveness and beseech thee to pardon my offence." The Shaykh said, "Will you fetch me down from the highest heaven to earth and demand a pledge from me in return for a thousand dínárs? If you wish me to be pleased with you, give me the money now, and you will see how little it weighs in the scales of my lofty spirit!" Bú 'Amr immediately went home and brought back two purses, each containing five hundred Níshápúrí dínárs. The Shaykh handed them to me and said, "Buy oxen and sheep. Make a hotchpotch (*harísa*) of the beef and a *zíra-bá* of the mutton, seasoned with saffron and otto of roses. Get plenty of *lawzína* and rose-water and aloes-wood, and light a thousand candles in the daytime. Lay the tables at Púshangán (a beautiful village, which is a pleasure resort of the people of Níshápúr), and proclaim in the city that all are welcome who wish to eat food that entails neither obligation in this world nor calling to account in the next." More than two thousand men assembled at Púshangán. The Shaykh came with his disciples and entertained high and low and with his own blessed hand sprinkled rose-water over his guests while they partook of the viands.

Abú Sa'íd's methods of raising money are further illustrated by the story in which it is recorded that, while preaching in public, he held up a sash and declared that he must have three hundred dínárs in exchange for it, which sum was at once offered by an old woman in the congregation[1]. On another occasion, being in debt to the amount of five hundred dínárs, he sent a message to a certain Abu 'l-Faḍl Furátí that he was about to visit him. Abu 'l-Faḍl entertained him sumptuously for three days, and on the fourth day presented him with five hundred dínárs, adding a hundred for travelling expenses and a hundred more as a gift. The Shaykh said, "I pray that God may take from thee the riches of this world." "Nay," cried Abu 'l-Faḍl, "for had I lacked riches, the blessed feet of the Shaykh would never have come here, and I should never have waited upon him and gained from him spiritual power and peace." Abú Sa'íd then said, "O God! do not let him be a prey to worldliness: make it a means of his spiritual advancement, not a plague!" In consequence of this prayer Abu 'l-Faḍl and his family prospered greatly and reached high positions in church and state[2]. Apparently, Abú Sa'íd did not scruple to employ threats when the prospective donor disappointed him. And his threats were not to be despised! For example, there was the Amír Mas'úd who, after once paying the Shaykh's debts, obstinately

[1] A 280, 3. [2] A 299, 16.

refused to comply with a second demand; whereupon Abú Sa'íd caused the following verse to be put into his hands by Ḥasan-i Mu'addib:

> Perform what thou hast promised, else thy might
> And valour will not save thy life from me!

The Amír flew into a rage and drove Ḥasan from his presence. On being told of this Abú Sa'íd uttered no word. That same night Mas'úd, as is the custom of Oriental princes, slipped out from his tent in disguise to make a round of the camp and hear what the soldiers were saying. The royal tent was guarded by a number of huge Ghúrí dogs, kept in chains by day but allowed to roam at night, of such ferocity that they would tear to pieces any stranger who approached. They did not recognise their master, and before any one could answer his cries for help he was a mangled corpse[1].

Stories of this type, showing the saint as a minister of divine wrath and vengeance, must have influenced many superstitious minds. The average Moslem's fatalism and belief in clairvoyance lead him to justify acts which to us seem desperately immoral. Abú Sa'íd is said to have corresponded with his famous contemporary, Ibn Síná (Avicenna)[2]. I cannot regard as historical the account of their meeting in the monastery at Níshápúr, or the report that after they had conversed with each other for three days and nights the philosopher said to his pupils, "All that I know he sees," while the mystic declared, "All that I see he knows[3]." Even less probable is the statement that Avicenna's mystical writings were the result of a miracle wrought by Abú Sa'íd, which first opened his eyes to the reality of saintship and Ṣúfism[4].

Among the eminent Persian mystics of this epoch none was so nearly akin to Abú Sa'íd in temperament and character as Abu 'l-Ḥasan of Kharaqán[5]. Before leaving Níshápúr and

[1] A 236, 21.

[2] The Arabic text of a letter written by Avicenna in reply to one from Abú Sa'íd is given in H 65, 3.

[3] A 251, 16.

[4] A 252, 12.

[5] See his biography in 'Aṭṭár's *Tadhkiratu 'l-Awliyá*, II. 201–255. Some of his sayings are translated in my *Mystics of Islam*, p. 133 foll.

finally settling at Mayhana, Abú Sa'íd paid him a visit, which is described with great particularity[1]. A complete version would be tedious, but I have translated the most interesting passages in full. When Abú Ṭáhir, the eldest son of Abú Sa'íd, announced his intention of making the pilgrimage to Mecca, his father with a numerous following of Ṣúfís and disciples resolved to accompany him. As soon as the party left Níshápúr behind them, Abú Sa'íd exclaimed, "Were it not for my coming, the holy man could not support this sorrow." His companions wondered whom he meant. Now, Aḥmad the son of Abu 'l-Ḥasan Kharaqání had just been arrested and put to death on his wedding-eve. Abu 'l-Ḥasan did not know until next morning, when, hearing the call to prayer, he came forth from his cell and trod upon the head of his son, which the executioners had flung away. On arriving at Kharaqán, Abú Sa'íd went into the convent and entered the private chapel where Abu 'l-Ḥasan usually sat. Abu 'l-Ḥasan rose and walked halfway down the chapel to meet him, and they embraced each other. Abu 'l-Ḥasan took Abú Sa'íd's hand and led him to his own chair, but he declined to occupy it; and since Abu 'l-Ḥasan was equally averse to take the place of honour, both seated themselves in the middle of the chapel. While they sat there weeping, Abu 'l-Ḥasan begged Abú Sa'íd to give him a word of counsel, but Abú Sa'íd said, "It is for thee to speak." Then he bade the Koran-readers who were with him read the Koran aloud, and during their chant the Ṣúfís wept and wailed. Abu 'l-Ḥasan threw his gaberdine (*khirqa*) to the readers. After that, the bier was brought out, and they prayed over the dead youth and buried him with manifestations of ecstasy. When the Ṣúfís had retired to their cells, a dispute arose between them and the readers for the possession of Abu 'l-Ḥasan's *khirqa*, which the Ṣúfís claimed in order that they might tear it to pieces. Abu 'l-Ḥasan sent a message by his servant to say that the readers should keep the *khirqa*, and he gave the Ṣúfís another *khirqa*, to be torn to pieces and distributed among them. A separate chamber was prepared for Abú Sa'íd, who lodged with Abu

[1] A 175–191.

'l-Ḥasan three days and nights. In spite of his host's entreaties he refused to speak, saying, "I have been brought hither to listen." Then Abu 'l-Ḥasan said, "I implored God that He would send to me one of His friends, with whom I might speak of these mysteries, for I am old and feeble and could not come to thee. He will not let thee go to Mecca. Thou art too holy to be conducted to Mecca. He will bring the Ka'ba to thee, that it may circumambulate thee." Every morning Abu 'l-Ḥasan came to the door of Abú Sa'íd's room and asked—addressing the mother of Khwája Muẓaffar, whom Abú Sa'íd had brought with him on this journey—"How art thou, O *faqíra*? Be sage and vigilant, for thou consortest with God. Here nothing of human nature remains, nothing of the flesh (*nafs*) remains. Here all is God, all is God." And in the daytime when Abú Sa'íd was alone, Abu 'l-Ḥasan used to come to the door and draw back the curtain and beg leave to come in and beseech Abú Sa'íd not to rise from his couch; and he would kneel beside him and put his head close to him, and they would converse in low tones and weep together; and Abu 'l-Ḥasan would slip his hand underneath Abu Sa'íd's garment and lay it upon his breast and cry, "I am laying my hand upon the Everlasting Light...." Abu 'l-Ḥasan said, "O Shaykh, every night I see the Ka'ba circumambulating thy head: what need for thee to go to the Ka'ba? Turn back, for thou wast brought hither for my sake. Now thou hast performed the pilgrimage." Abú Sa'íd said, "I will go and visit Bisṭám and return here." "Thou wishest to perform the '*umra*," said Abu 'l-Ḥasan, "after having performed the *ḥajj*." Then Abú Sa'íd set out for Bisṭám, where he visited the shrine of Báyazíd-i Bisṭámí. From Bisṭám the pilgrims journeyed westward to Dámghán, and thence to Rayy. Here Abú Sa'íd made a halt and declared that he would go no farther in the direction of Mecca. Bidding farewell to those who still persisted in their intention of performing the pilgrimage, the rest of the party, including Abú Sa'íd and his son Abú Ṭáhir, turned their faces towards Kharaqán and Níshápúr.

The last years of Abú Sa'íd's life were spent in retirement

at Mayhana. We are told that his final departure from Níshápúr was deeply regretted by the inhabitants, and that the chief men of the city urged him in vain to alter his decision[1]. With advancing years he may have felt that the duties which devolved upon him as a director of souls (not to speak of bodies) were too heavy a burden: in his old age he could not rise without being helped by two disciples who took hold of his arms and lifted him from his seat[2]. He left no money in the convent, saying that God would send whatever was necessary for its upkeep. According to the biographer, this prediction was fulfilled, and although the convent never possessed a sure source of income (*ma'lúm*), it attracted a larger number of dervishes and received more spiritual and material blessings than any other religious house in Níshápúr, until it was destroyed by the invading Ghuzz[3].

Abú Sa'íd lived 1000 months (83 years + 4 months). He died at Mayhana on the 4th of Sha'bán, A.H. 440 = 12th of January, A.D. 1049, and was buried in the mosque opposite his house[4]. His tomb bore the following lines in Arabic, which he himself had chosen for an epitaph:

> I beg, nay, charge thee: Write on my gravestone,
> "This was love's bondsman," that when I am gone,
> Some wretch well-versed in passion's ways may sigh
> And give me greeting, as he passes by[5].

Apart from several allusions to his corpulence, the only description of Abú Sa'íd's personal appearance that his biographers have preserved is the following, which depicts him as he was seen by an old man whom he saved from dying of thirst in the desert:

tall, stout, with a white skin and wide eyes and a long beard falling to the navel; clad in a patched frock (*muraqqa'*); in his hands a staff and a ewer; a prayer-rug thrown over his shoulder, also a razor and toothpick; a Ṣúfí cap on his head, and on his feet shoes of cotton soled with linen-rags (*jumjum*); light was shining from his face[6].

[1] A 193, 18. [2] A 110, 16. [3] A 195, 3. [4] A 67, 1.
[5] H 78, 19. A 445, 12, [6] A 80, 14.

This sketch of his life has shown us the saint and the abbot in one. Before coming into closer touch with the former character, I should like to refer to a few passages of specially monastic interest.

The first gives ten rules which Abú Sa'íd caused to be put in writing, in order that they might be observed punctiliously by the inmates of his convent. In the original, after every rule there follow some words of the Koran on which it is based.

I. Let them keep their garments clean and themselves always pure.

II. Let them not sit[1] in the mosque or in any holy place for the sake of gossiping.

III. In the first instance[2] let them perform their prayers in common.

IV. Let them pray much at night.

V. At dawn let them ask forgiveness of God and call unto Him.

VI. In the morning let them read as much of the Koran as they can, and let them not talk until the sun has risen.

VII. Between evening prayers and bedtime prayers let them occupy themselves with repeating some litany (*wirdí ú dhikrí*).

VIII. Let them welcome the poor and needy and all who join their company, and let them bear patiently the trouble of (waiting upon) them.

IX. Let them not eat anything save in participation with one another.

X. Let them not absent themselves without receiving permission from one another.

Furthermore, let them spend their hours of leisure in one of three things: either in the study of theology or in some devotional exercise (*wirdí*) or in bringing comfort to some one. Whosoever loves this community and helps them as much as he can is a sharer in their merit and future recompense[3].

[1] Reading ننشينند.

[2] باوّل وقت, *i.e.*, I suppose, at the commencement of their monastic life.

[3] A 416, 5.

Pír Abú Ṣáliḥ Dandání, a disciple of Shaykh Abú Sa'íd, used continually to stand beside him with a pair of nail-scissors in his hand. Whenever the Shaykh looked at his woollen gaberdine and saw the nap (*purz*) on it, he would pull the nap with his fingers, and then Abú Ṣáliḥ would at once remove it with the nail-scissors, for the Shaykh was so absorbed in contemplation of God that he did not wish to be disturbed by perceiving the state of his clothes. Abú Ṣáliḥ was the Shaykh's barber and used regularly to trim his moustache. A certain dervish desired to be taught the proper way of doing this. Abú Ṣáliḥ smiled and said, "It is no such easy matter. A man needs seventy masters of the craft to instruct him how the moustache of a dervish ought to be trimmed." This Abú Ṣáliḥ related that the Shaykh, towards the end of his life, had only one tooth left. "Every night, after supper, I used to give him a toothpick, with which he cleansed his mouth; and when he washed his hands, he would pour water on the toothpick and lay it down. One evening I thought to myself, 'He has no teeth and does not require a toothpick: why should he take it from me every night?' The Shaykh raised his head and looked at me and said, 'Because I wish to observe the Sunna and because I hope to win divine mercy. The Prophet has said, *May God have mercy upon those of my people who use the toothpick in their ablutions and at their meals*!' I was overcome with shame and began to weep[1]."

Pír Ḥubbí was the Shaykh's tailor. One day he came in with a garment belonging to the Shaykh which he had mended. At that moment the Shaykh was taking his noonday siesta and reclining on a couch, while Khwája 'Abdu 'l-Karím, his valet, sat beside his pillow and fanned him. Khwája 'Abdu 'l-Karím exclaimed, "What are you doing here?" Pír Ḥubbí retorted, "Wherever there is room for you, there is room for me." The valet laid down the fan and struck him again and again. After seven blows the Shaykh said, "That is enough." Pír Ḥubbí went off and complained to Khwája Najjár, who said to the Shaykh, when he came out for afternoon prayers, "The young men lift their hands against the elders: what says the Shaykh?" The Shaykh replied, "Khwája 'Abdu 'l-Karím's hand is my hand," and nothing more was said about it[2].

[1] A 146, 4.
[2] A 271, 5.

II.

In describing Abú Sa'íd's mystical doctrines and their relation to the historical development of Ṣúfism, European scholars have hitherto relied almost exclusively on the quatrains which he is said to have composed and of which more than six hundred have been published[1]. As I have shown above (p. 4, note 3), it is doubtful whether Abú Sa'íd is the author of any of these poems, and we may be sure that in the main they are not his work and were never even quoted by him. To repeat what has been already said, they form a miscellaneous anthology drawn from a great number of poets who flourished at different periods, and consequently they reflect the typical ideas of Persian mysticism as a whole. Abú Sa'íd helped to bring its peculiar diction and symbolism into vogue, by quoting Ṣúfí poetry in his sermons and allowing it to be chanted in the *samá'*, but we may hesitate to accept the view that he invented this style (which occurs, full-blown, in the odes of his contemporary, Bábá Kúhí of Shíráz) or was the first to embody it in quatrains.

The mysticism which his sayings and sermons unfold has neither the precision of a treatise nor the coherence of a system. It is experimental, not doctrinal or philosophical. It does not concern itself with abstract speculations, but sets forth in simple and untechnical language such principles and maxims as bear directly on the religious life and are the fruit of dearly-bought experience. As we read, we seem to hear the voice of the teacher addressing his disciples and expounding for their benefit the truths that had been revealed to him. Abú Sa'íd borrows much from his predecessors, sometimes mentioning them by name, but often appropriating

[1] 92 by H. Ethé in *Sitzungsberichte der königl. bayer. Akademie der Wissenschaften, philosophisch-philologische Classe* (1875), pp. 145–168 and (1878), pp. 38–70; 400 by Mawlaví 'Abdu 'l-Walí in the *Journal of the Asiatic Society of Bengal*, vol. v, No. 11 (December, 1909) and vol. VII, No. 10 (November, 1911); and 112 by H. D. Graves Law in the same journal (according to an offprint given to me by the author in 1913, which refers to 'Abdu 'l-Walí's work as "comparatively recent"; but I cannot find the article in the volumes issued in 1912 and 1913. It is entitled "Some new quatrains of Abû Sa'îd ibn Abi 'l-Khair").

their wisdom without a word of acknowledgement[1]. Amongst Moslems, this kind of plagiarism is considered respectable, even when the culprit is not a saint.

The sayings of Abú Sa'íd include several definitions of Ṣúfism, which it will be convenient to translate before going further.

1. To lay aside what thou hast in thy head, to give what thou hast in thy hand, and not to recoil from whatsoever befalls thee[2].

2. Ṣúfism is two things: to look in one direction and to live in one way[3].

3. Ṣúfism is a name attached to its object; when it reaches its ultimate perfection, it is God (*i.e.* the end of Ṣúfism is that, for the Ṣúfí, nothing should exist except God)[4].

4. It is glory in wretchedness and riches in poverty and lordship in servitude and satiety in hunger and clothedness in nakedness and freedom in slavery and life in death and sweetness in bitterness[5].

5. The Ṣúfí is he who is pleased with all that God does, in order that God may be pleased with all that he does[6].

6. Ṣúfism is patience under God's commanding and forbidding, and acquiescence and resignation in the events determined by divine providence[7].

7. Ṣúfism is the will of the Creator concerning His creatures when no creature exists[8].

8. To be a Ṣúfí is to cease from taking trouble (*takalluf*); and there is no greater trouble for thee than thine own self (*tu'í-yi tu*), for when thou art occupied with thyself, thou remainest away from God[9].

9. He said, "Even this Ṣúfism is polytheism (*shirk*)." "Why,

[1] One of his sayings, which is given both in Arabic and Persian and is ascribed to "a certain sage," reveals the source (hitherto, I believe, unidentified) of Sir William Jones's lines *To an Infant newly born*:

"On parent's knees, a naked new-born child,
Weeping thou sat'st while all around thee smiled;
So live, that sinking in thy long last sleep,
Calm thou mayst smile, while all around thee weep."

The original is in prose and runs as follows: "Thou wast born weeping, whilst thy folk smiled. Endeavour to die smiling, whilst thy folk weep" (A 317, 14).

[2] A 373, 7. [3] A 373, 16. [4] A 375, 11. [5] A 380, 2.
[6] A 381, 5. [7] A 383, 1. [8] A 386, 4. [9] A 389, 16.

O Shaykh?" they asked. He answered, "Because Ṣúfism consists in guarding the soul from what is other than God; and there is nothing other than God[1].

The quietism and pantheistic self-abandonment, on which these definitions lay so much stress, forms only the negative side of Abú Sa'íd's mystical teaching. His doctrine of *faná*, the passing-away from self, is supplemented by an equally characteristic positive element, of which I shall have more to say presently. Both aspects are indicated in the following maxim: "A man ought to be occupied with two things:—he ought to put away all that keeps him apart from God, and bring comfort to dervishes[2]."

Innumerable are the ways to God[3], yet the Way is but a single step: "take one step out of thyself, that thou mayst arrive at God[4]." To pass away from self (*faná*) is to realise that self does not exist, and that nothing exists except God (*tawḥíd*). The Tradition, "He who knows himself knows his Lord," signifies that he who knows himself as not-being (*'adam*) knows God as Real Being (*wujúd*)[5]. This knowledge cannot be obtained through the intellect, since the Eternal and Uncreated is inaccessible to that which is created[6]; it cannot be learned, but is given by divine illumination. The organ which receives it is the "heart" (*qalb* or *dil*), a spiritual faculty, not the heart of flesh and blood. In a remarkable passage Abú Sa'íd refers to a divine principle, which he calls *sirr Allah*, *i.e.* the conscience or consciousness of God, and describes it as something which God communicates to the "heart."

Answering the question, "What is sincerity (*ikhláṣ*)?" he said:

The Prophet has said that *ikhláṣ* is a divine *sirr* in man's heart and soul, which *sirr* is the object of His pure contemplation and is replenished by God's pure contemplation thereof. Whosoever declares God to be One, his belief in the divine Unity depends on that *sirr*.

[1] A 319, 8. [2] A 380, 6. [3] A 380, 9. [4] A 74, 13.
[5] A 402, 3. [6] A 397, 8.

Being asked to define it, he continued as follows:

That *sirr* is a substance of God's grace (*laṭífa*)—for He is gracious (*laṭíf*) unto His servants (Koran, 42, 18)—and it is produced by the bounty and mercy of God, not by the acquisition and action of man. At first, He produces a need and longing and sorrow in man's heart; then He contemplates that need and sorrow, and in His bounty and mercy deposits in that heart a spiritual substance (*laṭífa*) which is hidden from the knowledge of angel and prophet. That substance is called *sirr Allah*, and that is *ikhláṣ*[1]....That pure *sirr* is the Beloved of Unitarians. It is immortal and does not become naught, since it subsists in God's contemplation of it. It belongs to the Creator: the creatures have no part therein, and in the body it is a loan. Whoever possesses it is "living" (*ḥayy*), and whoever lacks it is "animal" (*ḥayawán*). There is a great difference between the "living" and the "animal"[2].

Students of medieval Christian mysticism will find many analogies to this *sirr Allah*, *e.g.* the "synteresis" of Gerson and Eckhart's "spark" or "ground of the soul."

I will now translate some of Abú Sa'íd's discourses and sayings on the Way to God through self-negation.

He was asked, "When shall a man be freed from his wants?"

"When God shall free him," he replied; "this is not effected by a man's exertion, but by the grace and help of God. First of all, He brings forth in him the desire to attain this goal. Then He opens to him the gate of repentance (*tawba*). Then He throws him into self-mortification (*mujáhada*), so that he continues to strive and, for a while, to pride himself upon his efforts, thinking that he is advancing or achieving something; but afterwards he falls into despair and feels no joy. Then he knows that his work is not pure, but tainted, he repents of the acts of devotion which he had thought to be his own, and perceives that they were done by God's grace and help, and that he was guilty of polytheism (*shirk*) in attributing them to his own exertion. When this becomes manifest, a feeling of joy enters his heart. Then God opens to him the gate of certainty (*yaqín*), so that for a time he takes anything from any one and accepts contumely and endures abasement, and knows for certain

[1] A 383, 15. [2] A 385, 3.

by Whom it is brought to pass, and doubt concerning this is removed from his heart. Then God opens to him the gate of love (*maḥabba*), and here too egoism shows itself for a time and he is exposed to blame (*malâma*), which means that in his love of God he meets fearlessly whatever may befall him and recks not of reproach; but still he thinks 'I love' and finds no rest until he perceives that it is God who loves him and keeps him in the state of loving, and that this is the result of divine love and grace, not of his own endeavour. Then God opens to him the gate of unity (*tawḥíd*) and causes him to know that all action depends on God Almighty. Hereupon he perceives that all is He, and all is by Him, and all is His; that He has laid this self-conceit upon His creatures in order to prove them, and that He in His omnipotence ordains that they shall hold this false belief, because omnipotence is His attribute, so that when they regard His attributes they shall know that He is the Lord. What formerly was hearsay now becomes known to him intuitively as he contemplates the works of God. Then he entirely recognises that he has not the right to say 'I' or 'mine.' At this stage he beholds his helplessness; desires fall away from him and he becomes free and calm. He wishes that which God wishes: his own wishes are gone, he is emancipated from his wants, and has gained peace and joy in both worlds....First, action is necessary, then knowledge, in order that thou mayst know that thou knowest naught and art no one. This is not easy to know. It is a thing that cannot be rightly learned by instruction, nor sewn on with needle nor tied on with thread. It is the gift of God[1]."

The heart's vision is what matters, not the tongue's speech. Thou wilt never escape from thy self (*nafs*) until thou slay it. To say "There is no god but Allah" is not enough. Most of those who make the verbal profession of faith are polytheists at heart, and polytheism is the one unpardonable sin. Thy whole body is full of doubt and polytheism. Thou must cast them out in order to be at peace. Until thou deny thy self thou wilt never believe in God. Thy self, which is keeping thee far from God and saying, "So-and-so has treated thee ill," "such and such a one has done well by thee," points the way to creatureliness; and all this is polytheism. Nothing depends on the creatures, all depends on the Creator. This thou must know and say, and having said it thou must stand

[1] A 376, 11.

firm. To stand firm (*istiqáma*) means that when thou hast said "One," thou must never again say "Two." Creator *and* creature are "Two."...Do not double like a fox, that ye may suddenly start up in some other place: that is not right faith. Say "Allah!" and stand firm there. Standing firm is this, that when thou hast said "God" thou shouldst no more speak or think of created things, so that it is just as though they were not....Love that One who does not cease to be when thou ceasest, in order that thou mayst be such a being that thou never wilt cease to be[1]!

So long as any one regards his purity and devotion, he says "Thou and I," but when he considers exclusively the bounty and mercy of God, he says "Thou! Thou!" and then his worship[2] becomes a reality[3].

He was asked, "What is evil and what is the worst evil?" He replied, "Evil is 'thou'; and the worst evil is 'thou,' when thou knowest it not[4]."

Abú Sa'íd's belief that he had escaped from the prison of individuality was constantly asserting itself. Once he attended a party of mourners (*ta'ziya*), where the visitors, as they arrived, were announced by a servant (*mu'arrif*) who with a loud voice enumerated their titles of honour (*alqáb*). When Abú Sa'íd appeared, the *mu'arrif* inquired how he should announce him. "Go," said he, "and tell them to make way for Nobody, the son of Nobody[5]." In speaking of himself, he never used the pronouns "I" or "we," but invariably referred to himself as "they" (*íshán*). The author of the *Asráru 'l-tawḥíd* apologises for having restored the customary form of speech, pointing out that if he had retained "they" in such cases, the meaning of the text would have been confused and unintelligible to most[6].

While the attainment of selflessness is independent of

[1] A 371, 5 (abridged in translation).

[2] *Bandagí* (Arabic '*ubúdiyya*) is properly man's relation as a slave to his Lord. Cf. R. Hartmann, *Al-Kuschairîs Darstellung des Ṣûfîtums*, p. 5 foll.

[3] A 410, 16.

[4] A 403, 3.

[5] A 348, 3.

[6] A 12, 7. Probably for the same reason, Abú Sa'íd discarded the imperative, using the impersonal form instead (A 68, 12). He always said, "It is necessary to do so-and-so" (*chunín báyad kard*), not "Do so-and-so" (*chunín bikun*).

human initiative, the mystic participates, to some extent, in the process by which it is attained. A power not his own draws him on towards the goal, but this divine attraction (*kashish*) demands, on his part, an inward striving (*kúshish*), without which there can be no vision (*bínish*)[1]. Like many Ṣúfís, Abú Sa'íd admits freewill in practice but denies it in theory. As a spiritual director, he could not teach what, as a pantheist, he was bound to believe—that the only real agent is God. Speaking from the standpoint of the religious law, he used often to say: "O God! whatever comes from me to Thee I beseech Thee to forgive, and whatever comes from Thee to me, Thine is the praise[2]!" On the other hand, he says that had there been no sinners, God's mercy would have been wasted[3]; and that Adam would not have been visited with the tribulation of sin unless forgiveness were the dearest of all things to God[4]. In the following passage he suggests that although sin is an act of disobedience to the divine commandment (*amr*), it is none the less determined by the divine will (*iráda*).

On the Day of Resurrection Iblís (Satan) will be brought to judgment with all the devils, and he will be charged with having led multitudes of people astray. He will confess that he called on them to follow him, but will plead that they need not have done so. Then God will say, "Let that pass! Now worship Adam, in order that thou mayst be saved." The devils will implore him to obey and thereby deliver himself and them from torment, but Iblís will answer, weeping, "Had it depended on my will, I would have worshipped Adam at the time when I was first bidden. God commands me to worship him, but does not will it. Had He willed it, I should have worshipped him then[5]."

It is significant that Abú Sa'íd lets Iblís have the last word, whereas Ḥalláj, who was faced with the same dilemma, insisted that the saint must fulfil the divine command (*amr*) at whatever cost of suffering to himself.

The "inward striving" after selflessness is identical with

[1] A 387, 9. [2] A 408, 14. [3] A 398, 10. [4] A 401, 17.
[5] A 332, 14. For a full discussion of the doctrine of *amr* and *iráda* see Massignon's edition of the *Kitáb al-Ṭawásín*, p. 145 foll.

the state which Abú Sa'íd calls "want" (*niyáz*). There is no way nearer to God than this[1]. It is described as a living and luminous fire placed by God in the breasts of His servants in order that their "self" (*nafs*) may be burned; and when it has been burned, the fire of "want" becomes the fire of "longing" (*shawq*) which never dies, neither in this world nor in the next, and is only increased by vision[2].

Complete negation of individuality involves complete affirmation of the real and universal Self—a fact which is expressed by Ṣúfís in the formula, "Abiding after passing-away" (*al-baqá ba'd al-faná*). The perfect mystic abides in God, and yet (as Ruysbroeck says) "he goes out towards created things in a spirit of love towards all things, in the virtues and in works of righteousness[3]." He is not an ecstatic devotee lost in contemplation of the Oneness, nor a saintly recluse shunning all commerce with mankind, but a philanthropist who in all his words and actions exhibits and diffuses amongst those around him the divine life with which he has been made one. "The true saint," said Abú Sa'íd, "goes in and out amongst the people and eats and sleeps with them and buys and sells in the market and marries and takes part in social intercourse, and never forgets God for a single moment[4]." His ideal of charity and brotherhood was a noble one, however he may have abused it. He declared that there is no better and easier means of attaining to God than by bringing joy to the heart of a Moslem[5], and quoted with approval the saying of Abu 'l-'Abbás Bashshár, "When a disciple performs an act of kindness to a dervish, it is better for him than a hundred genuflexions; and if he gives him a mouthful of food, it is better for him than a whole night spent in prayer[6]." His purse was always open, and he never quarrelled with any one[7], because he regarded all creatures with the eye of the Creator, not with the eye of the creatures[8]. When his followers wished to chastise a bigot who had cursed

[1] A 328, 10.
[2] A 388, 10.
[3] Cf. my *Mystics of Islam*, p. 162 foll.
[4] A 259, 5.
[5] A 380, 11.
[6] A 329, 12.
[7] A 306, 17; 220, 3.
[8] A 382, 9.

him, he restrained them, saying, "God forbid! He is not cursing me, but he thinks that my belief is false and that his own belief is true: therefore he is cursing that false belief for God's sake[1]." He seldom preached on Koranic texts describing the pains of Hell, and in his last years, when reciting the Koran, he passed over all the "verses of torment" (*áyát-i 'adháb*). "O God!" he cried, "inasmuch as men and stones have the same value in Thy sight, feed the flames of Hell with stones and do not burn these miserable wretches[2]!" Although Abú Sa'íd's charity embraced all created beings, he makes a clear distinction between the Ṣúfís and the rest of his fellow-men. The Ṣúfís are God's elect and are united by a spiritual affinity which is more binding than any ties of blood.

Four thousand years before God created these bodies, He created the souls and kept them beside Himself and shed a light upon them. He knew what quantity of light each soul received and He was showing favour to each in proportion to its illumination. The souls remained all that time in the light until they became fully nourished. Those who in this world live in joy and agreement with one another must have been akin to one another in yonder place. Here they love one another and are called the friends of God, and they are brethren who love one another for God's sake. These souls know each other by the smell, like horses. Though one be in the East and the other in the West, yet they feel joy and comfort in each other's talk, and one who lives in a later generation than the other is instructed and consoled by the words of his friend[3].

Abú Sa'íd said:

Whoever goes with me in this Way is my kinsman, even though he be many degrees removed from me, and whoever does not back me in this matter is nobody to me, even though he be one of my nearest relatives[4].

To many Christians the description of Abú Sa'íd as a Moslem saint will seem doubly paradoxical. The Mohammedan notion of saintship, which is founded on ecstasy[5],

[1] A 120, 2. [2] A 261, 1; 359, 15. [3] A 399, 14.
[4] A 391, 12. [5] See *The Mystics of Islam*, p. 120 foll.

justifies the noun; but we may still wonder that the adjective should be applied to a man who on one occasion cried out in a transport of enthusiasm, "There is nothing inside this coat except Allah[1]!" I need not discuss here the causes which gradually brought about such a revolution that, as Professor D. B. Macdonald says, "the devout life within the Muslim church led to a more complete pantheism than ever did the Christian trinity[2]." At any rate, the question whether Abú Sa'íd was a Moslem cannot be decided against him on this count, unless we are prepared to excommunicate most of the saints, some of the profoundest theologians, and wellnigh all the earnestly religious thinkers of Islam. This was recognised by his orthodox opponents, who ignored his theosophical doctrines and attacked him as an innovator in matters connected with the religious law. Within reasonable limits, he might believe and say what he liked, they would take notice only of his overt acts. The following pages, which set forth his attitude towards positive religion, will prove to every impartial reader that in their treatment of heretics the medieval Christian divines had much to learn from their Moslem contemporaries. Upon toleration also *ex Oriente lux*.

At the time of Abú Sa'íd's residence in Níshápúr Shaykh Bú 'Abdallah Bákú was in the convent of Shaykh Abú 'Abd al-Raḥmán al-Sulamí, of which he became the director after the death of Abú 'Abd al-Raḥmán. (Bákú is a village in the district of Shirwán.) This Bú 'Abdallah Bákú used frequently to talk with Shaykh Abú Sa'íd in a controversial spirit and ask him questions about the Ṣúfí Path. One day he came to him and said, "O Shaykh! we see you doing some things that our Elders never did." "What are these things?" Abú Sa'íd inquired. "One of them," said he, "is this, that you let the young men sit beside the old and put the juniors on a level with their seniors in all affairs and make no difference between them; secondly, you permit the young men to dance and sing; and thirdly, when a dervish throws off his gaberdine (in ecstasy), you sometimes direct that it should be

[1] H 6, 5. A 262, 5.
[2] *The religious attitude and life in Islam*, p. 39.

given back to him, saying that the dervish has the best right to his own gaberdine. This has never been the practice of our Elders." "Is there anything else?" said Abú Sa'íd. "No," he replied. Abú Sa'íd said, "As regards the juniors and seniors, none of them is a junior in my opinion. When a man has once entered on the Path of Ṣúfism, although he may be young, his seniors ought to consider that possibly he will receive in a single day what they have not received in seventy years. None who holds this belief will look upon any person as a junior. Then, as to the young men's dancing in the *samá'*, the souls of young men are not yet purged of lust: indeed it may be the prevailing element; and lust takes possession of all the limbs. Now, if a young dervish claps his hands, the lust of his hands will be dissipated, and if he tosses his feet, the lust of his feet will be lessened. When by this means the lust fails in their limbs, they can preserve themselves from great sins, but when all lusts are united (which God forfend!), they will sin mortally. It is better that the fire of their lust should be dissipated in the *samá'* than in something else. As regards the gaberdine which a dervish throws off, its disposal rests with the whole company of dervishes and engages their attention. If they have no other garment at hand, they clothe him again in his own gaberdine, and thereby relieve their minds from the burden of thinking about it. That dervish has not taken back his own gaberdine, but the company of dervishes have given him *their* gaberdine and have thus freed their minds from thought of him. Therefore he is protected by the spiritual concentration (*himma*) of the whole company. This gaberdine is not the same one which he threw away." Bú 'Abdallah Bákú said, "Had I never seen the Shaykh, I should never have seen a real Ṣúfí[1]."

This interesting passage represents Abú Sa'íd as having departed in certain respects from the ancient Ṣúfistic tradition. His innovations, by destroying the influence and authority of the more experienced dervishes, would naturally tend to relax discipline. Early Ṣúfí writers, *e.g.* Sarráj, Qushayrí, and Hujwírí, do not agree with him in thinking that the practice of *samá'* is beneficial to the young; on the contrary, they urge the necessity of taking care lest novices should be demoralised

[1] A 269, 2.

by it. According to the same writers, the doctrines of Ṣúfism are contained in, and derived from, the Koran and the Traditions, of which the true meaning has been mystically revealed to the Ṣúfís alone. This theory concedes all that Moslems claim as to the unique authority of the Koran and reduces the difference between Moslem and Ṣúfí to a question of interpretation. Abú Sa'íd, however, found the source of his doctrine in a larger revelation than the Word which was given to the Prophet.

The author of the *Asrár* says:

My grandfather, Shaykhu 'l-Islám Abú Sa'íd, relates that one day, whilst Abú Sa'íd was preaching in Níshápúr, a learned theologian who was present thought to himself that such doctrine is not to be found in the seven sevenths (*i.e.* the whole) of the Koran. Abú Sa'íd immediately turned towards him and said, "Doctor, thy thought is not hidden from me. The doctrine that I preach is contained in the eighth seventh of the Koran." "What is that?" the theologian inquired. Abú Sa'íd answered: "The seven sevenths are, *O Apostle, deliver the message that hath been sent down to thee* (Kor. 5, 71), and the eighth seventh is, *He revealed unto His servant that which He revealed* (Kor. 53, 10). Ye imagine that the Word of God is of fixed quantity and extent. Nay, the infinite Word of God that was sent down to Mohammed is the whole seven sevenths of the Koran; but that which He causes to come into the hearts of His servants does not admit of being numbered and limited, nor does it ever cease. Every moment there comes a messenger from Him to the hearts of His servants, as the Prophet declared, saying, 'Beware of the clairvoyance (*firása*) of the true believer, for verily he sees by the light of God.'" Then Abú Sa'íd quoted the verse:

Thou art my soul's joy, known by vision, not by hearsay.
Of what use is hearsay to one who hath vision?

In a Tradition (he went on) it is stated that the Guarded Tablet (*lawḥ-i maḥfúẓ*)[1] is so broad that a fleet Arab horse would not be able to cross it in four years, and the writing thereon is finer than a hair. Of all the writing which covers it only a single line has been

[1] Mohammedans believe that everything that shall happen till the Last Day is inscribed on a Tablet under the Throne of God.

communicated to God's creatures. That little keeps them in perplexity until the Resurrection. As for the rest, no one knows anything about it[1].

Here Abú Sa'íd sets aside the partial, finite, and temporal revelation on which Islam is built, and appeals to the universal, infinite, and everlasting revelation which the Ṣúfís find in their hearts. As a rule, even the boldest Mohammedan mystics shrink from uttering such a challenge. So long as the inner light is regarded only as an interpreter of the written revelation, the supremacy of the latter is nominally maintained, though in fact almost any doctrine can be foisted upon it: this is a very different thing from claiming that the inner light transcends the Prophetic Law and possesses full authority to make laws for itself. Abú Sa'íd does not say that the partial and universal revelations are in conflict with each other: he does not repudiate the Koran, but he denies that it is the final and absolute standard of divine truth. He often quotes Koranic verses in support of his theosophical views. Only when the Book fails him need he confound his critics by alleging a secret communication which he has received from the Author.

The foregoing anecdote prepares us for mysticism of an advanced and antinomian type. Not that Abú Sa'íd acted in logical accordance with his beliefs. With one exception, which will be noted presently, he omitted no religious observance that a good Moslem is required to perform. But while he thus shielded himself under the law, he showed in word and deed how little he valued any external ceremony or traditional dogma.

There was at Qá'in a venerable Imám, whose name was Khwája Muḥammad Qá'iní. When Abú Sa'íd arrived at Qá'in, Khwája Muḥammad spent most of his time in waiting upon him, and he used to attend all the parties to which Abú Sa'íd was invited. On one of these occasions, during the *samá'* which followed the feast, Abú Sa'íd and all the company had fallen into transports of ecstasy. The muezzin gave the call to noonday

[1] H 49, 22. A 132, 3.

prayers, but Abú Sa'íd remained in the same rapture and the dervishes continued to dance and shout. "Prayers! Prayers!" cried the Imám Muḥammad Qa'iní. "We *are* at prayers," said Abú Sa'íd; whereupon the Imám left them in order to take part in the prayer-service. When Abú Sa'íd came out of his trance, he said, "Between its rising and setting the sun does not shine upon a more venerable and learned man than this"—meaning Muḥammad Qá'iní—"but his knowledge of Ṣúfism is not so much as the tip of a hair[1]."

Although it would be wrong to use this story as evidence of Abú Sa'íd's habitual practice, we may at least affirm that in his eyes the essence of prayer was not the formal act, but the "passing away from self" which is completely attained in ecstasy. "Endeavour," he said, "to have a mystical experience (*wárid*), not a devotional exercise (*wird*)[2]." One day he said to a dervish, who in order to show the utmost respect stood before him in the attitude of prayer, "This is a very respectful posture, but thy not-being would be still better[3]."

He never made the pilgrimage to Mecca, which every Moslem is bound to make at least once. Many Ṣúfís who would have gladly dispensed with this semi-pagan rite allegorised it and attached a mystical significance to each of the various ceremonies[4]; but they saved their orthodoxy at the expense of their principles. Abú Sa'íd had no such reputation to keep up. His refusal to perform the Ḥajj is not so surprising as the contemptuous language in which he refers to one of the five main pillars of Islam.

Abú Sa'íd was asked, "Who has been thy Pír? for every Pír has had a Pír to instruct him; and how is it that thy neck is too big for thy shirt-collar, while other Pírs have emaciated themselves by austerities? And why hast thou not performed the Pilgrimage, as they have done?" He replied, "Who has been my Pír? *This* (doctrine that I teach) *is part of what my Lord hath*

[1] A 293, 12.
[2] A 403, 15.
[3] A 375, 13.
[4] Cf. *Kashf al-Maḥjúb* (translation), p. 327 foll.; *Kitáb al-Luma'*, 172, 3 foll. The allegorical interpretation of the Pilgrimage seems to have been borrowed by the Ṣúfís from the Ismá'ílís. See Professor Browne's *Literary History of Persia*, vol. II, p. 241 foll.

taught me (Kor. 12, 37). How is it that my neck is too big for my shirt-collar? I marvel how there is room for my neck in the seven heavens and earths after all that God hath bestowed upon me. Why have I not performed the Pilgrimage? It is no great matter that thou shouldst tread under thy feet a thousand miles of ground in order to visit a stone house. The true man of God sits where he is, and the *Bayt al-Ma'múr*[1] comes several times in a day and night to visit him and perform the circumambulation above his head. Look and see!" All who were present looked and saw it[2].

The mystic's pilgrimage takes place within himself[3]. "If God sets the way to Mecca before any one, that person has been cast out of the Way to the Truth[4]." Not content with encouraging his disciples to neglect the Ḥajj, Abú Sa'íd used to send those who thought of performing it to visit the tomb of Abu 'l-Faḍl Ḥasan at Sarakhs, bidding them circumambulate it seven times and consider that their purpose was accomplished[5]. One sees what a menace to Mohammedan institutions the cult of the saints had already become.

The saint lost in contemplation of God knows no religion, and it is often his fate to be classed with the freethinkers (*zanádiqa*), who, from the Moslem point of view, are wholly irreligious, though some of them acknowledge the moral law. Abú Sa'íd said, "Whoever saw me in my first state became a *ṣiddíq*, and whoever saw me in my last state became a *zindíq*[6]," meaning that those who accused him of being a freethinker thereby made themselves guilty of the very thing which they imputed to him. I will translate the biographer's commentary on this saying.

His first state was self-mortification and asceticism, and since most men look at the surface and regard the outward form, they saw the austerity of his life and how painfully he advanced on the Way to God, and their sincere belief (*ṣidq*) in this Way was increased and they attained to the degree of the Sincere (*ṣiddíqán*). His last state was contemplation, a state in which the fruit of self-

[1] The celestial archetype of the Ka'ba. See E. J. W. Gibb, *History of Ottoman Poetry*, vol. I, p. 37.

[2] A 347, 7. [3] A 360, 11. [4] A 374, 15.

[5] H 15, 12. [6] A 41, 19.

mortification is gathered and the complete unveiling (*kashf*) comes to pass; accordingly, eminent mystics have said that states of contemplation are the heritage of acts of self-mortification (*al-musháhadát mawáríthu 'l-mujáhadát*). Those who saw him in this state, which is necessarily one of enjoyment and happiness, and were ignorant of his former state denied that which was true (*ḥaqq*); and whoever denies the Truth (*Ḥaqq*) is a freethinker (*zindíq*). There are many analogies to this in the sensible world. For example, when a man seeks to win the favour of a king and to become his companion and intimate friend, before attaining to that rank he must suffer all sorts of tribulation and patiently endure injuries and insults from high and low, and submit with cheerfulness to maltreatment and abuse, giving fair words in return for foul; and when he has been honoured with the king's approval and has been admitted to his presence, he must serve him assiduously and hazard his life in order that the king may place confidence in him. But after he has gained the king's confidence and intimacy, all this hard and perilous service belongs to the past. Now all is grace and bounty and favour; everywhere he meets with new pleasures and delights; and he has no duty but to wait upon the king always, from whose palace he cannot be absent a single moment by day or night, in order that he may be at hand whenever the king desires to tell him a secret or to honour him with a place by his side[1].

Asceticism and positive religion are thus relegated to the lower planes of the mystical life. The Ṣúfí needs them and must hold fast to them while he is serving his spiritual apprenticeship and also during the middle stage which is marked by longer or shorter intervals of illumination; but in his "last state," when the unveiling is completed, he has no further use for ascetic practices and religious forms, for he lives in permanent communion with God Himself. This leads directly to antinomianism, though in theory the saint is above the law rather than against it. One who sees the reality within cannot judge by appearances. Being told that a disciple of his was lying blind-drunk on a certain road, Abú Sa'íd said, "Thank God that he has fallen on the way, not

[1] A 42, 1.

off the Way[1]." Some one asked him, "Are the men of God in the mosque?" "They are in the tavern too," he replied[2].

His pantheistic vision blotted out the Mohammedan afterworld with its whole system of rewards and punishments. "Whoever knows God without mediation worships Him without recompense[3]." There is no Hell but selfhood, no Paradise but selflessness: "Hell is where thou art and Paradise where thou art not[4]." He quoted the Tradition, "My people shall be split into more than seventy sects, of which a single one shall be saved, while the others shall be in the Fire," and added, "that is to say, in the fire of their own selves[5]."

As I have already remarked, Abú Sa'íd speaks with two voices: now as a theosophist, now as a Moslem. Hence the same terms bear their ordinary religious meaning in one passage and are explained mystically in another, while the purest pantheism runs side by side with popular theology. To our minds it seems absurd to suppose that he believed in both; yet probably he did, at least so far as to have no difficulty in accepting the Mohammedan scheme when it suited him. For example, he preaches the doctrine of the intercession of saints, in which (though the Koran does not support it) Paradise, Hell, the Day of Judgment, etc., are what the Koran says they are. A few of his sayings on this subject may be quoted here, especially as it is closely connected with his miracles and legend which will be discussed in the following pages.

The man who is being carried off to Hell will see a light from afar. He will ask what it is and will be told that it is the light of such and such a Pír. He will say, "In our world I used to love him." The wind will bear his words to the ears of that Pír, who will plead for him in the divine presence, and God will release the sinner on account of the intercession of that holy man[6].

Whoever has seen me and has done good work for my family and disciples will be under the shadow of my intercession hereafter[7].

I have prayed God to forgive my neighbours on the left, on the

[1] H 76, 7. [2] A 373, 4. [3] A 406, 1.
[4] A 266, 16; 375, 16. [5] A 392, 16.
[6] A 380, 16. [7] A 418, 4.

right, in front, and behind, and He has forgiven them for my sake." Then he said, "My neighbours are Balkh and Merv and Níshápúr and Herát. I am not speaking of those who live here (Mayhana)[1]."

"I need not say a word on behalf of those around me. If any one has mounted an ass and passed by the end of this street, or has passed my house or will pass it, or if the light of my candle falls on him, the least thing that God will do with him is that He will have mercy upon him[2]."

III.

Ṣúfism is at once the religious philosophy and the popular religion of Islam. The great Mohammedan mystics are also saints. Their lives belong to the Legend and contain, besides their lofty and abstruse speculations, an account of the miracles which they wrought. They are the object of endless worship and adoration, their tombs are holy shrines whither men and women come as pilgrims to beseech their all-powerful aid, their relics bring a blessing that only the rich can buy. Whilst still living, they are canonised by the people; not posthumously by the Church. Their title to saintship depends on a peculiarly intimate relation to God, which is attested by fits of ecstasy and, above all, by thaumaturgic gifts (*karámát* = χαρίσματα, grazie). Belief in such gifts is almost universal, but there is disagreement as to the importance which should be attached to them. The higher doctrine, that they are of small value in comparison with the attainment of spiritual perfection, was ignored by the mass of Moslems, who would have considered a saint without miracles to be no saint at all. Miracles there must be; if the holy man failed to supply them, they were invented for him. It is vain to inquire how far the miracles of Abú Sa'íd may have been the work of popular imagination, but the following extracts show that the question is not an irrelevant one, even if we take for granted the reality of these occult and mysterious powers.

It is related by Ustád 'Abdu 'l-Raḥmán, who was Abú

[1] A 418, 6. [2] A 418, 9.

Sa'íd's principal Koran-reader (*muqrí*), that when Abú Sa'íd was living in Níshápúr a man came to him and saluted him and said:

"I am a stranger here. On my arrival I found the whole city full of thy fame. They tell me thou art a man who has the gift of miracles and does not hide it. Now show me one." Abú Sa'íd replied: "When I was at Ámul with Abu 'l-'Abbás Qaṣṣáb, some one came to him on the same errand and demanded of him the same thing which you have just demanded of me. He answered, 'What do you see that is not miraculous? A butcher's son (*pisar-i qaṣṣábí*), whose father taught him his own trade, has a vision, is enraptured, is brought to Baghdád and falls in with Shaykh Shiblí; from Baghdád to Mecca, from Mecca to Medina, from Medina to Jerusalem, where Khaḍir appears to him, and God puts it in Khaḍir's heart to accept him as a disciple; then he is brought back here and multitudes turn towards him, coming forth from taverns and renouncing wickedness and taking vows of penitence and sacrificing wealth. Filled with burning love they come from the ends of the world to seek God from me. What miracle is greater than this?' The man replied that he wished to see a miracle at the present moment. 'Is it not a miracle,' said Abu 'l-'Abbás, 'that a goat-killer's son is sitting in the seat of the mighty and that he does not sink into the earth and that this wall does not fall upon him and that this house does not tumble over his head? Without goods and gear he possesses saintship, and without work or means of support he receives his daily bread and feeds many people. Is not all this a gift of miracles?' Good sir (Abú Sa'íd continued), your experience with me is the same as that man's with Abu 'l-'Abbás Qaṣṣáb." "O Shaykh!" said he, "I ask thee for miracles and thou tellest of Shaykh Abu 'l-'Abbás." Abú Sa'íd said, "Whosoever belongs entirely to the Giver (*Karím*), all his acts are gifts (*karámát*)."

Then he smiled and said in verse:

Every wind that comes to me from the region of Bukhárá
Breathes the perfume of roses and musk and the scent of jessamine.
Every man and woman on whom that wind is blowing
Thinks it is surely blowing from Khoten.
Nay, nay! From Khoten bloweth no such delicious gale:

That wind is coming from the presence of the Beloved.
Each night I gaze towards Yemen, that thou mayst rise;
For thou art Suhayl (Canopus), and Suhayl rises from Yemen.
Adored One! I endeavour to hide thy name from all,
In order that thy name may not come into folk's mouths;
But whether I will or no, whenever I speak to any one,
Thy name is the first word that comes to my lips.

When God makes a man pure and separates him from his selfhood, all that he does or abstains from doing, all that he says and all that he feels becomes a wondrous gift (*karámát*). God bless Mohammed and the whole of his Family[1].

In another passage the extraordinary feats performed by saints are reduced to their proper insignificance.

They said to him, "So-and-so walks on the water." He replied, "It is easy enough: frogs and waterfowl do it." They said, "So-and-so flies in the air." "So do birds and insects," he replied. They said, "So-and-so goes from one town to another in a moment of time." "Satan," he rejoined, "goes in one moment from the East to the West. Things like these have no great value"; and he proceeded to give the definition of the true saint which has been quoted already[2]—a man who lives in friendly intercourse with his fellow-creatures, yet is never forgetful of God[3].

Abú Sa'íd looked with disfavour on the composition of marvellous tales concerning himself. One day he summoned his famulus, Khwája 'Abdu 'l-Karím, and inquired what he had been doing. 'Abdu 'l-Karím answered that he had been writing some anecdotes of his master for a certain dervish who wanted them. "O 'Abdu 'l-Karím!" said the Shaykh, "do not be a writer of anecdotes: be such a man that anecdotes will be told of thee." The biographer observes that Abú Sa'íd's fear lest a legend of his miracles should be published and widely circulated accords with the practice of the most eminent Ṣúfís, who have always concealed their mystical experiences[4]. Abú Sa'íd placed the hidden and unrecognised saint above the saint manifest and known to the people: the former is he whom God loves, the latter he who loves God[5].

[1] A 369, 5. [2] See p. 55. [3] A 258, 17. [4] A 243, 18. [5] A 381, 1.

Such protests may have retarded, although they did not check, the constantly increasing glorification of popular saints by themselves and their devotees. At any rate, the ancient Lives of Abú Sa'íd are modest and subdued if we compare them with some famous legends of the same kind.

As I have mentioned, his recorded miracles are mostly instances of *firása*, a term equivalent to clairvoyance. Being an effect of the light which God sets in the purified heart, *firása* is reckoned among the "gifts" (*karámát*) of the saint and is accepted as evidence of holiness. There were two friends, a tailor and a weaver, who obstinately asserted that Abú Sa'íd was an impostor. One day they said, "This man pretends to have the gift of miracles. Let us go to him, and if he knows what trade each of us follows, we shall then know that his claim is true." They disguised themselves and went to the Shaykh. As soon as his eye fell on them, he said:

> On the *falak* are two craftsmen[1],
> One a tailor, one a weaver.

Then he said, pointing to the tailor:

> This one fashions robes for princes.

And pointing to the weaver:

> This one weaves black woollens only.

Both were covered with confusion and fell at the Shaykh's feet and repented of their disbelief[2].

Moslems attribute to *firása*, and therefore to a divine source, all the phenomena of telepathy, thought-reading, and second sight. In the course of this essay I have had occasion to translate several testimonies that Abú Sa'íd was richly endowed with these "gifts" and that he made his reputation as a saint by exhibiting them in public. That he really possessed them or, at least, persuaded a great number of people to think so, is beyond dispute—otherwise, traditions attesting

[1] The *falak* is a pole on which the feet are tied when bastinado is administered. The words "on the *falak*" refer, no doubt, to the anxious suspense in which the two sceptics awaited the result of their experiment. Cf. our phrase "on the rack."

[2] A 240, 9.

them would not have occupied so much of his legend; but when we come to examine particular cases, we find that the evidence is weak from a scientific point of view as well as on common grounds of probability. Such considerations, I need hardly say, not only have no influence upon the Moslem's belief in occult phenomena but do not even enter his mind. Many stories illustrating Abú Sa'íd's powers of *firása* occur in the preceding pages, and it would be useless to give further specimens. The following extracts commemorate some miracles of a different class.

In Níshápúr there lived a woman of noble family, whose name was Íshí Nílí. She was a great ascetic, and on account of her piety the people of Níshápúr used to seek blessings from her. It was forty years since she had gone to the warm baths or set foot outside of her house. When Abú Sa'íd came to Níshápúr and the report of his miracles spread through the city, she sent a nurse, who always waited upon her, to hear him preach. "Remember what he says," said she, "and tell me when you come back." The nurse, on her return, could recollect nothing of Abú Sa'íd's discourse, but repeated to her mistress some bacchanalian verses she had heard him recite[1]. Íshí cried, "Go and wash your mouth! Do ascetics and divines speak such words as these?" Now, Íshí was in the habit of making eye-salves which she gave to the people. That night she saw a frightful thing in her sleep and started up. Both her eyes were aching. She treated them with eye-salves, but was no better; she betook herself to all the physicians, but found no cure: she moaned in pain twenty days and nights. Then one night she slept and dreamed that if she wished her eyes to be better, she must satisfy the Shaykh of Mayhana and win his exalted favour. Next day she put in a purse a thousand dirhems, which she had received as alms, and bade the nurse take it to Abú Sa'íd and present it to him as soon as he should have finished his sermon. When the nurse laid it before him, he was using a toothpick—for it was his rule that at the end of the sermon a disciple brought some bread and a toothpick, which he would use after eating the bread. He said to her, as she was about to depart, "Come, nurse, take this toothpick and give it to thy lady. Tell her

[1] I have not attempted to translate this *rubá'í*. Its general drift is plain, but there are textual difficulties.

that she must stir some water with it and then wash her eyes with the water, in order that her outward eye may be cured. And tell her to put out of her heart all suspicious and unfriendly feelings towards the Ṣúfís, in order that her inward eye too may be cured." Íshí carefully followed his directions. She dipped the toothpick in water and washed her eyes and was cured immediately. Next day she brought to the Shaykh all her jewelry and ornaments and dresses, and said, "O Shaykh! I have repented and have put every hostile feeling out of my heart." "May it bring thee blessing!" said he, and bade them conduct her to the mother of Bú Ṭáhir[1], that she might robe her in the gaberdine (*khirqa*). Íshí went in obedience to his command and donned the gaberdine and busied herself with serving the women of this fraternity (the Ṣúfís). She gave up her house and goods, and rose to great eminence in this Path, and became a leader of the Ṣúfís[2].

During the time when Abú Sa'íd was at Níshápúr, disciples came to him of all sorts, well and ill bred. One of his converts was a rough peasant with iron-soled mountain-shoes, which made a disagreeable noise whenever he entered the monastery; he was always knocking them against the wall and annoying the Ṣúfís by his rudeness and violence. One day the Shaykh called him and said, "You must go to a certain valley (which he named—it lies between the hills of Níshápúr and Ṭús, and a stream descending from it falls into the Níshápúr river). After going some distance you will see a big rock. You must perform an ablution on the bank of the stream and a prayer of two genuflexions on the rock, and wait for a friend of mine, who will come to you. Give him my greeting, and there is something I wish you to tell him, for he is a very dear friend of mine: he has been with me seven years." The dervish set off with the utmost eagerness, and all the way he was thinking that he was going to see one of the saints or one of the Forty Men who are the pivot of the world and upon whom depends the order and harmony of human affairs. He was sure that the holy man's blessed look would fall on him and make his fortune both in this world and in the next. When he came to the place indicated by the Shaykh, he did what the Shaykh had ordered; then he waited a while. Suddenly there was a dreadful clap and the mountain quaked. He looked and saw a black dragon,

[1] The eldest son of Abú Sa'íd.

[2] A 91, 18.

the largest he had ever seen: its body filled the whole space between two mountains. At the sight of it his spirit fled; he was unable to move and fell senseless to the earth. The dragon advanced slowly towards the rock, on which it laid its head reverently. After a little while, the dervish recovered himself somewhat, and observing that the dragon had come to a halt and was motionless, he said, though in his terror he scarcely knew what he said, "The Shaykh greets thee." The dragon with many signs of reverence began to rub its face in the dust, whilst tears rolled from its eyes. This, and the fact that it attempted nothing against him, persuaded the dervish that he had been sent to meet the dragon; he therefore delivered the Shaykh's message, which it received with great humility, rubbing its face in the dust and weeping so much that the rock where its head lay became wet. Having heard all, it went away. As soon as it was out of sight, the dervish came to himself and once more fell in a swoon. A long time passed before he revived. At last he rose and slowly descended to the foot of the hill. Then he sat down, picked up a stone, and beat the iron off his clogs. On returning to the monastery, he entered so quietly that none was aware of his coming, and spoke the salaam in such a low voice that he was barely heard. When the elders saw his behaviour, they desired to know who was the Pír to whom he had been sent; they wondered who in half a day had wrought in his pupil a change that can generally be produced only by means of long and severe discipline. When the dervish told the story, every one was amazed. The elder Ṣúfís questioned the Shaykh, who replied, "Yes, for seven years he has been my friend, and we have found spiritual joy in each other's society." After that day none ever saw the dervish behave rudely or heard him speak loudly. He was entirely reformed by a single attention which the Shaykh bestowed on him[1].

When Shaykh Abú Sa'íd was at Níshápúr, holding splendid feasts and musical entertainments and continually regaling the dervishes with luxurious viands, such as fat fowls and *lawzína* and sweetmeats, an arrogant ascetic came to him and said, "O Shaykh! I have come in order to challenge you to a forty days' fast (*chihila*)." The poor man was ignorant of the Shaykh's novitiate and of his forty years' austerities: he fancied that the

[1] A 128, 11.

Shaykh had always lived in this same manner. He thought to himself, "I will chasten him with hunger and put him to shame in the eyes of the people, and then I shall be the object of their regard." On hearing his challenge, the Shaykh said, "May it be blessed!" and spread his prayer-rug. His adversary did the like, and they both sat down side by side. While the ascetic, in accordance with the practice of those who keep a fast of forty days, was eating a certain amount of food, the Shaykh ate nothing; and though he never once broke his fast, every morning he was stronger and fatter and his complexion grew more and more ruddy. All the time, by his orders and under his eyes, the dervishes feasted luxuriously and indulged in the *samá'*, and he himself danced with them. His state was not changed for the worse in any respect. The ascetic, on the other hand, was daily becoming feebler and thinner and paler, and the sight of the delicious viands which were served to the Ṣúfís in his presence worked more and more upon him. At length he grew so weak that he could scarcely rise to perform the obligatory prayers. He repented of his presumption and confessed his ignorance. When the forty days were finished, the Shaykh said, "I have complied with your request: now you must do as I say." The ascetic acknowledged this and said, "It is for the Shaykh to command." The Shaykh said, "We have sat forty days and eaten nothing and gone to the privy: now let us sit forty days and eat and never go to the privy." His adversary had no choice but to accept the challenge, but he thought to himself that it was impossible for any human being to do such a thing[1].

In the end, of course, the Shaykh proves to be an overman, and the ascetic becomes one of his disciples.

It is related that an eminent Shaykh who lived in Abú Sa'íd's time went on a warlike expedition to Rúm (Asia Minor), accompanied by a number of Ṣúfís. Whilst he was marching in that country, he saw Iblís. "O accursed one!" he cried, "what art thou doing here?—for thou canst not cherish any design against us." Iblís replied that he had come thither involuntarily. "I was passing by Mayhana," said he, "and entered the town. Shaykh Abú Sa'íd came out of the mosque. I met him on the way to his house and he gave a sneeze which cast me here[2]."

[1] A 160, 18. [2] A 361, 5.

A tomb and sepulchre (*turbatí ú mashhadí*) was the only memorial of Abú Sa'íd in his native town that the Ghuzz hordes did not utterly destroy[1]. Concerning his relics, that is to say, garments and other articles which were venerated on account of some circumstance that gave them a peculiar sanctity or simply because they once had belonged to him, we find valuable details in three passages of the *Asrár*.

One day, whilst Shaykh Abú Sa'íd was preaching at Níshápúr, he grew warm in his discourse and being overcome with ecstasy exclaimed, "There is naught within this vest (*jubba*) except Allah!" Simultaneously he raised his forefinger (*angusht-i musabbiḥa*), which lay on his breast underneath the *jubba*, and his blessed finger passed through the *jubba* and became visible to all. Among the Shaykhs and Imáms present on that occasion were Abú Muhammad Juwayní, Abu 'l-Qásim Qushayrí, Ismá'íl Ṣábúní, and others whom it would be tedious to enumerate. None of them, on hearing these words, protested or silently objected. All were beside themselves, and following the Shaykh's example they flung away their gaberdines (*khirqahá*). When the Shaykh descended from the pulpit, his *jubba* and their gaberdines were torn to pieces (and distributed)[2]. The Shaykhs were unanimously of opinion that the piece of silk (*kazhpára*) which bore the mark of his blessed finger should be torn off from the breast of the *jubba* and set apart, in order that in the future all who came or went might pay a visit to it. Accordingly, it was set apart just as it was, with the cotton and lining, and remained in the possession of Shaykh Abu 'l-Fatḥ and his family. Those who came from all parts of the world as pilgrims to Mayhana, after having visited his holy shrine used to visit that piece of silk and the other memorials of the Shaykh and used to see the mark of his finger, until the Ghuzz invasion, when that blessing and other precious blessings of his were lost[3].

Bú Naṣr Shirwání, a rich merchant of Níshápúr, was converted by Abú Sa'íd. He gave the whole of his wealth to the Ṣúfís and

[1] A 6, 4.

[2] "The tearing up and distributing is to distribute the blessing that is supposed to cleave to them from having been worn by some one in an especially blessed state. So the garments of saints acquire miraculous power; compare Elijah's mantle" (Prof. D. B. Macdonald in *JRAS*, 1902, p. 10; see also Richard Hartmann, *Al-Ḳuschairî's Darstellung des Ṣûfîtums*, p. 141 foll. and cf. pp. 43 and 58 *supra*).

[3] A 262, 5.

showed the utmost devotion to the Shaykh. When the latter left Níshápúr to return to Mayhana, he bestowed on Bú Naṣr a green woollen mantle (*labácha*) of his own, saying, "Go to thy country and set up my banner there." Accordingly Bú Naṣr went back to Shirwán, became the director and chief of the Ṣúfís in that region, and built a convent, which exists to-day and is known by his name. The Shaykh's mantle is still preserved in the convent, where Bú Naṣr deposited it. Every Friday at prayer-time the famulus hangs it from a high place in the building, and when the people come out of the Friday mosque they go to the convent and do not return home until they have paid a visit to the Shaykh's mantle. No citizen neglects this observance. If at any time famine, pestilence, or other calamity befall the country, they place the mantle on their heads and carry it afield, and the whole population go forth and reverently invoke its intercession. Then God, the glorious and exalted, in His perfect bounty and in honour of the Shaykh removes the calamity from them and brings their desires to pass. The inhabitants of that country say that the mantle is a proved antidote (*tiryák-i mujarrab*) and they make immense offerings to the followers of the Shaykh. At the present time, through the blessings of the Shaykh's spirit (*himma*) and the people's excellent belief in the Ṣúfís, this province can show more than four hundred well-known monasteries, where dervishes obtain refreshment[1].

When the fame of Abú Sa'íd reached Mecca, the Shaykhs of the Holy City, wishing to know what kind of man he was, sent Bú 'Amr Bashkhwání, who was a great ascetic and had resided in Mecca for thirty years, to Mayhana in order that he might bring back a trustworthy report of Abú Sa'íd's character and mystical endowments. Bú 'Amr journeyed to Mayhana and had a long conversation with Abú Sa'íd in private. After three days, when he was about to return to Mecca, Abú Sa'íd said to him, "You must go to Bashkhwán: you are my deputy in that district. Ere long the bruit of your renown will be heard in the fourth heaven." Bú 'Amr obeyed and set out for Bashkhwán. As he was taking leave, Abú Sa'íd gave him three toothpicks which he had cut with his own blessed hand, and said, "Do not sell one of these for ten dínárs nor for twenty, and if thirty dínárs are offered"—(here he stopped short and Bú 'Amr went on his way). On arriving at Bashkhwán,

[1] A 173, 15.

he lodged in the room which is now (part of) his convent, and the people honoured him as a saint. Every Thursday he began a complete recitation of the Koran, in which he was joined by his disciples and the men of Bashkhwán and all the notables of the neighbouring hamlets; and when the recitation was finished, he would call for a jug of water and dip in it one of the toothpicks which he had received from Shaykh Abú Sa'íd. The water was then distributed amongst the sick, and it healed them by means of the blessed influence of both Shaykhs. The headman of Bashkhwán, who was always suffering from colic, begged Bú 'Amr to send him some of the holy water. No sooner had he drunk it than the pain ceased. Next morning he came to Bú 'Amr and said, "I hear that you have three of these toothpicks. Will you sell me one, for I am very often in pain?" Bú 'Amr asked him how much he would give. He offered ten dínárs. "It is worth more," said Bú 'Amr. "Twenty dínárs." "It is worth more." "Thirty dínárs." "No, it is worth more." The headman said nothing and would not bid any higher. Bú 'Amr said, "My master, Shaykh Abú Sa'íd, stopped at the same amount." He gave him one of the toothpicks in exchange for thirty dínárs, and with that money he founded the convent which now exists. The headman kept the toothpick as long as he lived. On his deathbed he desired that it should be broken and that the pieces should be placed in his mouth and buried with him. As regards the two remaining toothpicks, in accordance with Bú 'Amr's last injunctions they were placed in his shroud and interred in his blessed tomb[1].

I have set before my readers a picture of Abú Sa'íd as he appears in the oldest and most authentic documents available. These do not always show him as he was, but it would be absurd to reproach his biographers with their credulity and entire lack of critical judgment: they write as worshippers, and their work is based upon traditions and legends which breathe the very spirit of unquestioning faith. Only an alloy can be extracted from such materials, however carefully they are analysed. The passages in which Abú Sa'íd describes his early life, conversion, and novitiate are perhaps less open to suspicion than the numerous anecdotes concerning his

[1] A 201, 12.

miracles. Here pious invention plays a large part and is not limited by any sense of natural law. Even the sceptics converted by Abú Sa'íd feel sure that miracles occur, and only doubt his ability to perform them. The mystical sayings attributed to him have a power and freedom beyond speculative theosophy and suggest that he owed his fame, in the first instance, to an enthusiastic personality and to the possession of "psychic" gifts which he knew how to exhibit impressively. He was a great teacher and preacher of Ṣúfism. If the matter of his doctrine is seldom original, his genius gathered up and fused the old elements into something new. In the historical development he stands out as a leading exponent of the pantheistic, poetical, anti-scholastic, and antinomian ideas which had been already broached by his predecessor, Báyazíd of Bisṭám, and Abu 'l-Ḥasan Kharaqání. It may be said of Abú Sa'íd that he, perhaps more than any one else, gave these ideas the distinctive form in which they are presented to us by the later religious philosophy of Persia. Their peculiarly *Persian* character is just what we should expect, seeing that Báyazíd, Abu 'l-Ḥasan, and Abú Sa'íd himself were born and passed their lives in Khurásán, the cradle of Persian nationalism. Abú Sa'íd also left his mark on another side of Ṣúfism, its organisation as a monastic system[1]. Although he founded no Order, the convent over which he presided supplied a model in outline of the fraternities that were established during the 12th century; and in the ten rules which he, as abbot, drew up and caused to be put into writing[2] we find, so far as I know, the first Mohammedan example of a *regula ad monachos*.

[1] Cf. Qazwíní, *Áthdru 'l-bilád* (ed. Wüstenfeld), p. 241, 3 fr. foot.
[2] See p. 46 *supra*.

CHAPTER II

THE PERFECT MAN[1]

Man, is not he Creation's last appeal,
The light of Wisdom's eye? Behold the wheel
Of universal life as 'twere a ring,
But Man the superscription and the seal.

OMAR KHAYYAM.

Οὕτως, φησίν, ἐστι πάνυ βαθεῖα καὶ δυσκατάληπτος ἡ τοῦ τελείου ἀνθρώπου γνῶσις. Ἀρχὴ γάρ, φησίν, τελειώσεως γνῶσις ἀνθρώπου· θεοῦ δὲ γνῶσις ἀπηρτισμένη τελείωσις. HIPPOLYTUS.

Ἄνθρωπος θεοῦ τοῦ ἀϊδίου λόγος. PHILO.

WHAT do Ṣúfís mean when they speak of the Perfect Man (*al-insánu 'l-kámil*), a phrase which seems first to have been used by the celebrated Ibnu 'l-'Arabí, although the notion underlying it is almost as old as Ṣúfism itself[2]? The question

[1] The title is borrowed from Jílí's work, the *Insánu 'l-kámil*, of which a brief but illuminating exposition will be found in Dr Muḥammad Iqbál's *Development of metaphysics in Persia* (London, 1908), p. 150 foll. I may also refer to two articles written by myself: "A Moslem philosophy of religion" (*Muséon*, Cambridge, 1915, p. 83 foll.) and "The Ṣúfí doctrine of the Perfect Man" (*Quest*, 1917, p. 545 foll.); passages from both have been incorporated in this essay, with or without alteration. The following abbreviations are used: K = the edition of the *Insánu 'l-kámil* published at Cairo in A.H. 1300; Comm. K = the commentary by Aḥmad ibn Muḥammad al-Madaní on chapters 50–54 of the *Insánu 'l-kámil* (Loth's *Catalogue of the Arabic manuscripts in the Library of the India Office*, No. 667); M = the commentary by Jílí on the 559th chapter of Ibnu 'l-'Arabí's *Futúḥátu 'l-Makkiyya* (Loth's *Catalogue*, No. 693[1]).

[2] In the first chapter of the *Fuṣúṣu 'l-ḥikam* (Cairo, A.H. 1321) Ibnu 'l-'Arabí (ob. A.D. 1240) says that when God willed that His attributes should be displayed, He created a microcosmic being (*kawn jámi'*), the Perfect Man, through whom "God's consciousness (*sirr*) is manifested to Himself." Abú Yazíd al-Bisṭámí (ob. A.D. 875) defines "the perfect and complete man" (*al-kámilu 'l-támm*), who after having been invested with Divine attributes becomes unconscious of them (Qushayrí, *Risála*, Cairo, A.H. 1318, p. 140, l. 12 foll.), *i.e.*, enters fully into the state of *faná*; but here the term does not bear the peculiar significance attached to it by Ibnu 'l-'Arabí and Jílí.

might be answered in different ways, but if we seek a general definition, perhaps we may describe the Perfect Man as a man who has fully realised his essential oneness with the Divine Being in whose likeness he is made. This experience, enjoyed by prophets and saints and shadowed forth in symbols to others, is the foundation of the Ṣúfí theosophy. Therefore, the class of Perfect Men comprises not only the prophets from Adam to Mohammed, but also the superlatively elect (*khuṣúṣu 'l-khuṣúṣ*) amongst the Ṣúfís, *i.e.*, the persons named collectively *awliyá*, plural of *walí*, a word originally meaning "near," which is used for "friend," "*protégé*," or "devotee." Since the *walí* or saint is the popular type of Perfect Man, it should be understood that the essence of Mohammedan saintship, as of prophecy, is nothing less than Divine illumination, immediate vision and knowledge of things unseen and unknown, when the veil of sense is suddenly lifted and the conscious self passes away in the overwhelming glory of "the One true Light." An ecstatic feeling of oneness with God constitutes the *walí*. It is the end of the Path (*ṭaríqa*) in so far as the discipline of the Path is meant to predispose and prepare the disciple to receive this incalculable gift of Divine grace, which is not gained or lost by anything that a man may do, but comes to him in proportion to the measure and degree of spiritual capacity with which he was created.

Two special functions of the *walí* further illustrate the relation of the popular saint-cult to mystical philosophy—(1) his function as a mediator, (2) his function as a cosmic power. The Perfect Man, as will be explained in the course of our argument, unites the One and the Many, so that the universe depends on him for its continued existence. In Mohammedan religious life the *walí* occupies the same middle position: he bridges the chasm which the Koran and scholasticism have set between man and an absolutely transcendent God. He brings relief to the distressed, health to the sick, children to the childless, food to the famished, spiritual guidance to those who entrust their souls to his care, blessing to all who visit his tomb and invoke Allah in his name. The *walís*, from the highest to the lowest, are arranged in a graduated hierarchy, with the *Quṭb* at their head, forming "a saintly board of administration by which the invisible government of the world is carried on[1]." Speaking of the *Awtád*—four saints whose rank is little inferior to that of the *Quṭb* himself—Hujwírí says:

> It is their office to go round the whole world every night, and if there be any place on which their eyes have not fallen, next day some flaw will appear in that place; and they must then inform the *Quṭb*, in order that he may direct his attention to the weak spot, and that by his blessing the imperfection may be remedied[2].

Such experiences and beliefs were partly the cause and partly the consequence of speculation concerning the nature of God and man, speculation which drifted far away from Koranic monotheism into pantheistic and monistic philosophies. The Ṣúfí reciting the Koran in ecstatic prayer and seeming to hear, in the words which he intoned, not his own voice but the voice of God speaking through him, could no longer acquiesce in the orthodox conception of Allah as a Being utterly different from all other beings. This dogma was supplanted by faith in a Divine Reality (*al-Ḥaqq*), a God who is the creative principle and ultimate ground of all that exists. While Ṣúfís, like Moslems in general, affirm the transcendence of God and reject the notion of infusion or incarnation (*ḥulúl*), it is an interesting fact that one of the first attempts in Islam to indicate more precisely the meaning of mystical union was founded on the Christian doctrine of two natures in God. Ḥalláj, who dared to say *Ana 'l-Ḥaqq*, "I am the *Ḥaqq*[3]," thereby announced that the saint in his deification "becomes the living and personal witness of God." The Jewish tradition that God created Adam in His own image reappeared as a *ḥadíth* (saying of the Prophet) and was put to strange uses by Mohammedan theosophists.

[1] Prof. D. B. Macdonald, *The religious attitude and life in Islam*, p. 163.

[2] Hujwírí, *Kashf al-Maḥjúb*, p. 228 of my translation.

[3] Massignon renders, "I am the Creative Truth" (*Kitáb al-Ṭawásín*, p. 175). *Al-Ḥaqq* is the Creator as opposed to the creatures (*al-khalq*) and this seems to be the meaning in which Ḥalláj understood the term, but it is also applied to God conceived pantheistically as the one permanent reality. Cf. the article "Ḥaḳḳ" by Prof. D. B. Macdonald in *Encycl. of Islam*.

Even the orthodox Ghazálí hints that here is the key of a great mystery which nothing will induce him to divulge[1]. According to Ḥalláj, the essence of God's essence is Love. Before the creation God loved Himself in absolute unity and through love revealed Himself to Himself alone. Then, desiring to behold that love-in-aloneness, that love without otherness and duality, as an external object, He brought forth from non-existence an image of Himself, endowed with all His attributes and names. This Divine image is Adam, in and by whom God is made manifest—divinity objectified in humanity[2]. Ḥalláj, however, distinguishes the human nature (*násút*) from the Divine (*láhút*). Though mystically united, they are not essentially identical and interchangeable. Personality survives even in union: water does not become wine, though wine be mixed with it. Using a more congenial metaphor, Ḥalláj says in verses which are often quoted:

> I am He whom I love, and He whom I love is I.
> We are *two* spirits dwelling in one body[3],
> If thou seest me, thou seest Him;
> And if thou seest Him, thou seest us both.

The markedly Christian flavour of the Ḥallájian doctrine condemned it in Moslem eyes, and while later Ṣúfís develop its main ideas and venerate Ḥalláj himself as a martyr who was barbarously done to death because he had proclaimed the Truth, they interpret his *Ana 'l-Ḥaqq* in the light of an idealistic monism which reduces all antitheses—including *láhút* and *násút*—to necessarily correlated aspects of the universal Essence. His doctrine in its original form has only

[1] *Iḥyá* (Búláq, A.H. 1289), vol. IV, p. 294.

[2] Massignon, *Kitáb al-Ṭawásín*, p. 129.

[3] Contrast this with the monistic expression of the same thought by Jílí (K I. 51, 1): "We are the spirit of One, though we dwell by turns in two bodies." So, too, Jalálu'ddín Rúmí (*Dīvāni Shamsi Tabrīz*, p. 153):

> "Happy the moment when we are seated in the palace, thou and I,
> With two forms and with two figures, but with one soul, thou and I."

Cf. K II. 121, 11 foll.: "Essential love is love in Oneness, so that each of the lovers appears in the form of the other and represents the other. Inasmuch as the love of the body and the soul is essential, the soul is pained by the body's pain in this world, while the body is pained by the soul's pain in the other world: then each of them appears in the other's form."

recently been recovered and given to the world by M. Louis Massignon, to whose learned and brilliant monograph every student of Ṣúfism is deeply indebted.

'Abdu 'l-Karím ibn Ibráhím al-Jílí, author of *al-Insánu 'l-kámil fí ma'rifati 'l-awákhir wa 'l-awá'il* ("The Man perfect in knowledge of the last and first things"), was born in A.D. 1365–6 and probably died some time between A.D. 1406 and 1417. His surname, which is derived from Jílán or Gílán, the province south of the Caspian, commemorates his descent from the founder of the Qádirite order of dervishes, 'Abdu 'l-Qádir al-Jílí (Gílání), who died almost exactly 200 years before the date of Jílí's birth[1]. In the *Insánu 'l-kámil* he more than once refers to 'Abdu 'l-Qádir as "our Shaykh," so that he must have been a member of the fraternity. The Moslem biographers leave him unnoticed, but he himself tells us that he lived at Zabíd in Yemen with his Shaykh, Sharafu'ddín Ismá'íl ibn Ibráhím al-Jabartí, and had previously travelled in India[2]. Of his mystical writings twenty are known to be extant, and it is not unlikely that as many have been lost.

Jílí begins his work with a statement of his object in composing it[3]. That object is God (*al-Ḥaqq*): therefore he must treat in the first place, of the Divine names, then of the Divine attributes, and lastly of the Divine essence. "I will call attention," he says, "to mysteries which no author has ever put into a book[4], matters concerning the gnosis of God and of the universe, and will tread a path between reserve and divulgation." He writes throughout as one reporting what has been communicated to him in mystical converse (*muká-*

[1] I do not know on what authority Dr Goldziher in his article on Jílí in the *Encycl. of Islam* (vol. I, p. 46) connects the *nisba* with Jíl, a village in the district of Baghdád. Jílí calls himself الكيلانى نسبًا البغدادى اصلًا (Loth, *Cat. of Arabic MSS. in the India Office Library*, p. 182, col. 1, l. 7 from foot). He traced his descent to a *sibṭ* of 'Abdu 'l-Qádir, *i.e.*, to a son of the Shaykh's daughter.

[2] He mentions (K II. 43, 20 foll.) that in A.H. 790 = A.D. 1388 he was in India at a place named Kúshí, where he conversed with a man under sentence of death for the murder of three notables. The earliest date referring to his stay at Zabíd is A.H. 796 = A.D. 1393–4 (K II. 61, 20), and the latest A.H. 805 = A.D. 1402–3 (Loth, *op. cit.* p. 183).

[3] K I. 6, 4 foll.

[4] Cf. K I. 63, penult. and foll.

lama), so that "the hearer knows it intuitively to be the word of God[1]." These private revelations are supported, he asserts, by the Koran and the Sunna, and he warns his readers not to charge him with errors which may arise from their own want of understanding; but while he professes belief in the Mohammedan articles of faith[2], he interprets them by an allegorising method that yields any and every meaning desired. As a writer, he is not without talent, though his work belongs to mysticism rather than to literature. Besides many poems which he seems to have admired inordinately[3], he introduces *maqámas* in rhymed prose and specimens of the Platonic myth. Thus he tells how the stranger, whose name is the Spirit, returned from long exile and imprisonment to the world known as Yúḥ, and entered a spacious city where Khaḍir rules over "the Men of the Unseen" (*rijálu 'l-ghayb*) —exalted saints and angels, of whom six classes are described[4].

The characteristic of the *Insánu 'l-kámil* is the idea of the Perfect Man, "who as a microcosmos of a higher order reflects not only the powers of nature but also the divine powers 'as in a mirror' (comp. the γενικὸς ἄνθρωπος of Philo)[5]." On this basis Jílí builds his mystical philosophy. It will be better grasped as a whole, if before coming to details I endeavour to sketch it in outline.

Jílí belongs to the school of Ṣúfís who hold that Being is one[6], that all apparent differences are modes, aspects, and manifestations of reality, that the phenomenal is the outward expression of the real. He begins by defining essence as that

[1] Jílí often uses logical arguments, but "the paradoxes proved by his logic are really the paradoxes of mysticism, and are the goal which he feels his logic must reach if it is to be in accordance with insight" (Bertrand Russell, "Mysticism and Logic" in the *Hibbert Journal*, vol. XII, No. 4, p. 793).

[2] K I. 4, 10 foll.

[3] K I. 39, 20 foll.

[4] K II. 34, 23 foll. Cf. K I. 8, 6 foll. In the *Futúḥátu 'l-Makkiyya*, ch. 559, Ibnu 'l-'Arabí likens the Divine Spirit in man to Yúḥ, "which is a name of the sun and refers to God (*al-Ḥaqq*), for He is the light of the heavens and the earth, and Man is a perfect and complete copy of Him" (M 34 *a*).

[5] Goldziher in *Encycl. of Islam*. The heavenly man is the *summum genus*, the earthly man the *summa species* (M 40 *a*).

[6] This doctrine is called "the unity of Being" (*waḥdatu 'l-wujúd*).

to which names and attributes are referred; it may be either existent or non-existent, *i.e.*, existing only in name, like the fabulous bird called *'Anqá*. Essence that really exists is of two kinds: Pure Being, or God, and Being joined to not-being, *i.e.*, the world of created things. The essence of God is unknowable *per se*; we must seek knowledge of it through its names and attributes. It is a substance with two accidents, eternity and everlastingness; with two qualities, creativeness and creatureliness; with two descriptions, uncreatedness and origination in time; with two names, Lord and slave (God and man); with two aspects, the outward or visible, which is the present world, and the inward or invisible, which is the world to come; both necessity and contingency are predicated of it, and it may be regarded either as non-existent for itself but existent for other, or as non-existent for other but existent for itself[1].

Pure Being, as such, has neither name nor attribute; only when it gradually descends from its absoluteness and enters the realm of manifestation, do names and attributes appear imprinted on it. The sum of these attributes is the universe, which is "phenomenal" only in the sense that it shows reality under the form of externality. Although, from this standpoint, the distinction of essence and attribute must be admitted, the two are ultimately one, like water and ice. The so-called phenomenal world—the world of attributes—is no illusion: it really exists as the self-revelation or other self of the Absolute. In denying any real difference between essence and attribute, Jílí makes Being identical with Thought. The world expresses God's idea of Himself, or as Ibnu 'l-'Arabí puts it, "we ourselves are the attributes by which we describe God; our existence is merely an objectification of His existence. God is necessary to us in order that we may exist, while we are necessary to Him in order that He may be manifested to Himself[2]."

Jílí calls the simple essence, apart from all qualities and relations, "the dark mist" (*al-'Amá*). It develops conscious-

[1] K I. 20, 23 foll.
[2] *Fuṣúṣ* (Cairo, A.H. 1312), 19, 78, 181, etc.

ness by passing through three stages of manifestation, which modify its simplicity. The first stage is Oneness (*Aḥadiyya*), the second is He-ness (*Huwiyya*), and the third is I-ness (*Aniyya*). By this process of descent Absolute Being has become the subject and object of all thought and has revealed itself as Divinity with distinctive attributes embracing the whole series of existence. The created world is the outward aspect of that which in its inward aspect is God. Thus in the Absolute we find a principle of diversity, which it evolves by moving downwards, so to speak, from a plane beyond quality and relation, beyond even the barest unity, until by degrees it clothes itself with manifold names and attributes and takes visible shape in the infinite variety of Nature. But "the One remains, the Many change and pass." The Absolute cannot rest in diversity. Opposites must be reconciled and at last united, the Many must again be One. Recurring to Jílí's metaphor, we may say that as water becomes ice and then water once more, so the Essence crystallised in the world of attributes seeks to return to its pure and simple self. And in order to do so, it must move upwards, reversing the direction of its previous descent from absoluteness. We have seen how reality, without ceasing to be reality, presents itself in the form of appearance: by what means, then, does appearance cease to be appearance and disappear in the abysmal darkness of reality?

Man, in virtue of his essence, is the cosmic Thought assuming flesh and connecting Absolute Being with the world of Nature.

While every appearance shows some attribute of reality, Man is the microcosm in which all attributes are united, and in him alone does the Absolute become conscious of itself in all its diverse aspects. To put it in another way, the Absolute, having completely realised itself in human nature, returns into itself through the medium of human nature; or, more intimately, God and man become one in the Perfect Man—the enraptured prophet or saint—whose religious function as a mediator between man and God corresponds with his metaphysical function as the unifying principle by means of which the opposed terms of reality and appearance are harmonised. Hence the upward movement of the Absolute from the sphere of manifestation back to the unmanifested Essence takes place in and through the unitive experience of the soul; and so we have exchanged philosophy for mysticism.

Jílí distinguishes three phases of mystical illumination or revelation (*tajallí*), which run parallel, as it were, to the three stages—Oneness, He-ness, and I-ness—traversed by the Absolute in its descent to consciousness.

In the first phase, called the Illumination of the Names, the Perfect Man receives the mystery that is conveyed by each of the names of God, and he becomes one with the name in such sort that he answers the prayer of any person who invokes God by the name in question.

Similarly, in the second phase he receives the Illumination of the Attributes and becomes one with them, *i.e.*, with the Divine Essence as qualified by its various attributes: life, knowledge, power, will, and so forth. For example, God reveals Himself to some mystics through the attribute of life. Such a man, says Jílí, is the life of the whole universe; he feels that his life permeates all things sensible and ideal, that all words, deeds, bodies, and spirits derive their existence from him. If he be endued with the attribute of knowledge, he knows the entire content of past, present, and future existence, how everything came to be or is coming or will come to be, and why the non-existent does not exist: all this he knows both synthetically and analytically. The Divine attributes are classified by the author under four heads: (1) attributes of the Essence, (2) attributes of Beauty, (3) attributes of Majesty, (4) attributes of Perfection. He says that all created things are mirrors in which Absolute Beauty is reflected. What is ugly has its due place in the order of existence no less than what is beautiful, and equally belongs to the Divine perfection: evil, therefore, is only relative. As was stated above, the Perfect Man reflects all the Divine attributes, including even the Essential ones, such as unity and eternity, which he shares with no other being in this world or the next.

The third and last phase is the Illumination of the Essence.

Here the Perfect Man becomes *absolutely* perfect. Every attribute has vanished, the Absolute has returned into itself.

In the theory thus outlined we can recognise a monistic form of the myth which represents the Primal Man, the first-born of God, as sinking into matter, working there as a creative principle, longing for deliverance, and, at last finding the way back to his source[1]. Jílí calls the Perfect Man the preserver of the universe, the *Quṭb* or Pole on which all the spheres of existence revolve. He is the final cause of creation, *i.e.*, the means by which God sees Himself, for the Divine names and attributes cannot be seen, as a whole, except in the Perfect Man. He is a copy made in the image of God; therefore in him is that which corresponds to the Essence with its two correlated aspects of He-ness and I-ness, *i.e.*, inwardness and outwardness, or divinity and humanity. His real nature is threefold, as Jílí expressly declares in the following verses, which no one can read without wondering how a Moslem could have written them:

If you say that it (the Essence) is One, you are right; or if you say that it is Two, it is in fact Two.
Or if you say, "No, it is Three," you are right, for that is the real nature of Man[2].

Here we have a Trinity consisting of the Essence together with its two complementary aspects, namely, Creator and creature—God and man. Now, all men are perfect potentially, but few are actually so. These few are the prophets and saints. And since their perfection varies in degree according to their capacity for receiving illumination, one of them must stand out above all the rest. Jílí remains a Moslem in spite of his philosophy, and for him this absolutely Perfect Man is the Prophet Mohammed. In the poem from which I have quoted he identifies the Three-in-One with Mohammed and addresses him as follows:

O centre of the compass! O inmost ground of the truth! O pivot of necessity and contingency!

[1] See Bousset, *Hauptprobleme der Gnosis*, p. 160 foll.
[2] K I. 10, 21 fol.

O eye of the entire circle of existence! O point of the Koran and the *Furqán*![1]

O perfect one, and perfecter of the most perfect, who have been beautified by the majesty of God the Merciful!

Thou art the Pole (*Quṭb*) of the most wondrous things. The sphere of perfection in its solitude turns on thee.

Thou art transcendent; nay, thou art immanent; nay, thine is all that is known and unknown, everlasting and perishable.

Thine in reality is Being and not-being; nadir and zenith are thy two garments.

Thou art both the light and its opposite; nay, but thou art only darkness to a gnostic that is dazed[2].

Jílí also holds that in every age the Perfect Men are an outward manifestation of the essence of Mohammed[3], which has the power of assuming whatever form it will; and he records the time and place of his own meeting with the Prophet, who appeared to him in the guise of his spiritual director, Sharafu-'ddín Ismá'íl al-Jabartí. In the 60th chapter of the *Insánu 'l-kámil* he depicts Mohammed as the absolutely perfect man, the first-created of God and the archetype of all other created beings. This, of course, is an Islamic Logos doctrine[4]. It brings Mohammed in some respects very near to the Christ of the Fourth Gospel and the Pauline Epistles. But if the resemblance is great, so is the difference. The Fatherhood of God, the Incarnation, and the Atonement suggest an infinitely rich and sympathetic personality, whereas the Mohammedan Logos tends to identify itself with the active principle of revelation in the Divine essence. Mohammed is

[1] See *Studies in Islamic Poetry*, p. 174, note 3. [2] K I. 11, 1 foll.

[3] So in the pseudo-Clementine writings Adam or Christ, the true prophet and perfect incarnation of the Divine spirit, is represented as manifesting himself personally in a whole series of subsequent bearers of Revelation. Bousset, *op. cit.* p. 172, quotes the following passages: "nam et ipse verus propheta ab initio mundi per saeculum currens festinat ad requiem," and "Christus, qui ab initio et semper erat, per singulas quasque generationes piis latenter licet semper tamen aderat." On the transmission of the Light of Mohammed see Goldziher's article cited in the next note.

[4] An excellent survey of the doctrine concerning the pre-existence of Mohammed, of the consequences drawn from it, and of the sources from which it was derived, will be found in Goldziher's *Neuplatonische und gnostische Elemente im Ḥadīṯ* (*Zeitschrift für Assyriologie*, vol. 22, p. 317 foll.).

loved and adored as the perfect image or copy of God: "he that has seen me has seen Allah," says the Tradition[1]. Except that he is not quite co-equal and co-eternal with his Maker, there can be no limit to glorification of the Perfect Man[2]. I need hardly say that Mohammed gave the lie direct to those who would have thrust this sort of greatness upon him: his apotheosis is the triumph of religious feeling over historical fact.

These ideas in part go back to Ḥalláj but were first worked out and systematised by the most prolific of Moslem theosophists and one of the most original, Muḥyi'ddín Ibnu 'l-'Arabí, of whose influence on the course of later Ṣúfí speculation the traces are so broad and deep that he well deserves the honorary title of *doctor maximus* (*al-shaykhu 'l-akbar*), by which he is frequently designated. Although Jílí does not follow him everywhere, he has learned much from his predecessor's manner of philosophising; he looks at things from a similar standpoint, and his thought moves in the same circle of mystical phantasies struggling to clothe themselves with forms of logic. Ibnu 'l-'Arabí would be better known to us, if he had written more briefly, lucidly, and methodically. In all these respects Jílí has the advantage: we can say of the *Insánu 'l-kámil* what cannot be said of the *Futúḥátu 'l-Makkiyya* or the *Fuṣúṣu 'l-ḥikam*—that the author is not so difficult as the subject. The philosophy of Ibnu 'l-'Arabí requires a volume for itself, but I will attempt to give my readers some account of the *Fuṣúṣ*, where he treats particularly of the Divine attributes displayed by the prophetic class of Perfect Men[3].

The *Insánu 'l-kámil*, though strongly marked with a character and expression of its own, is one of those books which gather up the threads of a whole system of thought and serve as a clue to it. After having explored the visionary world of reality through which the author conducts us step by step,

[1] Borrowed from St John, ch. xiv. *v*. 9.

[2] Jílí declares that wherever in his writings the expression "the Perfect Man" is used absolutely, it refers to Mohammed (K II. 59, 6).

[3] See Appendix II.

we at least know where we are when hierophants of the same guild beckon us to their company and bid us soar with them

Into the height of Love's rare universe.

I trust that the following analysis and exposition is full enough to bring out the principal features of the work and open an avenue for further study. The subject-matter of Jílí's sixty-three chapters has been arranged under a few heads in the way that seemed most suitable.

I. Essence, Attribute, and Name

The Absolute Essence (*Dhát*), or the Essence of God, is that to which names and attributes belong in their real nature, not as they appear in existence[1]. It denotes the self (*nafs*) of God whereby He exists, for He is self-subsistent. It is endowed with all the names and ideas which His perfection demands. Amongst these are infinity and incomprehensibility. No words can express or hint what the Essence is, since it has no opposite or like. In its absoluteness it annuls all the contradictions which, as the universal ground of individualisation, it includes[2].

I am convinced that It (the Essence) is non-existence, since by existence It was manifested[3].
Thought hath beheld It from afar as a power exerting itself in existence.
It is not other than a wall, wherein is set for thee a store of treasures.
I am that wall, and It is the hidden treasure—hidden in order that I may find it by digging.
Take It then, to be a body in respect of an outward form (which It assumes), while to that body It is a spirit, that thou mayst regard it (the body).

[1] K I. 18.
[2] Cf. the passage (I. 20, 23 foll.) translated on p. 83.
[3] The concept of existence involves non-existence as its logical complement. God, in virtue of His name, "the Outward" (*al-Ẓáhir*), is identical with all existing objects, while in virtue of His name, "the Inward" (*al-Báṭin*) He is non-existent externally. Cf. the saying of Hegel, "Being and not-Being are identical," *i.e.*, no distinctions are absolute.

God made Its comeliness (*ḥusn*) complete[1], and by the beauty (*jamál*) of God It became celebrated (known to all).
It never subsisted (as an object) but in thee alone[2]: perceive the Word (*Amr*)[3], that thou mayst see its diverse forms[4].

I am the existent and the non-existent and the naughted and the everlasting.
I am the awared and the imagined and the snake and the charmer.
I am the loosed and the bound and the wine and the cupbearer.
I am the treasure, I am poverty, I am my creatures and my Creator.

* * * * * *

Neither affirm my existence nor deny it, O immortal one!
Do not suppose thyself different from me or deem thyself the eye of my eye-corners.

* * * * * *

And say, "That am I, yet in respect of my qualities and natural dispositions That I am not[5]."

Jílí defines the attribute (*ṣifat*) of a thing as that which conveys knowledge of its state to the understanding[6]. The attributes of the Essence are the forms of thought by which it is manifested and made known. In the world of appearance we distinguish the forms from the reality underlying them, but the distinction is not ultimate: the attributes in their real nature are identical with the Essence which manifests itself as "other," *i.e.*, under the aspect of externality, to our perceptions[7]. What is called in theology the creation of the world is just this manifestation, accompanied by division and plurality, of the Essence as the attributes, or of Being as the object of thought; and in reality the Essence *is* the attributes (*al-Dhát 'aynu 'l-ṣifát*). The universe is an idea—"such stuff as dreams are made on," although the idea cannot properly be differentiated from the "thing-in-itself," except for convenience of understanding. Here let me translate part of the

[1] *Jamál* denotes the attribute of Divine Beauty, *ḥusn* its outward manifestation. Cf. Jílí's verse (in his *'Ayniyya*):

اذا قيل قُلْ لا قُلْتُ غَيْرَ جمالها * وإن قيل إلّا قلتُ حُسْنُك شائع

[2] In Man, the microcosm. [3] *I.e.* the Logos. [4] K I. 8, 18 foll.
[5] K I. 9, 11 foll. [6] K I. 27, 26. [7] Cf. K I. 81, 2 foll.

57th chapter, "Concerning thought (*khayál*), how it is the material (*hayúlá*, ὕλη) of the Cosmos[1]."

Thought is the life of the spirit of the universe: it is the foundation of that life, and its (Thought's) foundation is Man.
To him that knows Thought through the power of the Almighty, existence is nothing but a thought.
Sensation, before its appearance, is an object of thought to thee, and if it goes it resembles a dream.
And, similarly, the time during which it is felt inheres in our consciousness upon a foundation (of thought).
Be not deceived by sensation, for it is an object of thought (*mukhayyal*), and so is the reality (which every form expresses) and the whole universe,
And likewise, to him that knows the truth, the worlds of *malakút* and *jabarút*, and the divine nature (*láhút*) and the human nature (*násút*).
Do not despise the rank of Thought, for it is the very gist of the notion[2] of the Being who disposes all.

Know that Thought is the origin of existence and is the essence wherein God is manifested perfectly. Consider your own belief in God and in His having the attributes and names which belong to Him. Where is the *locus* (*maḥall*) of this belief, in which God is made manifest to you? It is Thought. Therefore we said that Thought is the essence wherein He becomes manifest in perfection. If you recognise this, it will be plain to you that Thought is the origin of the whole universe, because God is the origin of all things, and their most perfect manifestation occurs nowhere but in a *locus* which is the origin (of His manifestation); and that *locus* is Thought. Mark how the Prophet considered the sensible world to be a dream—and dream is a thought—and said, "Mankind are asleep, and when they die, they awake," *i.e.*, the reality in which they were during their earthly life is manifested to them, and they

[1] K II. 32, last line. *Khayál* is imaginal thought (phantasy). It includes all that is perceived by the mind in an ideal or material form. Mystics hold that God reveals Himself in five planes (*ḥaḍarát*): (1) the plane of the Essence, (2) the plane of the Attributes, (3) the plane of the Actions, (4) the plane of Similitudes and Phantasy (*khayál*), (5) the plane of sense and ocular vision. Each of these is a copy of the one above it, so that whatever appears in the sensible world is the symbol of an unseen reality. Cf. *Fuṣúṣ*, 110.

[2] *Ḥaqíqa*, *i.e.*, the attributes by which Pure Being is individualised.

perceive that they were asleep. Not that death brings a complete awakening. Forgetfulness (*ghaflat*) of God prevails over those in the intermediate state (*barzakh*) and those in the place of Judgment and those in Hell and Paradise, until God reveals Himself to them on the Hill to which the inhabitants of Paradise go forth and behold Him. This forgetfulness is the sleep (mentioned by the Prophet). The universe, then, has its origin in a thought, and for this reason Thought determines the individuals therein: all, whatever their sphere of existence, are determined by Thought. For example, the people of this world are determined by thought of their life as it is now or as it shall be hereafter; in either case, they are forgetful of presence with God (*al-ḥuḍúr ma' Allah*): they are asleep. He that is present with God is awake according to the measure of his presence....The sleep of the inhabitants of the next world is lighter, but although they are with God in respect that He is with all beings and says (in the Koran), "He is with you wheresoever ye be," yet are they with Him in sleep, not in waking. One that, by divine predestination, enjoys in this world what shall at last be shown on the Hill to the people of Paradise, so that God reveals Himself to him and he knows God—that man is (truly) awake. If you perceive that those in every world are judged to be asleep, then judge that all those worlds are a thought, inasmuch as Sleep is the world of Thought.

The comparison with dream-experience does not imply that the universe is unreal, but that it is reality *as presented to itself through and in the cosmic consciousness of the Perfect Man*, which holds all the attributes of reality together. This, we have already noted, is the central doctrine of the work before us. Other men lack such consciousness: they regard the sum of attributes constituting the "material" world as something different from the Essence and from themselves.

In the unitive state there is immediate perception of the Essence, but no mystic perceives the attributes as they really are: you can feel intuitively that you are He, that the Divine essence is consubstantial (*'ayn*) with your own, and thereby attain to knowledge of the Essence; you cannot, however, perceive and know the attributes of the Essence any more than you can perceive and know the qualities latent in yourself, which are only visible in their effects. Consequently it may be said that the Essence is imperceptible, in the sense of its being identical with the attributes[1].

The name (*ism*) objectifies the named (*musammá*) in the understanding, pictures it in the mind, presents it to the judgment, moves it in reflection and keeps it in memory[2]. It serves to make unknown things known; therefore, its relation to the named is that of the outward to the inward, and in this respect it is identical with the named. Some things exist in name and not otherwise; thus, the existence of the *'Anqá* is entirely nominal: the "named" in this case is not-being. God, on the contrary, is real Being; and just as our knowledge of the *'Anqá* is derived from its name, so we reach knowledge of God through the name Allah, in which all the Divine names and attributes are comprised[3].

God made this name a mirror for man, so that when he looks in it, he knows the true meaning of "God was and there was naught beside Him," and in that moment it is revealed to him that his hearing is God's hearing, his sight God's sight, his speech God's speech, his life God's life, his knowledge God's knowledge, his will God's will, and his power God's power, and that God possesses all these attributes fundamentally; and then he knows that all the aforesaid qualities are borrowed and metaphorically applied to himself, whereas they really belong to God[4].

The Divine names are either names of the Essence, *e.g.*, *al-Aḥad* (the One), or names of the attributes, *e.g.*, *al-Raḥmán* (the Merciful), *al-'Alím* (the Knowing). Each of them—except *al-Aḥad*, which transcends relationship—brings forth the effect (*athar*) inherent in that particular aspect of the Essence of which it is, so to speak, the embodiment. Good and evil, faith and infidelity, all mundane life, thought, feeling, and action proceed inevitably from the Divine names[5].

[1] K I. 28, 21 foll. [2] K I. 21, 4 fr. foot.

[3] Cf. the theory and practice of *dhikr*. The doctrine that the "named" is revealed by means of the name, which is its obverse or outward self, has played a great part in Ṣúfism.

[4] K I. 22, 20 foll.

[5] Cf. Ibnu 'l-'Arabí's definition of *ism* (*Ta'rífát* of Jurjání, ed. by Flügel, p. 293) as "the Divine name that rules a passing state of mystical feeling

II. The Descent of the Absolute[1].

Pure Being, devoid of qualities and relations, is called by Jílí "the dark mist" or "blindness" (*al-'Amá*), a term which the Prophet is said to have used in answering the question, "Where was God before the creation?[2]" Dr Iqbal remarks that *al-'Amá*, translated into modern phraseology, would be "the Unconsciousness," and that our author here anticipates the theories of Schopenhauer and Von Hartmann[3]. The parallel seems to me little more than verbal. Jílí's ontology is based on logic, and in developing it he follows a method which curiously resembles the Hegelian dialectic. According to Hegel,

the Absolute Idea itself is the resolution of the antithesis of Nature and Mind. The Idea is articulated as abstract, self-identical unity, negation of this by a plural "other" of particularity and differences, and as concrete identity-in-difference and unity-in-plurality, wherein it affirms itself with a richer content....The "result" in question, however, must not be expressed amiss. It does not occur at the end of a time-process. "Moments" severed for us are together for the Absolute Idea, the conscious Reason, the Notion which knows all as itself. The tail of the serpent is in the serpent's mouth. This self-sundering of the Idea is the Hegelian form of the mystic Jacob Böhme's view that "without self-diremption" the being of the Eternal would be not-being. Conscious knowledge, it is urged, implies antithesis within the Spiritual Ground[4].

(*ḥál*)," and the definitions of terms like *'abdullah*, *'abdu 'l-Raḥím*, *'abdu 'l-Malik*, etc., in the *Iṣṭiláḥátu 'l-Ṣúfiyya* of 'Abdu 'l-Razzáq al-Káshání, ed. by Sprenger, p. 91 foll.

1 "Descent" (*nuzúl*, *tanazzul*) is equivalent to "individualisation" (*ta'ayyun*) and denotes the process by which Pure Being gradually becomes qualified.

2 K I. 43, 2 foll. Cf. Lane under عَمَاءٌ and Nyberg, *Kleinere Schriften des Ibn al-'Arabī*, Introd., p. 154. Jílí says that the word signifies the Essence without its complementary attributes of *Ḥaqq* (Creator) and *khalq* (creatures), *i.e.*, the Essence viewed apart from its "self-diremption."

3 *Development of Metaphysics in Persia*, p. 165 fol. I have assumed that Dr Iqbal is referring to these philosophers. His exact words are "anticipates metaphysical doctrines of modern Germany."

4 E. D. Fawcett, *The World as imagination*, p. 102.

Similar principles determine Jílí's line of thought, although he never states them formally.

The *'Amá*, as he describes it, is not a blind unconscious power, but it is the absolute inwardness (*buṭún*) and occultation (*istitár*) in which the opposite concept of outwardness (*ẓuhúr*)—*i.e.*, all relations of the Essence to itself as "other"—is somehow absorbed and negated, like starlight in sunlight[1]. Jílí compares the *'Amá*, as the eternal and unchangeable ground of Being, to the fire which, in a sense, is always latent in the flint whence it flashes forth[2]. Thus the *'Amá* may be regarded as the inmost self, the "immanent negativity" of the Essence; as such, it is logically correlated with *Aḥadiyya*[3], in which the Essence knows itself as transcendental unity; and both these aspects are reconciled in the Absolute, "whose outwardness is identical with its inwardness[4]."

Aḥadiyya, the abstract notion of oneness, although nothing else is manifested in it, marks the first approach of the Essence to manifestation[5]. Its nature is analogous to a wall viewed from a distance as a single whole without reference to the clay, wood, bricks, and mortar of which it is composed: the wall is "one" in respect of its being a name for the "murity" (*jidáriyya*)[6]. In the same way *Aḥadiyya* comprises all particulars as negated by the idea of unity. This absolute unity in turn resolves itself into a pair of opposites in order to become re-united in a third term which carries the process of individualisation a stage further. Thus we arrive at *Wáḥidiyya*

[1] K I. 43, 8 foll.; I. 44, 5 foll. Cf. I. 61, 4 foll.—"The Essence (*Dhát*) denotes Absolute Being stripped of all modes, relations, and aspects. Not that they are outside of Absolute Being; on the contrary, they belong to it, but they are in it neither as themselves nor as aspects of it; no, they are identical with the being of the Absolute. The Absolute is the simple essence in which no name or quality or relation is manifested. When any of these appears in it, that idea is referred to that which appears in the Essence, not to the pure Essence, inasmuch as *the Essence, by the law of its nature, comprehends universals, particulars, and relations, not as they are judged to exist, but as they are judged to be naughted under the might of the transcendental oneness of the Essence.*"

[2] K I. 42, 23 foll.

[3] Jílí says distinctly that the terms *'Amá* and *Aḥadiyya* are opposed to each other as inward and outward aspects of the Essence (K I. 43, 7 foll.).

[4] K I. 45, 7.

[5] K I. 61, 16 foll.

[6] K I. 36, 9 foll.

or relative unity, *i.e.*, unity in plurality. The intervening thesis and antithesis are named *Huwiyya* (He-ness)[1] and *Aniyya* (I-ness)[2]. *Huwiyya* signifies the *inward* unity (*al-aḥadiyyat al-báṭina*) in which the attributes of the Essence disappear; *Aniyya*, the obverse side or outward expression of *Huwiyya*, is that unity *revealing itself* in existence. Clearly, then, external manifestation is the result of a "self-diremption" which lies in the very nature of the Essence as Pure Thought[3]. The discord of *Huwiyya* (the Many submerged in the One) and *Aniyya* (the One manifested in the Many) is overcome in the harmony of *Wáḥidiyya* (the Many identical in essence with each other and with the One)[4]. In *Wáḥidiyya* "essence is manifested as attribute and attribute as essence," so that all distinction between the attributes is lost: one is the *'ayn* (identity) of the other, Mercy and Vengeance are the same. We shall see that from this point of view the plane of Divinity (*Iláhiyya*) is a descent from *Wáḥidiyya*, in so far as in the former the attributes, which were identical in the latter, become distinct and opposed. Before passing to theology, let

[1] See K I. 61, 20 foll. and 82, 11 foll. *Huwa*, the pronoun of the third person singular, is called in Arabic grammar "the absent one" (*al-ghá'ib*); therefore *Huwiyya* indicates the absence (*ghaybúbiyya*) of the attributes of the Essence (from manifestation and perception). It is the inmost consciousness of God (*sirr Allah*). Jílí demonstrates this (I. 82, 19 foll.) by analysing the name Allah, which in Arabic is written ALLH: take away the A, and there remains LLH=*lilláh*="to God"; then take away the first L, and you are left with LH=*lahú*="to Him"; remove the second L, and you have H=*Huwa*="He" (cf. my ed. of the *Kitáb al-Luma'*, p. 89, l. 3 foll.). God is often described by Ṣúfís as the *huwiyya* or inmost self of man and the universe, while man and the universe are the *huwiyya* (*ḥaqíqa*, objectified idea) of God. God is the absolute *Huwiyya* (Individuality), and everything has its own peculiar *huwiyya*, which makes it what it is (*Fuṣúṣ*, 146, 8 foll.). Cf. *Fuṣúṣ*, 46 and 194.

[2] K I. 61, 22; 83, 16. *Aniyya*, derived from *Ana*, "I," and indicating presence, is involved in the notion of *Huwiyya* as the rind is implied by the kernel.

[3] Cf. E. Caird, *Hegel*, p. 149: "As the lightning sleeps in the dewdrop, so in the simple and transparent unity of self-consciousness there is held in equilibrium that vital antagonism of opposites, which, as the opposition of thought and things, of mind and matter, of spirit and nature, seems to rend the world asunder."

[4] Cf. K I. 37, 8–9: "*Wáḥidiyya* is that (aspect) in which the Essence appears as unifying the difference of my attributes. Here the All is both One and Many. Marvel at the plurality of what essentially is One."

me put the author's scheme of ontological devolution in the form of a table.

A. Absolute Being or Pure Thought (*al-Dhát, al-Wujúd al-muṭlaq*).
  (*a*) Inward aspect: "the dark mist" (*al-'Amá*). Being, sunk in itself, bare potentiality.
  (*b*) Outward aspect: abstract Oneness (*Aḥadiyya*). Being, conscious of itself as unity.

B. Abstract Oneness (*Aḥadiyya*).
  (*a*) Inward aspect: He-ness (*Huwiyya*). Being, conscious of itself as negating the Many (attributes).
  (*b*) Outward aspect: I-ness (*Aniyya*). Being, conscious of itself as the "truth" of the Many.

C. Unity in plurality (*Wáḥidiyya*). Being, identifying itself as One with itself as Many.

III. THE ESSENCE AS GOD.

In the *Insánu 'l-kámil* we find the same contrast as in the Vedânta system between Being with attributes, *i.e.*, God, and Being which would not be absolute unless it were stripped of all qualities. The essence of God is Pure Being, but Divinity (*Iláhiyya*)—the domain of Allah, regarded as He who necessarily exists—is the highest *manifestation* of the Essence, embracing all that is manifested: "it is a name for the sum of the individualisations of Being, *i.e.*, Being in the relation of Creator (*al-Ḥaqq*) to created things (*al-khalq*), and for their maintenance in their respective order in that sum[1]." Here the full ideal content of every individualisation, existent or non-existent[2], is manifested according to its proper place in the series, and all opposites exhibit their relativity in the greatest possible perfection; thus, the Creator (*al-Ḥaqq*) appears in the form of the creature (*al-khalq*)[3], and conversely the creature in the form of the Creator[4]. Since Divinity represents the sum of the attributes, it is invisible to the eye,

[1] K I. 31, 4 fr. foot.

[2] The universal correlation of *Iláhiyya* links Being with Not-being (cf. p. 89, note 3), a truth which cannot be apprehended except by mystical intuition (K I. 33, 2 foll.).

[3] According to the Ḥadíth, "I saw my Lord in the form of a beardless youth."

[4] *E.g.* "God created Adam in His own image."

though visible everywhere in its effects, *i.e.*, in the sensible world; the Essence, on the other hand, is visible, though its *where* is unknown. Similarly, when you see a man, you know or believe that he has certain qualities, but you do not see them; his essence (*dhát*), however, you see as a whole, even if many of his qualities are unknown to you. Only the effects of his qualities are visible, the qualities themselves you cannot see, because the attribute must always remain hidden in the Essence; otherwise, it could be separated from the Essence, and that is impossible[1]. In a scale of existence where each lower individualisation marks a loss of simplicity, the difference-in-identity (*Iláhiyya*) in which the sunken riches of the Absolute are completely realised, might be expected to succeed the identity-in-difference which belongs to the stage of *Wáḥidiyya*. Jílí, as a mystical theologian, does not take this view. He enthrones Allah in the seat of the Absolute and gives the following line of descent[2]:

1. Divinity (*Iláhiyya*).
2. Abstract Oneness (*Aḥadiyya*).
3. Unity in plurality (*Wáḥidiyya*).
4. Mercifulness (*Raḥmániyya*).
5. Lordship (*Rubúbiyya*).

Mercifulness and Lordship are specialised aspects of Divinity. *Raḥmániyya*[3] manifests the creative attributes (*al-ṣifátu 'l-ḥaqqiyya*) exclusively[4], whereas *Iláhiyya* comprehends both the creative and the creaturely (*khalqí*). The first mercy (*raḥmat*) of God was His bringing the universe into existence from Himself[5]. His manifestation pervaded all that exists, and His perfection was displayed in every particle and atom of the whole, yet He remains One (*wáḥid*) in the Many which mirror Him and Single (*aḥad*) according to the necessity of His nature, for He is indivisible and He created the world

[1] K I. 34, 14 foll. Cf. p. 92 *supra*.

[2] K I. 32, 8 foll.

[3] K I. 38, 16 foll.

[4] *I.e.*, the attributes peculiar to the Essence (*Aḥadiyya, Wáḥidiyya*, etc.) as well as those of the Creator (*al-Ḥaqq*), which necessarily bear a relation to created beings, *viz.*, life, knowledge, power, will, speech, hearing, and sight.

[5] K I. 39, 6.

from Himself. It is wrong to say that God "lends" His attributes to things; the things are really His attributes, to which He lends the name of creatureliness (*khalqiyya*)[1], in order that the mysteries of Divinity and the antithesis inherent in it may be revealed. God is the substance (*hayúlá*) of the universe. The universe is like ice, and God is the water of which it is made: the name "ice" is "lent" to the congealed mass, but its true name is "water." Jílí pursues this analogy in four verses which he quotes from an ode of his own composition[2]. He says in the second verse that although Religion declares the ice and the water to be different, "we mystics know that they are the same." He asks how this doctrine—the permeation of existence by the Essence—can be confounded with *ḥulúl* (incarnation), which affirms contact, *i.e.*, non-identity[3]. In virtue of the name *al-Raḥmán*, God exists in all the things that He brought into being. His mercy towards His creatures was shown by His manifesting Himself in them and by causing them to appear in Himself. "In every idea that you form God is present as its Creator, and you are God in respect of its existence in you, for you must needs form ideas in God and find (feel the presence of) God in forming them[4]."

Lordship (*Rubúbiyya*) establishes a necessary relation between God and His creatures, since it typifies the class of attributes which involve a complementary term or require an object; *e.g.*, "lord" implies "slave," and "knower"[4] refers to something "known."

It will be understood that "comparison" (*tashbíh*), *i.e.*, the bringing of God into relation with created things, is

[1] Cf. Ibnu 'l-'Arabí, *Tarjumán al-ashwáq*, No. 41, vv. 11–13.

[2] K I. 39, 6 fr. foot. The title of the ode is *al-nawádiru 'l-'ayniyya fí 'l-bawádiri 'l-ghaybiyya*. Cf. No. 19 in the list of his works given by Brockelmann, II. 206.

[3] K I. 40, 5 foll.

[4] K I. 40, 9 foll. In another passage (I. 66, 3 fr. foot and foll.) Jílí argues that by means of man the impossible is judged to be necessary. If you suppose what is impossible, *e.g.*, a living being without knowledge, that being exists in your thought and is a creature of God, inasmuch as thought with its content is a creature of God: thus by means of man there came into existence in the world that which had its centre of thought elsewhere (*i.e.*, in the knowledge of God).

"a judgment about Him[1]" and does not affect His absolute transcendence (*tanzíh*) as He is in Himself, which He alone can conceive and know[2]. This fact is known intuitively by Perfect Men; for other mystics it is a truth apprehended by faith. While the Essential *tanzíh* has no opposite, the antithesis of *tanzíh* and *tashbíh* is associated with God in His creative and creaturely aspects by those who perceive that He is One and that the form of all existent things is the form of Divine excellence (*ḥusn*)[3]. Considered absolutely, the Divine nature does not admit of change. Change consists in the relations of God, *i.e.*, in the diverse aspects wherein He manifests Himself to us. His manifestation of Himself to Himself, and His occultation of Himself in Himself, is eternally one and the same[4]. The notion of eternity, without beginning and without end, when it is applied to God, involves no time-relation with His creatures, but only a judgment that His nature is necessarily timeless[5].

Jílí makes a fourfold division of the Divine attributes: (1) attributes of the Essence, *e.g.*, One, Eternal, Real; (2) attributes of Beauty (*jamál*), *e.g.*, Forgiving, Knowing, Guiding aright; (3) attributes of Majesty (*jalál*), *e.g.*, Almighty, Avenging, Leading astray; (4) attributes of Perfection (*kamál*), *e.g.*, Exalted, Wise, First and Last, Outward and Inward[6].

Every attribute has an effect (*athar*), in which its *jamál* or *jalál* or *kamál* is manifested. Thus, objects of knowledge are the "effect" of the Name *al-'Alím*, the Knower. All attributes of *jamál*, and some of *jalál*, are displayed by everything that exists. Paradise is the mirror of absolute *jamál*, Hell of absolute *jalál*, and the universe is the form of these Divine attributes. Evil, as such, does not exist, although it has its appointed place in the world of opposites. What we call evil is really the relation of some parts and aspects of the whole to other parts and aspects; in a word, all imperfection arises

[1] K I. 46, 21.
[2] K I. 45, 12 foll.
[3] True knowledge of God combines His transcendence with His immanence (*Fuṣúṣ*, 228).
[4] K I. 43, 10 foll.
[5] See the chapters on *azal*, *abad* and *qidam* (K I. 85–89).
[6] K I. 75 foll. A list of the attributes in each class is given in K I. 78

from our not looking at things *sub specie unitatis*. Sin is not evil except in so far as we judge it to be forbidden by God. The author's treatment of the seven principal attributes—Life, Knowledge, Will, Power, Speech, Hearing, and Sight—is marked by great subtlety, but the discussion is somewhat arid. I will give a few specimens.

Life[1]. The existence of a thing for itself is its complete life; its existence for another is its relative life. God exists for Himself. He is the Living One (*al-Ḥayy*), and His life is the life complete and immortal. Created beings in general exist for God: their life is relative and linked with death. While the Divine life in created beings is one and complete, some manifest it in a complete form, *e.g.*, the Perfect Man and the Cherubim; others incompletely, *e.g.*, the animal man (*al-insánu 'l-ḥayawání*), the inferior angels, the *jinn* (genies), animals, plants, and minerals. Yet, in a certain sense, the life of all created beings is complete in the measure suitable to their degree and necessary for the preservation of the order of the universe. Life is a single essence, incapable of diminution or division, existent for itself in everything; and that which constitutes a thing is its life, that is to say, the life of God whereby all things subsist: they all glorify Him in respect of all His names, and their glorification of Him in respect of His name "the Living" is identical with their existence through His life. The author states, as a fact known to few but revealed to him by mystical illumination, that everything exists in and for itself, and that its life is entirely free and self-determined. This—which, as he admits, does not tally with what has been said above—is confirmed by the Divine information that on the Day of Resurrection each of a man's deeds will appear in visible shape and will address him and say, "I am thy deed."

Knowledge[2]. Although every attribute is independent and uncompounded, knowledge is most nearly connected with life: whatever lives knows[3]. Jílí controverts the doctrine of Ibnu 'l-'Arabí that God's knowledge is given Him by the

[1] K I. 63, 25 foll. [2] K I. 64, 22 foll.

[3] Animals and insects have an inspirational knowledge (*'ilm ilhámí*).

objects which He knows[1]. God certainly decreed that every individual thing should be what its nature required it to be, but the consequence drawn by Ibnu 'l-'Arabí, namely, that His knowledge of things is derived from the necessity of their natures, is false: on the contrary, their natures were necessitated by His knowledge of them before they were created and brought into existence—it was His knowing them, not the necessity inherent in them of being what they are, that caused them to become objects of His knowledge. Afterwards (*i.e.*, when they were created), their natures required other than that which He knew of them at first, and He then for the second time decreed that they should be what their natures required, according to that which He knew of them.

Will[2]. The will of God is "His particularisation of the objects of His knowledge by existence, according to the requirements of His knowledge." Our will is identical with the Divine eternal will, but in relation to us it partakes of our temporality (*ḥudúth*), and we call it "created." Nothing but this (unreal) attribution prevents us from actualising whatever we propose: if we refer our will to God, all things become subject to it. Jílí enumerates nine phases of will, beginning with inclination (*mayl*) and ending with the highest and purest love (*'ishq*), in which there is no lover or beloved, since both have passed away in the love that is God's very essence[3]. The Divine will is uncaused and absolutely free, not, as Ibnu 'l-'Arabí holds, determined by the obligation of the Knower to act as His nature demands[4].

[1] See Appendix. [2] K I. 67, 23 foll.

[3] Here the lover is named the beloved, and *vice versâ*. Jílí quotes three verses by himself; the last runs: "Thou seest them as two separate individuals in the point of Love, which is one." Cf. p. 80.

[4] According to Ibnu 'l-'Arabí, all action is the necessary result of God's infinite nature as eternally known to Himself (see Appendix), and free-will in the ordinary sense is excluded. Jílí tries to make room for it by ascribing to God a power of origination (*ikhtirá'*) which affects the things written in the Guarded Tablet, so that sometimes that which comes to pass is the contrary of what was decreed. Although the actions required by the Divine nature correspond with the capacity of the recipient individual in whom they are manifested, yet in consequence of his weakness and imperfection they lose their unalterable character and become contingent, *i.e.*, God, who is All-wise, determines whether they shall happen or not (K II. 8, 20 foll.).

Power[1]. This is defined by Jílí as "the bringing of the non-existent into existence." Here again he disagrees with Ibnu 'l-'Arabí, who asserts that God did not create the world from not-being, but only brought it from being in His knowledge into actual being. But in that case, Jílí argues, the world would be co-eternal with God. It is not so: the judgment that God exists in Himself is logically prior to the judgment that things exist in His knowledge; and the former judgment involves the non-existence of things and the existence of God alone. God brought things from not-being into being and caused them to exist in His knowledge, *i.e.*, He knew them as brought into existence from not-being; *then* He brought them forth from His knowledge and caused them to exist externally. Does it follow, because they were produced from not-being, that they were unknown to Him before He caused them to exist in His knowledge? No; the priority is of logic, not of time. There is no interval between the not-being of things and their existence in His knowledge. He knows them as He knows Himself, but they are not eternal as He is eternal.

IV. The Heavenly Man.

Like Jacob Böhme[2], Jílí sets out from the principle that "in order that the truth may be manifested as a Something, there must be a contrary therein." He finds the ground of existence in a Being which, though essentially One, is of threefold nature, since it knows itself as the Creator (*al-Ḥaqq*) and the creatures (*al-khalq*).

In another passage (I. 72, I foll.) Jílí says that God imputes free-will to mankind in order that He may show His justice by punishing them with Hell, and His mercy by rewarding them with Paradise.

[1] K I. 69, 24 foll.

[2] Böhme's three principles, *viz.*, the Godhead, Divine Wrath, and Divine Love, are represented in Jílí's system by the Essence with its complementary and harmonious attributes of majesty (*jalál*) and beauty (*jamál*). The German mystic unites Wrath and Love in a form which he calls "Fire": it is "the *centrum naturae*, the point between the kingdom of light and that of darkness, between love and anger, between good and evil" (Professor Deussen's introd. to Böhme's *Three Principles of the Divine Essence* tr. by John Sparrow, p. lvi foll.). This exactly answers to the perfection (*kamál*) of the Perfect Man.

"The Essence," he says, "is 'Thou' and 'I'—'Thou' in respect of thy deepest self (*huwiyya*, He-ness), not in respect of the human attributes which the notion 'Thou' admits; and 'I' in respect of my individual self, not in respect of the Divine attributes which the notion 'I' admits. That is what is signified by the Essence (*al-Dhát*). 'I,' in respect of my 'I-ness' (*aniyya*), viewed in relation to the judgments which the notion 'I' is capable of, is God; and 'Thou,' in the creaturely aspect, is Man. Therefore consider your essence, if you will, as 'I,' or if you will, as 'Thou,' for there is nothing besides the universal reality....

If you say, that it (the Essence) is One, you are right; or if you say that it is Two, it is in fact Two.

Or if you say, 'No, it is Three,' you are right, for that is the real nature of Man.

Regard the Oneness (*aḥadiyya*) which is his essence: say, 'He is One relatively (*wáḥid*), One absolutely (*aḥad*), unique in glory.'

But if the two essences are considered, you will say that he is Two, because he is a slave (*'abd*) and a Lord (*rabb*).

And if you examine his real nature and what is united therein, namely, two things deemed to be contrary,

You will contemplate him with amazement: his lowness is such that you will not call him lofty, and his loftiness is such that you will not call him low.

Nay, name that (Man) a Third, because of a reality having two attributes inherent in the realities of its essence[1].

It (that reality) is he named Aḥmad as being that (Man), and Mohammed as being the true idea (*ḥaqíqa*) of all things that exist[2]."

As an introduction to the Logos doctrine foreshadowed here, which is interwoven with a mystical scheme of cosmology, I will translate part of the 60th chapter, "Of the Perfect Man: showing that he is our Lord Mohammed, and that he stands over against the Creator (*al-Ḥaqq*) and the creatures (*al-khalq*)[3]."

[1] The Perfect Man is neither Absolute Being nor Contingent Being, but a third metaphysical category, *i.e.*, the Logos. See Nyberg, *Kleinere Schriften des Ibn al-'Arabī*, Introd., p. 32 foll., 50.

[2] K I. 10, 12 foll. In the Koran (61, 6) Mohammed is named Aḥmad and identified with the Paraclete foretold by Christ.

[3] K II. 58, 22.

The Perfect Man is the *Quṭb* (axis) on which the spheres of existence revolve from first to last, and since things came into being he is one (*wáḥid*) for ever and ever. He hath various guises and appears in diverse bodily tabernacles (*kaná'is*): in respect of some of these his name is given to him, while in respect of others it is not given to him. His own original name is Mohammed, his name of honour Abu 'l-Qásim, his description 'Abdullah[1], and his title Shamsu'ddín[2]. In every age he bears a name suitable to his guise (*libás*) in that age. I once met him in the form of my Shaykh, Sharafu'ddín Ismá'íl al-Jabartí, but I did not know that he (the Shaykh) was the Prophet, although I knew that he (the Prophet) was the Shaykh. This was one of the visions in which I beheld him at Zabíd in A.H. 796. The real meaning of this matter is that the Prophet has the power of assuming every form. When the adept (*adíb*) sees him in the form of Mohammed which he wore during his life, he names him by that name, but when he sees him in another form and knows him to be Mohammed, he names him by the name of the form in which he appears. The name Mohammed is not applied except to the Idea of Mohammed (*al-Ḥaqíqatu 'l-Muḥammadiyya*). Thus, when he appeared in the form of Shiblí[3], Shiblí said to his disciple, "Bear witness that I am the Apostle of God"; and the disciple, being one of the illuminated, recognised the Prophet and said, "I bear witness that thou art the Apostle of God." No objection can be taken to this: it is like what happens when a dreamer sees some one in the form of another; but there is a difference between dreaming and mystical revelation, *viz.*, that the name of the form in which Mohammed appears to the dreamer is not bestowed in hours of waking upon the *Ḥaqíqatu 'l-Muḥammadiyya*, because interpretation is applicable to the World of Similitudes: accordingly, when the dreamer wakes he interprets the *ḥaqíqa* of Mohammed as being the *ḥaqíqa* of the dream-form. In mystical revelation it is otherwise, for if you perceive mystically that the *ḥaqíqa* of Mohammed is displayed in any human form, you must bestow upon the *ḥaqíqa* of Mohammed the name of that form and regard its owner with no less reverence than you would show to our Lord Mohammed, and after having seen him therein you may not behave towards it in the same

[1] The servant of God. [2] The Sun of the Religion.

[3] A famous Ṣúfí of Baghdád. He died in A.D. 945–6.

manner as before. Do not imagine that my words contain any tincture of the doctrine of metempsychosis. God forbid! I mean that the Prophet is able to assume whatever form he wishes, and the Sunna declares that in every age he assumes the form of the most perfect men, in order to exalt their dignity and correct their deviation (from the truth): they are his vicegerents outwardly, and he is their spiritual essence (*ḥaqíqa*) inwardly.

The Perfect Man in himself stands over against all the individualisations of existence. With his spirituality he stands over against the higher individualisations, with his corporeality over against the lower. His heart stands over against the Throne of God (*al-'Arsh*), his mind over against the Pen (*al-Qalam*), his soul over against the Guarded Tablet (*al-Lawḥu 'l-maḥfúẓ*), his nature over against the elements, his capability (of receiving forms) over against matter (*hayúlá*)....He stands over against the angels with his good thoughts, over against the genies and devils with the doubts which beset him, over against the beasts with his animality. ...To every type of existence he furnishes from himself an antitype. We have already explained that every one of the Cherubim is created from an analogous faculty of the Perfect Man. It only remains to speak of his correspondence with the Divine names and attributes.

You must know that the Perfect Man is a copy (*nuskha*) of God, according to the saying of the Prophet, "God created Adam in the image of the Merciful," and in another *ḥadíth*, "God created Adam in His own image." That is so, because God is Living, Knowing, Mighty, Willing, Hearing, Seeing, and Speaking, and Man too is all these. Then he confronts the Divine *huwiyya* with his *huwiyya*, the Divine *aniyya* with his *aniyya*, and the Divine *dhát* (essence) with his *dhát*—he is the whole against the whole, the universal against the universal, the particular against the particular....Further, you must know that the Essential names and the Divine attributes belong to the Perfect Man by fundamental and sovereign right in virtue of a necessity inherent in his essence, for it is he whose "truth" (*ḥaqíqa*) is signified by those expressions and whose spirituality (*laṭífa*) is indicated by those symbols: they have no subject in existence (whereto they should be attached) except the Perfect Man. As a mirror in which a person sees the form of himself and cannot see it without the mirror, such is the relation of God to the Perfect Man, who cannot possibly see his own form but in the mirror of the name Allah; and he is also a mirror to God, for God laid upon Himself the necessity that His names and attributes should not be seen save in the Perfect Man. This obligation to display the Divine attributes is the "trust" (*amána*) which God offered to the heavens and the earth: they were afraid to accept it, "but Man accepted it; verily he is unjust and ignorant" (Kor. 33, 72), *i.e.*, unjust to his own soul in letting it suffer degradation (from the things of this world) and ignorant of his real worth, because he is unaware of that with which he has been entrusted....Beyond the plane of the Names and Attributes, which are ranged on the right and left of him according to their kind, the Perfect Man feels through his whole being "a pervasive delight, which is named the delight of the Godhead" (*ladhdhatu 'l-iláhiyya*)....Here he is independent of his modes, *i.e.*, the Names and Attributes, and regards them not at all. He knows nothing in existence save his own nature (*huwiyya*), contemplates the emanation (*ṣudúr*) from himself of all that exists, and beholds the Many in his essence, even as ordinary men are conscious of their own thoughts and qualities; but the Perfect Man is able to keep every thought, great or small, far from himself: his power over things does not proceed from any secondary cause but is exercised freely, like other men's power of speaking, eating, and drinking.

These extracts bring out the germinal idea which is developed by Jílí into a psychological and cosmological system. The Perfect Man, as the copy of God and the archetype of Nature, unites the creative and creaturely aspects of the Essence and manifests the oneness of Thought with things. "He is the heaven and the earth and the length and the breadth[1]."

Mine is the kingdom in both worlds: I saw therein none but
myself, that I should hope for his favour or fear him.
Before me is no "before," that I should follow its condition, and
after me is no "after," that I should precede its notion.

[1] K I. 26, 3 fr. foot. "The length and the breadth" (*al-ṭúl wa 'l-'arḍ*) is a formula invented by Ḥalláj, which corresponds with *láhút* (Divinity) and *násút* (Humanity) and expresses his dualistic conception of the spiritual and material universe. Ibnu 'l-'Arabí and Jílí interpret the "two dimensions" in a monistic sense. See Massignon, *Kitáb al-Ṭawásín*, p. 141 foll.

I have made all kinds of perfection mine own, and lo, I am the beauty of the majesty of the Whole: I am naught but It.

Whatsoever thou seest of minerals and plants and animals, together with Man and his qualities,

And whatsoever thou seest of elements and nature and original atoms (*haba'*) whereof the substance is (ethereal as) a perfume,

And whatsoever thou seest of seas and deserts and trees and high-topped mountains,

And whatsoever thou seest of spiritual forms and of things visible whose countenance is goodly to behold,

And whatsoever thou seest of thought and imagination and intelligence and soul, and heart with its inwards,

And whatsoever thou seest of angelic aspect, or of phenomena whereof Satan is the spirit,

* * * * * *

Lo, I am that whole, and that whole is my theatre: 'tis I, not it, that is displayed in its reality.

Verily, I am a Providence and Prince to mankind: the entire creation is a name, and my essence is the object named.

The sensible world is mine and the angel-world is of my weaving and fashioning; the unseen world is mine and the world of omnipotence springs from me.

And mark! In all that I have mentioned I am a slave returning from the Essence to his Lord—

Poor, despised, lowly, self-abasing, sin's captive, in the bonds of his trespasses[1].

The concluding verses only say what Jílí repeats in many places, that while at supreme moments a man may lose himself in God, he can never be identified with God absolutely.

In the second part of his work the author treats of the Perfect Man as the Spirit whence all things have their origin. Accordingly he devotes successive chapters to the organs and faculties which make up the psychological and intellectual constitution of the Perfect Man—spirit, heart, intelligence, reflection, etc., with the corresponding celestial beings which are said to be "created" from them[2]. The highest hypostases of his psychology are the Holy Spirit (*Rúḥu 'l-Quds*) and the

[1] K I. 26, last line and foll.

[2] K II. 10 foll.

Spirit (*al-Rúḥ*); the latter is also described as "the angel named al-Rúḥ" and, in the technical language of the Ṣúfís, as "the *ḥaqq* by means of which the world is created" (*al-ḥaqqu 'l-makhlúq bihi*) and "the Idea of Mohammed" (*al-Ḥaqíqatu 'l-Muḥammadiyya*). How these two Spirits are related to each other is indicated in the following passage:

You must know that every sensible object has a created spirit which constitutes its form, and the spirit is to the form as the meaning to the word. The created spirit has a Divine spirit which constitutes it, and that Divine spirit is the *Rúḥu 'l-Quds*. Those who regard the *Rúḥu 'l-Quds* in man deem it created, because two eternal substances cannot exist: eternity belongs to God alone, whose names and attributes inhere in His essence because of the impossibility of their being detached; all else is created and originated. Man, for example, has a body, which is his form, and a spirit, which is his meaning, and a consciousness (*sirr*), which is *al-Rúḥ*, and an essential aspect (*wajh*), which is denoted by the terms *Rúḥu 'l-Quds* (the Holy Spirit), *al-sirru 'l-iláhí* (the Divine consciousness) and *al-wujúdu 'l-sárí* (the all-pervading Being)[1].

The *Rúḥu 'l-Quds* and the *Rúḥ* are one Spirit viewed as eternal in relation to God and non-eternal in relation to Man; as the inmost essence of things or as their form of existence[2]. The uncreated Spirit of God, sanctified above all phenomenal imperfections, is referred to in the verse, "I breathed of My Spirit into Adam" (Kor. 15, 29; 38, 72), and in the verse, "Wheresoever ye turn, there is the face (*wajh*) of Allah" (Kor. 2, 109), *i.e.*, the *Rúḥu 'l-Quds* exists, "individualised by its perfection," in every object of sense or thought. Jílí adds that inasmuch as the spirit of a thing is its self (*nafs*), existence is constituted by the "self" of God; and His "self" is His essence[3]. Union with the *Rúḥu 'l-Quds* comes only as the crown and consummation of the mystical life to "the holy one" (*qudsí*)[4] who unceasingly contemplates the

[1] K II. 11, 4 foll. [2] Cf. M, 4 *a*, 7 *b*.

[3] K II. 10, 6 fr. foot and foll.

[4] In M, 6 *b*, Jílí distinguishes the *qudsí* (holy one), who is illuminated by the Divine attributes, from the *aqdasí* (most holy one), who is united with the Essence.

Divine consciousness (*sirr*) which is his origin, so that its laws are made manifest in him and God becomes his ear, eye, hand and tongue: he touches the sick and they are healed, he bids a thing be and it is, for he has been strengthened with the Holy Spirit, even as Jesus was (Kor. 2, 81)[1].

It will now be seen that Jílí considers the created *Rúḥ* or the archetypal Spirit of Mohammed as a mode of the uncreated Holy Divine Spirit and as the medium through which God becomes conscious of Himself in creation[2].

God created the angel named *Rúḥ* from His own light, and from him He created the world and made him His organ of vision in the world. One of his names is the Word of Allah (*Amr Allah*)[3]. He is the noblest and most exalted of existent beings: there is no angel above him, and he is the chief of the Cherubim. God caused the mill-stone of existent beings to turn on him, and made him the axis (*quṭb*) of the sphere of created things. Towards every thing that God created he has a special aspect (*wajh*), in virtue of which he regards it and preserves it in its appointed place in the order of existence. He has eight forms, which are the bearers of the Divine Throne (*al-'Arsh*)[4]. From him were created all the angels, both the sublime and the elemental. The angels stand to him in the relation of drops of water to the sea, and the eight bearers of the *'Arsh* stand in the same relation to him as the eight faculties which constitute human existence to the spirit of man. These faculties are intelligence (*'aql*), judgment (*wahm*), reflection (*fikr*), phantasy (*khayál*), imagination (*al-muṣawwira*), memory (*al-ḥáfiẓa*), perception (*al-mudrika*), and the soul (*nafs*). The *Rúḥ* exercises a Divine guardianship, created in him by God, over the whole universe. He manifests himself in his perfection in the *Ḥaqíqatu 'l-Muḥammadiyya*: therefore the Prophet is the most excellent of mankind. While God manifests Himself in His attributes to all other created beings, He manifests Himself in His essence to this

[1] K II. 11, 7 fr. foot and foll. [2] K II. 12, 6 foll.

[3] For the use of *amr* (which is radically connected with the Jewish *mēmrā*) in the sense of Logos, see H. Hirschfeld, *New researches into the composition and exegesis of the Qoran*, p. 15. Cf. Kor. 17, 87.

[4] See Kor. 69, 17, and cf. Nyberg, *Kleinere Schriften des Ibn al-'Arabī*, Introd., p. 146. The *'Arsh* is the Universal Body (الجسم الكلّى) or the frame of the Cosmos (هيكل العالم وجسده), K II. 5–6.

angel alone. Accordingly the *Rúḥ* is the *Quṭb* of the present world and of the world to come. He does not make himself known to any creature of God but to the Perfect Man. When the saint (*walí*) knows him and truly understands the things which the *Rúḥ* teaches him, he becomes a pole (*quṭb*) on which the entire universe revolves; but the Poleship (*Quṭbiyya*) belongs fundamentally to the *Rúḥ*, and if others hold it, they are only his delegates[1]. He is the first to receive the Divine command, which he then delivers to the angels; and whenever a command is to be executed in the universe, God creates from him an angel suitable to that command, and the *Rúḥ* sends him to carry it out. All the Cherubim are created from him, *e.g.*, Seraphiel, Gabriel, Michael, and Azrael, and those above them, such as the angel named al-Nún[2], who is stationed beneath the Guarded Tablet, and the angel named the Pen (*al-Qalam*), and the angel named al-Mudabbir, whose station is beneath the *Kursí*[3], and the angel named al-Mufaṣṣil, who

[1] Jílí's identification of the *Rúḥ* with the *Quṭb*, taken in conjunction with the fact that the *Rúḥ* is essentially God regarded as the Holy Spirit or as the First Intelligence (see pp. 109 and 112), suggests an explanation of the mysterious doctrine broached by Ghazálí in the *Mishkátu 'l-Anwár*, where he asserts that in very truth the Mover of all is not Allah but a Being, described as "the Obeyed One" (*al-muṭá'*), "whose nature is left obscure, since our only information about him is that he is not the Real Being. Allah's relation to this Vicegerent, the supreme controller of the Universe, is compared to the relation of the impalpable light-essence to the sun, or of the elemental fire to a glowing coal" (W. H. T. Gairdner, *Al-Ghazālī's Mishkāt al-Anwār and the Ghazālī-problem* in *Der Islam*, 1914, p. 121 foll.). I agree with Canon Gairdner that Ghazálí would not have accepted the ordinary hierarchical *Quṭb* doctrine current amongst the Ṣúfís of the 5th century A.H., if not earlier. But an hypostatised *Quṭb* is another matter. The Perfect Man, though not himself the Absolute, in no way impairs the absolute Divine unity which he objectifies. It looks to me as if Ghazálí's esoteric teaching, which he keeps back from his readers because they "cannot bear it," was not different in substance from the Logos doctrine of the *Insánu 'l-kámil*. His allusions to ineffable arcana, centring in the tradition that Adam was created in the image of God, are extremely significant. [Cf. now Tor Andrae, *Die person Muhammeds*, p. 335 and Nyberg, *op. cit.*, Introd., p. 106 foll.]

[2] See Koran, 68, 1. Al-Nún symbolises the Divine knowledge (K II. 22, 3).

[3] The Footstool under the Divine Throne (*'Arsh*). Those who are not familiar with these and other details of Mohammedan cosmogony may consult E. J. W. Gibb's *History of Ottoman Poetry*, vol. I. p. 34 foll. According to Jílí, the creatures (*al-khalq*) are first individualised occultly and without differentiation in the Divine knowledge, then brought into existence,

stands beneath the Imámu 'l-Mubín[1]: these are the Sublime Angels, who were not commanded to worship Adam. God in His wisdom did not command them, for had they been commanded to worship, every one of Adam's descendants would have known them. Consider how, inasmuch as the angels were commanded to worship Adam, they appear to men in the forms of the Divine similitudes whereby God reveals Himself to the dreamer. All those forms are angels, who descend in diverse shapes by command of the angel entrusted with the making of similitudes. For this reason a man dreams that lifeless things speak to him: unless they were really spirits assuming the form of lifelessness, they would not have spoken. The Prophet said that a true dream is an inspiration from God—because an angel brings it—and also that a true dream is one of the forty-six parts of prophecy. Since Iblís, though he did not worship Adam, was amongst those commanded to worship, the devils who are his offspring were commanded to appear to the dreamer in the same forms as the angels: hence false dreams. According to this argument, the Sublime Angels are unknowable except by "the divine men" (*al-iláhiyyún*), on whom God bestows such knowledge as a gift after their release from the limitations of humanity.

The *Rúḥ* has many names according to the number of his aspects. He is named "The Most Exalted Pen" and "The Spirit of Mohammed" and "The First Intelligence" and "The Divine Spirit," on the principle of naming the original by the derivative, but in the presence of God he has only one name, which is "The Spirit" (*al-Rúḥ*).

Jílí gives a long account of a vision in which the *Rúḥ* conversed with him and spoke darkly concerning the mystery of his nature, saying, ' I am the child whose father is his son and the wine whose vine is its jar....I met the mothers who

synthetically and virtually, in the *'Arsh* (cf. K II. 5, 12 foll.), then manifested analytically in the *Kursí* (cf. K II. 6, 11 foll.). All these individualisations are "unseen" (*ghayb*), *i.e.*, in God, so to speak. The first *objective* individualisation takes place in the Pen (*al-Qalam*), which distinguishes the creatures from the Creator and imprints their forms of existence on the Guarded Tablet (*al-Lawḥ al-maḥfúẓ*), as the mind imprints ideas on the soul. Hence it is said in the Prophetic Tradition that the Pen or the Intelligence (*al-'aql*) was the first thing that God created (K II. 6, last line and foll.).

[1] The Imámu 'l-Mubín is identified with the First Intelligence (K II. 22, 1), and with the human spirit (M 7 *b*).

bore me, and I asked them in marriage, and they let me marry them[1]." In the course of this colloquy the Idea of Mohammed (*al-Ḥaqíqatu 'l-Muḥammadiyya*) says:

God created Adam in His own image—this is not doubted or disputed—and Adam was one of the theatres (*maẓáhir*) in which I displayed myself: he was appointed as a vicegerent (*khalífa*) over my externality. I knew that God made me the object and goal of all His creatures, and lo, I heard the most gracious allocution from the Most Great Presence: "Thou art the *Quṭb* whereon the spheres of beauty revolve, and thou art the Sun by whose radiance the full-moon of perfection is replenished; thou art he for whom We set up the pattern[2] and for whose sake We made fast the door-ring[3]; thou art the reality symbolised by Hind and Salmá and 'Azza and Asmá[4]. O thou who art endued with lofty attributes and pure qualities, Beauty doth not dumbfound thee nor Majesty cause thee to quake, nor dost thou deem Perfection unattainable: thou art the centre and these the circumference, thou art the clothed and these the splendid garments[5]."

In some aspects the spiritual organ which Ṣúfís call "the heart" (*qalb*) is hardly distinguished from the spirit (*rúḥ*): indeed Jílí says that when the Koran mentions the Divine spirit breathed into Adam, it is the heart that is signified. He

[1] K II. 14, 23 foll. The commentator explains that the *Rúḥ* is the object of Divine knowledge whose father (Divine knowledge) is produced by the object of knowledge and is therefore its son. Cf. the verse of Badru'ddín al-Shahíd:

> My mother bore her father—lo, that is a wondrous thing—
> And my father is a little child in the bosom of those who suckle it.

The mother is Nature. Adam, her son in one sense, is her father in another, because he (as the microcosm) is the origin of all created things, like the date-kernel which is both the seed of the palm and its fruit (Comm. K 17 *b*).

[2] *I.e.*, the First Intelligence, the archetype of created things, which in relation to the Perfect Man is named the Spirit of Mohammed (cf. K II. 6, penult. and foll.).

[3] *I.e.*, the Perfect Man is the door-keeper of the temple of the Godhead, and he alone can reveal its mysteries. The text has زرفونج, but according to Comm. K (foll. 19 *b*) the correct reading is زُرْقُونج = حلقة الباب, *i.e.*, the ring into which a chain was inserted, so that it served as a padlock. Cf. Vullers' Persian lexicon under زُرفين.

[4] These names are typical of the women whose charms are celebrated by Arabian poets.

[5] K II. 15, 10 foll.

describes it as "the eternal light and the sublime consciousness (*sirr*) revealed in the quintessence (*'ayn*) of created beings (Mohammed), that God may behold Man thereby[1]"; as "the Throne of God (*al-'Arsh*) and His Temple in Man...the centre of Divine consciousness and the circumference of the circle of all that exists actually or ideally[2]." It reflects all the Divine names and attributes at once, yet quickly changes under the influence of particular names. Like a mirror, it has a face and a back. The face is always turned towards a light called the attention (*al-hamm*), which is the eye of the heart, so that whenever a name becomes opposite to, or as we should say, strikes the attention, the heart sees it and receives the impression of it; then this name disappears and is succeeded by others. The "back" of the heart is the place from which the attention is absent[3]. Jílí illustrates his meaning by the diagram reproduced here:

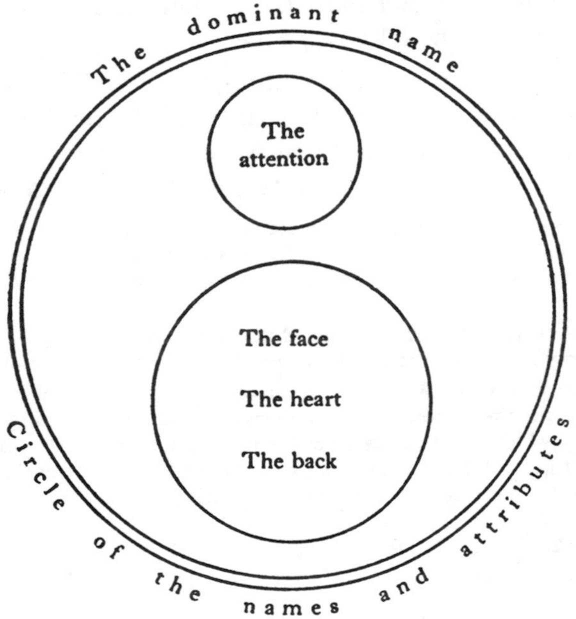

[1] K II. 18, 2. [2] K II. 16, 25 foll.

[3] The position of the *hamm* varies in different men. It may face upward or downward or to the right or to the left, *i.e.*, in the direction of the *nafs* (appetitive soul), which is located in the left rib. The hearts of profound mystics have no *hamm* and no back (*qafá*): these men face with their whole being the whole of the Divine names and attributes and are with God *essentially* (K II. 18, penult. and foll.).

The Divine names and attributes are the heart's true nature, in which it was created. Some men are so blessed that they have little trouble to keep it pure, but most of us must needs undergo painful self-mortifications in order to wash out the stains of the flesh[1]. Recompense for good works depends on the merit imputed by God to His creatures according to the original individualisations in which He created them: it is a necessary right, not an arbitrary gift[2]. The heart reflects the world of attributes, or rather, as Jílí holds, is itself reflected by the universe. "Earth and heaven do not contain Me, but the heart of My believing servant containeth Me": if the universe were primary and the heart secondary, *i.e.*, if the heart were only a mirror, then the power of containing and comprehending would have been ascribed to the universe, not to the heart; but in fact, it is the heart alone that comprehends God—by knowledge, by contemplation, and finally by transubstantiation[3].

When God created the whole world from the Light of Mohammed, He created from the heart of Mohammed the angel Isráfíl (Seraphiel), the mightiest of the angels and the nearest to God[4].

The faculty of Reason has three modes, *viz.*, the First Intelligence (*al-'aqlu 'l-awwal*), Universal Reason (*al-'aqlu 'l-kullí*), and ordinary reason (*'aqlu 'l-ma'ásh*)[5]. Jílí identifies the First Intelligence, as the faithful treasurer of Divine

[1] K II. 19, 15 foll.

[2] Therefore the illuminations (*tajalliyát*) of the Essence are not named "a gift" (II. 20, 10). Jílí quotes a verse of "our Shaykh, Shaykh 'Abdu 'l-Qádir al-Jílání":

I ceased not pasturing in the fields of quietism until I reached a dignity which is not bestowed by favour.

[3] K II. 20, 23 foll. This agrees with Ibnu 'l-'Arabí's doctrine in the *Fuṣúṣ*, 145 foll. The three kinds of comprehension are denoted by the terms *wus'u 'l-'ilm* (*'ilm* in this connexion is synonymous with *ma'rifa*), *wus'u 'l-musháhada*, and *wus'u 'l-khiláfa*. In the last stage Man is essentialised and becomes the *khalífa* or vicegerent of God. Jílí, however, maintains a distinction even here. The Perfect Man knows the perfection of the Divine nature as manifested in him, not the perfection of the Divine nature in itself, which is infinite and (since the Essence cannot be comprehended by one of its attributes) ultimately unknowable. We can only say that God knows Himself according to the necessity of His knowledge (*ḥaqqu 'l-ma'rifa*).

[4] K II. 21, 16 foll.

[5] K II. 22, 4.

Knowledge, with Gabriel, "the trusted Spirit" (*al-Rúḥu 'l-amín*)[1], and as a *locus* for the form of Divine Knowledge in existence—the first objective analysis of the Divine synthesis—with the Pen (*al-Qalam*) which transmits the particulars contained as a whole in God's consciousness to the Guarded Tablet (*al-Lawḥu 'l-maḥfúẓ*)[2]. Universal Reason is "the percipient luminous medium whereby the forms of knowledge deposited in the First Intelligence are made manifest[3]"; not the sum of individual intelligences, for in this case Reason would be plural, while in reality it is a single substance, the common element, so to speak, of human, angelic, and demonic spirits. Ordinary reason is "the light (of Universal Reason) measured by the rule of reflection (*fikr*), and does not apprehend save by means of reflection": therefore it cannot reach the unconditioned First Intelligence, often misses its mark, and fails to perceive many things. Universal Reason, on the other hand, is infallible, since it weighs all with the twin scales of Wisdom and Power[4], but it never penetrates beyond the sphere of creation. Neither universal (intuitive) nor ordinary (discursive) reason can attain to knowledge of God. The contrary doctrine has only a demonstrative and controversial value. True gnosis (*ma'rifa*) is given by faith, which does not depend on proofs and effects (*áthár*) but on the Divine attributes themselves[5].

The judgment (*wahm*) of Mohammed was created from the light of the Divine Name *al-Kámil* (the Perfect), and God created from the light of Mohammed's judgment Azrael, the Angel of Death[6]. *Wahm* is the strongest of the human faculties: it overpowers the understanding, the reflection, and the imagination[7]...nothing in the world apprehends more

[1] K II. 24, 5 foll. Gabriel was created from the First Intelligence regarded as the rational principle of Mohammed, who is therefore "the father of Gabriel."

[2] *I.e.*, Universal Soul (see K II. 7, 15 foll.).

[3] Universal Reason is a mode of Universal Soul (K II. 7, 3 fr. foot and foll.); it perceives the forms of existence imprinted on Universal Soul by the First Intelligence.

[4] Jílí likens the First Intelligence to the sun, Universal Reason to water irradiated by sunbeams, and ordinary reason to the light reflected from the water upon a wall (K II. 22, 4 fr. foot and foll.).

[5] K II. 23, 9 foll.

[6] K II. 24, 21 foll.

[7] Cf. *Fuṣúṣ*, 229.

quickly; it is what enables men to walk on the water and fly in the air; it is the light of certainty (*yaqín*) and the basis of dominion; he that has it at his command exercises sway over all things high and low, while he that is ruled by its might becomes stupefied and bewildered[1]. The spirit, on entering the body[2], either acquires angelic dispositions and ascends to Paradise, or assumes bestial dispositions and sinks to Hell: it ascends when it judges the limitations of its human form, *e.g.*, grossness and weakness, to be merely negative and capable of being thrown off, since the spirit always retains its original qualities potentially. At death Azrael appears to the spirit in a form determined by its beliefs, actions, and dispositions during life[3]. Or, again, he appears disembodied and invisible, so that a man may "die of a rose in aromatic pain" or of a stench[4]. When the spirit sees Azrael, it becomes enamoured of him, and its gaze is entirely withdrawn from the body[5], whereupon the body dies. The spirit does not quit its bodily form at once but abides in it for a while, like one who sleeps without seeing any vision[6]. After this dreamless sleep, which is its death (*mawtu 'l-arwáḥ*), the spirit passes into the intermediate state (*al-barzakh*).

Meditation (*himma*) is the noblest of the spiritual lights

[1] K II. 27, 14 foll. *Wahm* is generally defined as the "bodily" faculty which perceives the qualities of a sensible object and forms a judgment concerning it, *e.g.*, that the sheep runs away from the wolf. Jílí regards it as the faculty whereby things are judged intuitively to be what they really are: he says that by means of *wahm* God made His creatures worship Him as their Lord (*ta'abbada 'l-'álam*).

[2] *I.e.*, on becoming conscious of itself as the essence (*huwiyya*) of the body. "Spirits dwell in the place towards which they look, without being separated from their original centre" (K II. 25, 9 foll.).

[3] Sometimes in the form of the Prophet, which the Cherubim, having been created from his spiritual faculties, are able to assume, unlike Iblís and the devils who were created from his fleshly nature (K II. 26, 2 foll.).

[4] K II. 26, 22 foll.

[5] Jílí objects to the expression "goes forth from the body" on the ground that it implies *ḥulúl*.

[6] Against the opinion that no sleep is visionless, though some dreams are not remembered on waking, Jílí sets the fact, revealed to him (as he says) by Divine illumination, that it is possible to sleep dreamlessly for a period of two days or more, which seems to pass in the twinkling of an eye. Conversely, God may so extend a single moment of time that within it an individual lives many lives and marries and has children (K II. 27, 1 foll.).

(faculties), for it has no object but God[1]. Yet one must beware of resting in it in order to enjoy its fruits: the master-mystic will leave it before it has yielded all its secrets to him, lest it become a barrier to his further advance[2]. Michael, the angel created from it, is charged with the duty of dispensing the portions of fate allotted by eternal necessity to each recipient[3].

From the reflection (*fikr*) of Mohammed God created the spirits of the celestial and terrestrial angels, and appointed them to guard the higher and lower spheres of existence until the Last Day, when they shall be translated to the intelligible world[4]. One of the keys to that world is reflection, leading to true knowledge of the nature of Man, which is set with all its aspects over against the aspects of the Merciful (*al-Raḥmán*). But the pure region of *fikr* lies open to mystics alone: the path of speculative philosophy ends in a mirage[5].

As we have already seen[6], thought (*khayál*), *i.e.*, the faculty that retains what the fancy perceives of the forms of sensible objects after their substance has disappeared[7], is declared by Jílí to be the stuff of the universe. In Hegelian language "the things that we know about are appropriately described when we say that their being is established not on themselves, but on the Divine Idea." Nothing exists otherwise than as a dream in the perception of the dreamer, and the cosmos is "a thought within a thought within a thought" (*khayálun fí khayálin fí khayál*)[8]. It must be added, however, that while every thing, *i.e.*, every thought, expresses some reality, the Perfect Man (though he is not Reality itself) is the complete self-expression of Reality[9].

Imagination, memory, and perception, which the author

[1] K II. 28, 14. *Himma* denotes the utmost concentration of the heart (*qalb*) upon God. Cf. Jurjání's *Ta'rífát*, p. 278.

[2] K II. 30, 7 foll. [3] K II. 30, 13 foll. [4] K II. 32, 15 foll.

[5] K II. 31, 8 foll. Jílí confesses that he was once in danger of being engulfed in this "deadly science" and was only saved by the blessing of God and the watchful care of his Shaykh, Sharafu'ddín ibn Ismá'íl al-Jabartí (K II. 32, 4 foll.). [6] P. 91 *supra*.

[7] Jurjání, *Ta'rífát*, p. 107. [8] K II. 34, 16.

[9] The term *al-insánu 'l-kámil* signifies "the *manifestation* of the Divine essence, attributes, and names" (K I. 80, 14).

enumerated amongst the eight spiritual faculties[1], find no place in this discussion.

After a preliminary chapter on the Form of Mohammed (*al-ṣúratu 'l-Muḥammadiyya*), which I will omit for the present, he concludes his psychology with an account of the nature of the soul.

Ascetic and devotional Ṣúfism, in agreement with orthodox Islam, distinguishes sharply between the spirit (*rúḥ*) and the soul (*nafs*)[2]. The latter term may, indeed, be used to denote a man's spiritual "self"—"he that knows himself (*nafsahu*) knows his Lord"—but as a rule when Ṣúfís refer to the *nafs* they mean the appetitive soul, the sensual "self" which, from their point of view, is wholly evil and can never become one with God[3]. Jílí makes short work of this dualistic doctrine. The heading of his 59th chapter promises to show that the *nafs* is the origin of Iblís and all the devils, and he begins as follows:

> The *nafs* is the consciousness (*sirr*) of the Lord, and the essence (of God): through that Essence it hath in its essence manifold delights. It is created from the light of the attribute of Lordship: many, therefore, are its lordly qualities....God created the *nafs* of Mohammed from His own *nafs* (and the *nafs* of a thing is its essence); then He created the *nafs* of Adam as a copy of the *nafs* of Mohammed[4].

With great boldness Jílí argues that the Fall of Man is the necessary consequence of his Divine nature. Adam ate the forbidden fruit because his soul manifests a certain aspect of Deity, *viz.*, Lordship (*rubúbiyya*); for it is not in the nature of Lordship to submit to a prohibition. The soul knew that, if it ate the fruit[5], it would inevitably descend into the material

[1] P. 110 *supra*.

[2] Cf. Prof. D. B. Macdonald, *The religious attitude and life in Islam*, p. 224 foll.

[3] How far Ibnu 'l-'Arabí, Ibnu 'l Fáriḍ, and Jílí have advanced beyond the old Ṣúfism appears from the way in which they speak of the body. Although on account of its grossness it is an imperfect medium and therefore relatively a cause of evil, its faculties are necessary for the attainment of spiritual perfection. A man born blind could know nothing, either here or hereafter, of the Divine wisdom that is communicated through the eye (M 41). Cf. the *Tá'iyya*, *vv*. 677–9, and note *ad loc.*

[4] K II. 48, 2 foll.

[5] The forbidden fruit symbolises the darkness of Nature which is the

world and would suffer misery, but on the other hand it was aware of the blessedness of its inherent sovereignty. Thus it became perplexed, and its perplexity (*iltibás*) brought about its fall. The choice of the soul is at once determined and free: determined, because in the last resort its act proceeds from a fundamental difference in the nature of God; free, because the soul acts in accordance with its knowledge of itself and, had it not been blinded by pride, would have perceived that its true nature requires obedience to the Divine command, inasmuch as disobedience renders the spirit miserable, and misery is inconsistent with Lordship.

When God created the soul of Mohammed from His own Essence, which comprises all contraries, He created from the soul of Mohammed (1) the Sublime Angels in respect of His attributes of Beauty, Light, and Leading, and (2) Iblís and his followers in respect of His attributes of Majesty, Darkness, and Misleading[1]. Now, the name of Iblís was 'Azázíl: he had worshipped God for thousands of years before the creation of the world, and God had forbidden him to worship aught else. Therefore, when God created Adam and commanded the angels to bow down before him, Iblís refused, for he did not know that to worship by God's command is equivalent to worshipping God[2]. Instead of justifying his disobedience or repenting of it and asking God to forgive him, he silently acknowledged that God wills and acts in conformity with the eternal and unchangeable principles of His nature. Iblís was banished from the Divine presence and a curse was laid upon him "until the Day of Judgment" (Kor. 15, 35), *i.e.*, for a finite period[3]. After the Day of Judgment the creatureliness which hinders the spirit from knowing God as He really is

cause of disobedience, just as the light of Spirit is the cause of obedience; but Nature and Spirit, like their opposite effects, only differ correlatively.

[1] K II. 50, 7 foll.

[2] Jílí derives the name Iblís from the doubt and confusion (*talbís*) which was produced in the mind of 'Azázíl by the command to worship Adam.

[3] The Days of God (*ayyám Allah*) are the epiphanies by which He reveals His perfections (K I. 89, 25 foll.). The Day of Judgment signifies "an omnipotent epiphany before which all existent beings abase themselves" (K I. 111, 15), or in other words, the return of created things to God (K II. 50, last line).

will be counted amongst its perfections[1], and Iblís will then be restored to his place beside God[2].

Jílí mentions five phases of the soul, or ascending grades of spiritual life: (1) the animal soul, *i.e.*, the spirit regarded as governing the body; (2) the commanding (evil-prompting) soul[3], *i.e.*, the spirit regarded as subject to the passions; (3) the inspired soul, *i.e.*, the spirit which God inspires to do good; (4) the self-reproaching soul, *i.e.*, the spirit regarded as turning penitently towards God; (5) the tranquil soul, *i.e.*, the spirit regarded as at rest with God[4].

V. The Macrocosm.

As Man is created in the image of God, so the universe is created in the image of Man[5], who is its spirit and life[6]. In describing its creation Jílí combines mystical ideas with an old cosmological myth, in the following manner[7]:

Before the creation God was in Himself, and the objects of existence were absorbed (*mustahlik*) in Him so that He was not manifested in any thing. This is the state of "being a hidden treasure[8]" or, as the Prophet expressed it, "the dark mist above which is a void and below which is a void[9]," because the Idea

[1] Because the spirit, having regained its absoluteness, will be one with the Essence which is both Creator and creature.

[2] The view that Iblís suffered damnation rather than compromise the doctrine of the Divine unity (*tawḥíd*) is derived from Ḥalláj. See Massignon, *Kitáb al-Ṭawásín*, p. 5 and 41 foll.

[3] In so far as the soul does what its creaturely nature requires, it may be described as *ammára* (*bi 'l-sú'*), *i.e.*, "commanding itself (to do evil)."

[4] K II. 58, 3 foll.

[5] Mohammed, as the Logos, is the spiritual essence of Adam and of all things.

[6] Cf. K II. 79, 6 foll. "God caused Adam to dwell in the heaven of this world, because Adam is the world-spirit (*rúḥu 'l-'álam*): through him God beheld the existent things and had mercy on them and made them live by the life of Adam in them. The world will not cease to be living so long as humankind continues there. When humankind departs, the world will perish and collapse, as the body of an animal perishes when the spirit leaves it."

[7] K II. 77, 10 foll. Cf. Nyberg, *Kleinere Schriften des Ibn al-'Arabī*, Introd., p. 146 foll.

[8] According to the Ḥadíth, "I was a hidden treasure and I desired to be known, therefore I created the creatures in order that I might be known."

[9] See p. 94 fol.

of Ideas[1] is beyond all relations. The Idea of Ideas is called in another Tradition "the White Chrysolite[2], in which God was before He created the creatures." When God willed to bring the world into existence, He looked on the Idea of Ideas (or the White Chrysolite) with the look of Perfection, whereupon it dissolved and became a water; for nothing in existence, not even the Idea of Ideas, which is the source of all existence, can bear the perfect manifestation of God. Then God looked on it with the look of Grandeur, and it surged in waves, like a sea tossed by the winds, and its grosser elements were spread out in layers like foam, and from that mass God created the seven earths with their inhabitants. The subtle elements of the water ascended, like vapour from the sea, and from them God created the seven heavens with the angels of each heaven. Then God made of the water seven seas which encompass the world. This is how the whole of existence originated.

Jílí surveys the celestial, terrestrial and aqueous universe at considerable length[3], but I will not attempt to give more than an outline of his map. He takes first the seven heavens, which rise in concentric and gradually widening circles above the spheres of earth, water, air, and fire. Mystics, he remarks, have seen them and can interpret them to sublunary men.

1. The Heaven of the Moon.

This is not the earth-born vapour which we call the sky, but is invisible on account of its farness and subtlety. God created it from the nature of the Spirit (*al-Rúh*)[4], that it might have the same relation to the earth as the spirit has to the body; and He made it the dwelling-place of Adam[5]. Its colour is whiter than silver.

2. The Heaven of Mercury.

God created it from the nature of reflection (*fikr*) and placed in it all the angels who help craftsmen. Its colour is grey.

3. The Heaven of Venus.

It is created from the nature of phantasy (*khayál*) and is the locality of the World of Similitudes (*'álamu 'l-mithál*). Its colour

[1] *Ḥaqíqatu 'l-ḥaqá'iq*, *i.e.*, the whole content of God's knowledge, the Divine consciousness, the First Intelligence, the Logos. It is identical with the *Ḥaqíqatu 'l-Muḥammadiyya*. Cf. Nyberg, *op. cit.*, Introd., p. 33 foll. and 50. [2] *al-Yáqútatu 'l-bayḍá*. [3] K II. 78, 5—98, 22.

[4] See p. 108 foll. [5] Cf. p. 121, note 6.

is yellow. Jílí describes the various tasks assigned to the angels whom he saw in this heaven, where he also met the Prophet Joseph[1].

4. The Heaven of the Sun.

It is created from the light of the heart (*qalb*). The Sun in his heaven is like the heart in man—a mirror of Deity: while the heart displays the sublime degrees of existence connoted by the name Allah, the Sun is the source and principle of the elemental world. Idrís, Jesus, Solomon, David, and most of the prophets dwell in the heaven of the Sun; its ruling angel is Isráfíl.

5. The Heaven of Mars.

Azrael, the Angel of Death, presides over this blood-red heaven, which is created from the light of judgment (*wahm*).

6. The Heaven of Jupiter.

Its colour is blue. God created it from the light of meditation (*himma*). The angels of the Sixth Heaven, of whom Michael is the chief, are angels of mercy and blessing. Some have the shapes of animals and birds and men; others appear as substances and accidents which bring health to the sick or as solids and liquids which supply created beings with food and drink; others are formed half of fire and half of ice.

Here Jílí beheld Moses, "drunken with the wine of the revelation of Lordship," who explained to him the meaning of "*Thou shalt not see Me*" (Kor. 7, 139).

7. The Heaven of Saturn.

The Seventh Heaven was the first to be created. It was created from the light of the First Intelligence, and its colour is black. Between it and the Starless Heaven (*al-falaku 'l-aṭlas*) there are three heavens which have only a logical, not an actual, existence: the Heaven of Matter (*falaku 'l-hayúlá*), which is the highest of the three; the Heaven of Atoms (*falaku 'l-habá*)[2]; and the Heaven of the Elements (*falaku 'l-'anáṣir*); some philosophers add a fourth, *viz.*, the Heaven of Natural Properties (*falaku 'l ṭabá'i'*).

[1] K II. 83, 22 foll.

[2] The universe, being in space, requires a *locus* (*maḥall*). This *locus* is *al-habá*. It is "logical" (*ḥukmí*), since it cannot be homogeneous with the universe; otherwise it would need a *locus* for itself. Mystics call it "the First Intelligence" and "the Spirit of Mohammed" (M 35 *a*). Cf. Nyberg, *op. cit.*, Introd., p. 157.

The author proceeds to describe the seven limbos of the Earth[1].

1. The Earth of Souls (*arḍu 'l-nufús*).

God created it whiter than milk and sweeter than musk, but when Adam walked on it after the Fall it became dust-coloured, except one region in the North, never reached by any sinner, which is ruled by al-Khaḍir and inhabited by the Men of the Unseen World (*rijálu 'l-ghayb*)[2].

2. The Earth of Devotions (*arḍu 'l-'ibádát*).

In colour it resembles an emerald. Its inhabitants are those of the Jinn (genies) who believe in God: their night is our day, and their day our night. After the sun sets in our earth, they appear on it and fall in love with the children of men. Most of these spirits envy the disciples of the Mystic Way, and taking them unawares bring them to ruin. Jílí affirms that he had seen some Súfís who were in bondage to them and were made so deaf and blind that they could neither hear nor understand the Word of God, unless the reciter were one of the Jinn.

3. The Earth of Nature (*arḍu 'l-ṭab'*).

Its colour is saffron-yellow. The unbelieving Jinn who inhabit it appear in human shape amongst mankind and cause them to neglect the worship of God.

4. The Earth of Lust (*arḍu 'l-shahwa*).

Its colour is blood-red. It is inhabited by different sorts of devils who are the offspring of the soul of Iblís.

5. The Earth of Exorbitance (*arḍu 'l-ṭughyán*).

Its colour is indigo blue. 'Afríts and potent demons dwell in it, who busy themselves with seducing men to commit great sins.

6. The Earth of Impiety (*arḍu 'l-ilḥád*).

Its colour is black as night. It is the abode of the *márids* (the most evil and rebellious of the Jinn)[3].

[1] K II. 89, 18 foll.

[2] He says that it is near to the land of Bulghár and that in winter they are not obliged to perform the evening-prayer, because the dawn rises before sunset.

[3] Jílí inserts here a short passage in which he distinguishes four species of Jinn according as their nature is elemental, fiery, airy, or earthly. The "elementals" are akin to the angels and never go outside of the spiritual world.

7. The Earth of Misery (*arḍu 'l-shaqáwa*).

It is the floor of Gehenna (*Jahannum*) and is inhabited by enormous snakes and scorpions, which God placed there in order that it might be a pattern of the torments of Hell to the people of this world[1].

Concerning the Seven Seas, which were originally two—one of salt and the other of fresh water—Jílí has much to say[2], but his description of them is somewhat confused and we must now pass on to matters of greater interest.

VI. The Return to the Essence.

The gist of Jílí's philosophy, as I understand it, is the notion of One Being, which is One Thought, going forth from itself in all the forms of the universe, knowing itself as Nature and yet, amidst the multiformity of Nature, reasserting its unity in Man—in Man whom self-knowledge has enlightened and made perfect, so that ceasing to know himself as an individual he sinks into his Divine element, like a wave into the sea. This language, apart from its inadequacy, conveys a wrong impression by translating in terms of time and space what does not belong to these categories. All interpretations of ideal and mystical experience are more or less fictitious.

The word commonly used to denote the self-manifestation of God in His essence, attributes, and names is *tajallí*, which implies that something hidden before is now clearly seen, as the splendour of the sun emerging from eclipse or the beauty of a bride when she unveils. The Divine *tajallí*, in respect of the person to whom it is made, may be called an illumination, for it is the light whereby the mystic's heart has vision of God. Accordingly, the ontological descent from the Absolute and the mystical ascent or return to the Absolute are really the

[1] Similarly, God set over the Heaven of the Stars a prince (*ṭághiya*) like the people of Paradise to serve as a pattern of the joys of Paradise. Moreover, the images stored in the left side of the seat of *khayál* (see p. 91) in the human brain are a copy of the Earth of Misery, while those in the right side are a copy of the houris and other Paradisal pleasures. Otherwise, Jílí argues, the intellect could not know Paradise and Hell and would not be obliged to believe in them (K II. 92, 22 foll.).

[2] K II. 93, 9 foll.

same process looked at from different points of view[1]. The self-revelation of God necessarily involves the manifestation of His nature by those who possess an inborn capacity for realising it in themselves. Jílí divides the ascending movement of this consciousness into four stages—the Illumination of the Actions, the Illumination of the Names, the Illumination of the Attributes, and the Illumination of the Essence—which correspond in reverse order to the devolution of Pure Being from its primal simplicity to the manifestation of its effects in the sensible world.

(*a*) The Illumination of the Divine actions[2].

To one thus illumined it becomes plain that human agency is naught, that he has no power or will of his own, and that all things are done by the power of God who moves them and brings them to rest. Sometimes the Divine will is made known to him before the act: consequently, he may disobey the command of God in order to comply with His will; in which case his disobedience is essentially obedience and lies between him and God, though "it remains for us to exact from him the penalty which God has imposed in the Koran and the Sunna upon those who break His commandment[3]."

(*b*) The Illumination of the Divine names[4].

The mystic to whom God reveals Himself in one of His Names vanishes (from consciousness of individuality) under the radiance of the Name; and if you invoke God by that Name, the man will answer you, because the Name is applicable to him....If God reveal Himself in His Name Allah, the man will disappear and God will call to him, saying, "Lo, I am Allah"; and if you cry "O Allah!" the man will answer you with the words "At thy service (*labbayka*)!"[5] Then, if he mount higher[6] and God strengthen

[1] Cf. K I. 94, penult. "The Wise Koran (*al-Qur'ánu 'l-ḥakím*) is the descent (*tanazzul*) of the Divine individualisations (*ḥaqá'iq*) by means of the gradual ascent of man towards perfect knowledge of them in the Essence, according to the requirement of Divine Wisdom....He that is moulded after the Divine nature ascends in it and gains, step by step, such knowledge thereof as is revealed to him in a Divinely determined order."

[2] K I. 47, penult. [3] Cf. p. 54 and p. 120. [4] K I. 50, 10.

[5] *I.e.*, he is the unconscious centre of manifestation, *maẓhar*, of the Name Allah. Cf. the passage (K I. 22, 20 foll.) translated on p. 93.

[6] *I.e.*, from the plane of *Wáḥidiyya* (unity in plurality) to the plane of *Aḥadiyya* (abstract unity), together with *Wáḥidiyya* and the degrees below

him and let him abide in consciousness after his passing-away (*faná*), God will answer any one who calls the man, so that if you say, for instance, "O Muḥammad!" God will respond to you, saying, "At thy service!"[1] In proportion as he is strengthened to ascend, God will reveal Himself to him in His subordinate Names, *viz.*, the Merciful (*al-Raḥmán*), the Lord (*al-Rabb*), the King (*al-Malik*), the Omniscient (*al-'Alím*), the Omnipotent (*al-Qádir*), etc. The self-revelation of God in each of these Names is superior to His self-revelation in the Name preceding it, because as regards the Illumination of the Names analysis is superior to synthesis, and the manifestation of each lower Name is an analysis of the synthesis which is manifested by the one immediately above it.

As regards illuminations of the Essence, it is otherwise; here the more general is above the more particular: *al-Raḥmán* is superior to *al-Rabb*, and *Allah* to either. Finally, all the Divine Names seek to apply themselves to the illumined man, even as the name seeks the object named, and then he sings:

One calls Her by Her name and I answer him, and when I am called (by my own name) 'tis Laylá (the Beloved) that answers for me.
That is because we are the spirit of One, though we dwell by turns in two bodies—a marvellous thing!
Like a single person with two names: thou canst not miss by whichever name thou callest him.

Jílí only speaks of what he himself has experienced, since every Name is revealed in different ways to different individuals. From his account of these illuminations I take a passage which exhibits his characteristic blend of logic and mysticism:

it, or in other words, from *faná* (the naughting of all that is not God) to *baqá* (union with the Divine consciousness).

[1] Cf. K. II. 23, 1 foll.: "Then, when he becomes cleansed from the defilement of not-being and ascends to knowledge of the being of the Necessary (Absolute), and when God purifies him from the foulness of temporality by the manifestation of eternity, he becomes a mirror for the Name Allah, and in that moment he and the Name are like two opposite mirrors, each of which exists in the other. And in this vision it is God Himself that answers those who invoke him (the mystic); his anger is the cause of God's anger, and his satisfaction is the cause of God's satisfaction."

The way to the illumination of the Name *al-Qadím* (the Eternal) is through a Divine revelation whereby it is shown to any one that he existed in the knowledge of God before the Creation, inasmuch as he existed in God's knowledge through the existence of that knowledge, and that knowledge existed through the existence of God: the existence of God is eternal and the knowledge is eternal and the object of knowledge is inseparable from the knowledge and is also eternal, inasmuch as knowledge is not knowledge unless it has an object which gives to the subject the name of Knower. The eternity of existent beings in the knowledge of God necessarily follows from this induction, and the (illumined) man returns to God in respect of His Name, the Eternal. At the moment when the Divine eternity is revealed to him from his essence, his temporality vanishes and he remains eternal through God, having passed away from (consciousness of) his temporality[1].

(*c*) The Illumination of the Divine Attributes[2].

When God desires to reveal Himself to a man by means of any Name or Attribute, He causes the man to pass away (*faná*) and makes him naught and deprives him of his (individual) existence; and when the human light is extinguished and the creaturely spirit passes away, God puts in the man's body, without incarnation (*ḥulúl*), a spiritual substance, which is of God's essence and is neither separate from God nor joined to the man, in exchange for what He deprived him of; which substance is named the Holy Spirit (*rúḥu 'l-quds*)[3]. And when God puts instead of the man a spirit of His own essence, the revelation is made to that spirit. God is never revealed except to Himself, but we call that Divine spirit "a man" in respect of its being instead of the man. In reality there is neither "slave" nor "Lord," since these are correlated terms. When the "slave" is annulled, the "Lord" is necessarily annulled, and nothing remains but God alone.

Mystics receive these illuminations in proportion to their capacities, the abundance of their knowledge, and the strength of their resolution. Taking each of the seven chief attributes in turn, the author describes the effects of the illumination on himself or on others, and the different forms which it may

[1] K I. 51, 14 foll. [2] K I. 53, 7.

[3] This doctrine of substitution was taught by many Christian mystics in the Middle Ages. Cf. Inge, *Christian Mysticism*, p. 364.

assume. Concerning Life and Knowledge something has been said above[1]. Those endowed with Hearing hear the language of angels, animals, plants, and minerals[2]. As for the *mu-kallamún*, who receive the illumination of Speech, the Word (*kalám*) comes to them sometimes audibly and from a certain direction, sometimes from no direction and not through the ear, sometimes as an inner light having a definite shape; and in oneness with God they realise that all existent beings are *their* Word and that their words are without end[3]. According to Jílí, the illumination of Power is marked in its initial stages by a phenomenon characteristic of prophetic inspiration—the ringing of a bell (*ṣalṣalatu 'l-jaras*), which is produced, as he quaintly writes, by "the dashing of realities one against another in order that men's hearts may not dare to enter the presence of Divine Majesty[4]." "In this illumination," he says, "I heard the ringing of bells. My frame dissolved and my trace vanished and my name was rased out. By reason of the violence of what I experienced I became like a worn-out garment which hangs on a high tree, and the fierce blast carries it away piece by piece. I beheld naught but lightnings and thunders, and clouds raining lights, and seas surging with fire[5]."

(*d*) The Illumination of the Divine essence.

While every illumination of a Name or Attribute reveals the Essence in a particular relation, the Illumination of the absolute Essence is not identical with any or all of these illuminations. Jílí refers the difference to the Divine substance, which, as we have seen, God "puts instead of the man" so that the subject and object of illumination are really one. This substance may be either attributal (*ṣifátí*) or essential (*dhátí*). Only in the latter case does "the man" become the God-man. Such a one is

[1] See p. 101. [2] K I. 55, 3. [3] K I. 55, 8.

[4] K I. 90, penult. The Prophet declared that when inspiration descended upon him it was often like the ringing of a bell. Cf. Prof. D. B. Macdonald, *The religious attitude and life in Iṣlam*, p. 46.

[5] K I. 57, 9. A similar description occurs in the thirty-second chapter, "On the ringing of the bell." See K I. 91, 3 foll.

the Perfect Unit (*al-fardu 'l-kámil*) and the Microcosmic Pole (*al-ghawthu 'l-jámi'*) on whom the whole order of existence revolves; to him genuflexion and prostration in prayer are due, and by means of him God keeps the universe in being. He is denoted by the terms *al-Mahdí* and *al-Khátam* (the Seal)[1], and he is the Vicegerent (*khalífa*) indicated in the story of Adam[2]. The essences of all things that exist are drawn to obey his command, as iron is drawn to the magnet. He subdues the sensible world by his might and does what he will by his power. Nothing is barred from him, for when the Divine substance is in this *walí* as a simple essence, unconditioned by any degree appertaining to the Creator or to the creature, he bestows on every degree of existent things its *ḥaqq*, *i.e.* what it requires and is capable of receiving, and nothing can hinder him from doing so. That which hinders the Essence is merely its limitation by a degree or name or quality; but the simple Essence has nothing to hinder it: therefore with it all things are actual, not potential, while in other essences things are sometimes potential and sometimes actual.

It would seem, then, that the Illumination of the Absolute is given to the Heavenly Man (Mohammed) alone and transmitted through him to the Perfect Men who are his representatives on earth[3].

VII. Religion, Revelation and Prophecy.

Religious belief may be defined as man's thought about God, and we have learned that all things and thoughts in the universe are attributes of God, *i.e.*, aspects in which He reveals Himself to human minds. Moreover, the attributes are identical with the Essence in so far as they are nothing but the Essence regarded from every possible point of view. Therefore God is the essence of all thought; and all thought is

[1] The Perfect Man is the First and the Last: in his outward form he is the last of the Prophets and in his inward essence the last of the Saints, yet he is the source of all prophecy and all saintship (*Fuṣúṣ*, 34 foll.).

[2] Koran, 2, 28.

[3] Cf. *Fuṣúṣ*, 34. Therefore, while God is the essential being (*'ayn*) of all things, none of them is the *'ayn* of God except the Logos or Heavenly Man. Contemplation of the Perfect Man serves instead of contemplation of God (M 12 *a*).

about God. In the light of such principles the author's philosophy of religion is easy to understand.

Divine worship, he says, is the end for which all things are created[1], and therefore belongs to their original nature and constitution. The different forms of worship result from the variety of Names and Attributes by which God manifests Himself in creation. Every Name and Attribute produces its own characteristic effect. For example, God is the true Guide (*al-Hádí*); but He is also the Misleader (*al-Muḍill*), for the Koran says, "Allah shall lead the wicked into error." He is the Avenger (*al-Muntaqim*) as well as the Forgiver (*al-Mun'im*). If any one of His Names had remained ineffectual and unrealised, His self-manifestation would not have been complete. Therefore He sent His prophets, in order that those who followed them might worship Him as the One who guides mankind to salvation, and that those who disobeyed them might worship Him as the One who leads mankind to perdition[2].

All God's creatures worship Him in accordance with His will, and every form of worship expresses some aspect of His nature. Infidelity and sin are effects of the Divine activity and contribute to the Divine perfection. Satan himself glorifies God, inasmuch as his disobedience is subordinate to the eternal will. Yet some aspects in which God shows Himself, such as Majesty and Wrath, are relatively less perfect than others, such as Beauty and Mercy. And, again, the more completely and universally the idea of God is presented in any form of worship, the more perfect that form must be. Religions revealed through a prophet contain the fullest measure of truth, and amongst these the most excellent is Islam.

Jílí mentions ten principal "religious" sects from which all the rest are derived[3]. It is an odd catalogue, comprising (1) the Idolaters or Infidels; (2) the Physicists, who worship the four natural properties, namely, heat, cold, dryness and moisture; (3) the Philosophers, who worship the seven planets; (4) the Dualists, who worship light and darkness;

[1] Koran, 51, 56. [2] K II. 98 foll. [3] K II. 100.

(5) the Magians, who worship fire; (6) the Materialists (*Dahriyyún*), who abandon worship entirely; (7) the Brahmans (*Baráhima*), who claim to follow the religion of Abraham; (8) the Jews; (9) the Christians; (10) the Mohammedans.

The author proceeds to explain that God is the truth or essence of all these forms of belief[1]. The Infidels disbelieved in a Lord, because God, who is their essence, has no lord over Him, but on the contrary is Himself the absolute Lord. They worshipped God according to the necessity of their essential natures. Idolaters worship Him as the Being who permeates every atom of the material world without infusion or commixture. God is the "truth" of the idols which they worship, and they worship none but Him. This is the mystery of their following the Truth in themselves[2], because their hearts bore witness to them that the good lay in their so doing. On account of that spirit of belief in the reality of their worship, the thing as it really is shall be revealed to them in the next world. "Every sect is rejoicing in that which it hath" (Koran, 23, 55), *i.e.*, here they rejoice in their acts, and hereafter they shall rejoice in their spiritual states. Their joy is everlasting[3]. Therefore, even if the Infidels had known the torment which they must suffer in consequence of their worship, they would have persisted in it by reason of the spiritual delight which they experience therein; for when God wills to punish any one with torment in the life to come, He creates for him in that torment a natural pleasure of which his body becomes enamoured; and God does this in order that the sufferer may not have an unquestionable right to take refuge with Him from the torment, but may remain in torment so long as the pleasure continues to be felt by him. When God wills to alleviate his torment, He causes him to lose the sense of pleasure, and he then takes refuge in the mercy of God, "who answers the sorely distressed when they pray to Him" (Koran, 27, 63)[4].

[1] K II. 101 foll.

[2] Cf. Koran, 47, 3, where it is said of the Infidels that they followed Falsehood, and of the Believers that they followed "the Truth from their Lord," *i.e.* the Revelation given to Mohammed.

[3] This is inferred by the author from the form *fariḥún* (which implies continuance) in the Koranic text.

[4] K II. 101.

Similarly, the Physicists really worship the four essential attributes of God, namely, Life, Knowledge, Power, and Will; the Philosophers worship His names and attributes as manifested in the planets; the Dualists worship Him as Creator and creature in one; the Magians worship Him as the Unity in which all names and attributes pass away, just as fire destroys all natural properties and transmutes them to its own nature; the Materialists, who deny the existence of a Creator and believe in the eternity of Time, worship God in respect of His He-ness (*Huwiyya*), in which He is only potentially, but not actually, creative; the Brahmans worship Him absolutely, without reference to prophet or apostle[1].

As regards the future life, since all worship God by Divine necessity, all must be saved. But the seven sects above-mentioned (unlike the Jews, Christians and Moslems, who received their religions from a prophet) invented their forms of worship for themselves. Consequently, they are doomed to misery hereafter. That which constitutes their misery is the fact that their felicity, though ultimately assured, is far off and is not revealed to them until they have suffered retribution. On the other hand, those who worship God according to the mode ordained by a prophet enjoy immediate felicity, which is revealed to them continuously and gradually. It is true that the Jews and Christians suffer misery, but why is this? Because they have altered God's Word and substituted something of their own. Otherwise, they would have come under the rule that God never sent a prophet to any people without placing in his apostolic mission the felicity of those who followed him[2].

Here, perhaps, it will not be inopportune to give some details of the author's eschatology. We must remember that in his view all experience is perception by the human spirit

[1] Therefore the book which the Brahmans ascribe, as the author supposes, to Abraham did not come to them from God but was written by Abraham himself. Jílí says that it contains five parts. The fifth part on account of its profundity is forbidden to most Brahmans. He adds: "It is notorious among them that those who read this fifth part invariably become Moslems."

[2] K II. 104.

of the nature and destiny eternally stamped upon it. "I Myself am Heaven and Hell."

"Life" denotes the spirit's contemplation of its bodily form: the spirit assumes the form of the object contemplated, just as sunbeams falling on green or red glass take the form and colour of the glass. After death, *i.e.*, after the withdrawal of the spirit's gaze from the body, the spirit remains wholly in the spiritual world, while wearing the same corporeal aspect as it had before[1]. Those mystics who deny the resurrection of the body are in the wrong. "We know by Divine information that bodies are raised from the dead with their spirits." The death of the spirit consists in its detachment from the body and resembles the dreamless sleep which is akin to not-being[2], since the sleeper has neither perception of the sensible nor vision of the unseen[3].

During the intermediate state (*barzakh*) between death and resurrection every one moves in a world of phantasy (*khayál*) peopled by the forms, ideas, and essential characters of the actions which he or she committed in their earthly life[4]. The drunkard quaffs fiery wine in a cup of fire; the sinner whom God has forgiven passes into forms of good works, each fairer than the last; and he whose good works have been done in vain becomes imbued with the form of his eternal fate, ever-changing images of woe which his resurrection shall reveal to him as realities[5]. The present, intermediate, and future states are one existence (*wujúd wáḥid*), and you by virtue of your inmost nature (*huwiyya*) are the same in them all, but while the things of this world are free (*ikhtiyárí*), the things hereafter are determined by what happens here[6].

The world, having been created, must die: its death is its

[1] Ibnu 'l-'Arabí says (*Fuṣúṣ*, 211) that after death the spirit receives an immortal body homogeneous with the world to which it has been translated.

[2] Cf. p. 117.

[3] K II. 71, 15 foll.

[4] So long as the spirit remains in the *barzakh*, *i.e.*, limited by the properties of the body, it does not enjoy full freedom. Only after the Resurrection is it entirely free to act according to its nature, *i.e.*, to seek good or evil in conformity with its state in the present life (K II. 72, 20 foll.).

[5] K II. 73, 2 foll.

[6] K II. 74, 2 foll. As to the question of free-will, see p. 102, note 4.

passing away (*faná*) under the might of the Divine Reality which manifests itself in the guise of individuals; and its resurrection is the manifestation of that Reality with the signs foretold in the Koran[1]. The universal or greater resurrection (*al-sá'atu 'l-kubrá*) includes the particular or lesser resurrection (*al-sá'atu 'l-ṣughrá*), *i.e.*, the resurrection of every individual, and their signs correspond. For example, Dajjál (Antichrist) is an emblem of the flesh (*nafs*): as Dajjál shall be slain by Christ (the Spirit of God, *Rúḥ Allah*), so shall the flesh be destroyed by the spirit (*rúḥ*)[2]. Again, the coming of the Mahdí, who shall reign for forty years, symbolises the perfection of the Perfect Man uniting and consummating the forty grades of existence[3]. God beholds this world through the medium of Man; therefore, after the Resurrection, it will not exist otherwise than in God's knowledge, even as Paradise and Hell exist in His knowledge to-day. But when Man shall have been removed to the next world, God will behold Paradise and Hell through him, and they will then exist actually[4].

God created the Form of Mohammed (*al-ṣúratu 'l-Muḥammadiyya*) from the light of His Name the Almighty Maker (*al-Badí'u 'l-Qádir*), and regarded it with His Name the All-subduing Giver (*al-Mannánu 'l-Qáhir*); then He displayed Himself to it in His Name the Gracious Pardoner (*al-Laṭífu 'l-Gháfir*). Thereupon, because of this illumination, it split in two halves, and God created Paradise from the half on the right hand, and Hell from the half on the left hand[5].

Jílí's description of the Eight Paradises is not specially interesting[6]. In the first Paradise good works are rewarded, in the second good thoughts and beliefs concerning God. The third, which is gained solely by Divine grace, surpasses all the rest in magnitude and contains persons of every religion, sect, and nationality. Theoretically it is possible for any human being to enter this Paradise, if such fortune be vouchsafed to him in some Divine illumination, but the

[1] K II. 64, 21 foll. [2] K II. 69, 2. [3] K II. 69, 7 foll.
[4] K II. 65, 8 foll. [5] K II. 38, 15 foll. [6] K II. 44, 18 foll.

author adds: "We saw in mystical vision that only a few of each sect are there[1]." The four highest Paradises have no trees, pavilions, or houris, and are inhabited (except the highest of all) by contemplatives and saints in an ascending scale of holiness. The floor of the eighth Paradise is the roof of the Throne of God (*al-'Arsh*). Thither none may come—for it is the Paradise of the Essence, "the Lauded Station" (*al-Maqám al-maḥmúd*) which, as the Tradition tells us, was promised by God to Mohammed.

With the people of Paradise every idea immediately becomes an object of sensation. When Adam, whose form is a copy of the form of Mohammed, went down from Paradise, he lost the life of his form, *i.e.*, the power of materialising his thoughts. In the present world this power depends on the spirit, and since most of mankind are dead spiritually, belongs only to mystics endued with God's everlasting life[2].

Hell is the manifestation of Divine Majesty (*jalál*). When God created the Fire, He revealed Himself to it seven times, appearing each time in a different Name. These theophanies clove the Fire into seven valleys, which are the limbos of Hell[3].

Pantheism cannot allow evil to be permanent. Jílí cites the Tradition, "My Mercy preceded My Wrath," and infers that while the latter attribute is a mode of Divine Justice, Mercy is essential and prevails in the end[4]. Hell, according to him, is a temporary state[5], and not necessarily an altogether

[1] K II. 45, 12 foll.

[2] K II. 47, 18 foll. According to Ibnu 'l-'Arabí (*Fuṣúṣ*, 90 foll.), the gnostic (*'árif*) creates by means of his meditation (*himma*) ideas which have an objective existence in sensation, phantasy, or higher planes of perception. His creative power differs from that of God, inasmuch as his consciousness is not universal, *i.e.*, it does not comprehend every plane of perception simultaneously. Cf. Massignon, *Kitáb al-Ṭawásín*, p. 183.

[3] K II. 40, 21 foll.

[4] K II. 39, 10 foll.

[5] "Whenever God creates torment (*'adhdb*) by Hell-fire, He also creates in the sufferers the power of enduring it, for otherwise they would perish and so escape. Hence, their skins are periodically renewed (Koran, 4, 59), and they receive fresh powers of endurance, in virtue of which they feel a presentiment of new torments; but the powers with which they endured the former torments do not cease, inasmuch as these powers are given to them by God, and God never takes back His gifts. Thus their powers of endurance

undesirable one. Of course, he had been there in his visions, and he tells of a meeting with Plato, "whom the formal theologians account an infidel, but I saw that he filled the unseen world with light, and that his rank was such as few amongst the saints possess[1]." Some of the damned are more excellent than many of the Paradisal folk: God has placed them in Hell, that He may be revealed to them therein[2]. Jílí expatiates on the variety of pleasures enjoyed by those who burn in the Fire[3]. Some feel a pleasure comparable to the joy of battle, for although the soldier is conscious of pain he often has a keen delight in the fray into which "the Lordship lurking in his soul" impels him to plunge. Another of their pleasures resembles that felt when any one rubs an itch, even if he should chance to break the skin. Then they have subtler pleasures, like the self-satisfaction of the fanatic who persists in a wrong way of thinking, or the philosopher's happy sense of superiority in preferring his own wretched condition to the rich man's luxury and ignorance.

Their states are diverse: some, notwithstanding that they suffer the most intense torment, would not exchange it for Paradise; some long for a breath of the air of Eden and a draught of its water; some, having no pleasure in their pain, feel the utmost bitterness of loathing in themselves.

It is well known that Mohammed asserted the essential unity of Revelation. From the beginning of the world, as he believed, one and the same faith had been revealed to mankind through a succession of prophets, of whom he himself was the last. Abraham, Moses, David, and Jesus taught the same religion, the religion of Islam. It followed, in the first place, that the Pentateuch, the Psalms, and the Gospel are identical

continue to grow, until there appears in them a Divine power which extinguishes the Fire, because no one is doomed to misery after the Divine attributes become manifest in him" (K II. 38, 6 fr. foot and foll.). Elsewhere, on the ground that Hell-fire is an eternal object of God's knowledge, Jílí denies that it is extinguished absolutely (M 44 *b*). "You may say, if you wish, that it remains as it was, but that the torment of the damned is changed to pleasure" (K II. 40, 2).

[1] K II. 43, 9. [2] K II. 44, 15. [3] K II. 43, 16 foll.

in substance with the Koran, and secondly, that since the Jews and Christians would neither accept Islam nor acknowledge Mohammed as the prophet foretold in their books, they must be giving a false account of what these books actually contained. The *argumentum ad homines* needed firm handling. Uninspired Moslems would rather say that the books in their present form are corrupt or incomplete. From quite another standpoint the Ṣúfís agree with their Prophet that the Word of God is essentially one. For them, indeed, all that exists is His Word, which is revealed to His prophets and saints under different aspects and in varying degrees of perfection. The historical and temporal is only a symbol of the mystical and eternal revelation. As, in the former, Christianity occupies the middle place between Judaism and Islam, so in the latter, where these religions typify the progressive ascent of the soul to God, the Illumination of the Names is denoted by the Pentateuch, the Illumination of the Attributes by the Gospel, and the Illumination of the Essence by the Koran[1].

No one who reads the *Insánu 'l-Kámil* can fail to discern that its author was profoundly influenced by Christian ideas, though it is not always possible to separate these from the Jewish, Gnostic and other elements with which they are intermingled[2]. I need only allude to the Trinitarian basis of the Divine nature[3] and the prominence given to the Holy Spirit as the source and, in relation to man, the organ and

[1] K I. 104, I foll.

[2] Naturally, the main original source is Philo, from whom many parallels might be quoted. The Logos, made in the image of God, is described both as an ἀρχέτυπος ἰδέα and as a seal (σφραγίς, χαρακτὴρ) impressing itself on things. He is called an archangel, the instrument (ὄργανον) of creation, the heavenly man (cf. Corinthians, 15, 45 foll.), God's interpreter and prophet (ἑρμηνεὺς καὶ προφήτης). As a mediator between man and God, he is compared with the High-priest (ἀρχιερεὺς) who, like the Moslem saint, passes away in God: "he shall be no man when he goeth in to the Holy of Holies," according to Philo's rendering of Leviticus, 16, 17 (Siegfried, *Philo von Alexandria*, p. 224 foll.).

[3] Cf. Ibnu 'l-'Arabí's verse (*Tarjumán al-ashwáq*, XII. 4): "My Beloved is three although He is one, even as the (three) Persons (of the Trinity) are made one Person in essence"; and his statement that of all the Divine names only three are cardinal, *viz.*, Allah, al-Raḥmán, and al-Rabb (*op. cit.* p. 71). For his doctrine of "triplicity" (*tathlíth*) see Appendix II.

sustaining principle of spiritual life[1]. Jílí criticises the Christian doctrine, but so mildly and apologetically that one passage of his work is declared by the Moslem editor to be an interpolation which only a heretic could have written[2]. The Pentateuch, he says, was sent down to Moses in nine tables[3], two of which, containing the mysteries of Lordship and Power, he was forbidden to communicate to any one; and as the Jews remained ignorant of their contents, Moses was the last of that people to gain perfect knowledge of God. On the other hand, both Jesus and Mohammed revealed the mystery of Lordship; but whereas Mohammed cloaked it in symbols and made it an esoteric matter[4], Jesus proclaimed it openly, with the result that his followers became infidels and worshipped him as the third of three Divine Persons, namely, the Father, the Mother, and the Son[5]. This form of Trinity, by the way, appears in the Koran[6]; it is not a grotesque blunder on the part of Mohammed, but a Christian heresy which still survives amongst the tribes of the Syrian desert[7].

[1] Massignon points out (*Kitáb al-Ṭawásín*, p. 134, note 3) that in the treatises of the Ikhwánu 'l-Ṣafá (Bombay, A.H. 1306, IV. 107 fol.) "the inbreathing of the Spirit" (*nafkhu 'l-Rúḥ*) is mentioned as a doctrine specially characteristic of Christian mysticism.

[2] K I. 105. Ibnu 'l-'Arabí (*Fuṣúṣ*, 176 foll.) is more critical and orthodox than Jílí.

[3] Amongst the matters contained in the fourth table Jílí mentions (K I. 101, 13 foll.) the science of High Magic (*al-siḥru 'l-'álí*), which resembles the miracles of the saints and does not depend on drugs, formulae, etc., but solely on the magical powers in man. "In the way of Divine unity," he says, "I have had some experience of this, and if I had desired I could have assumed any shape in the world and done any deed, but I knew it to be pernicious and therefore abandoned it. Then God endowed me with the secret potency which He placed between K and N" (*i.e.* His creative Word, *Kun* = "Be!").

[4] There is a Tradition to the effect that Mohammed, on the night of his ascension, received three kinds of knowledge: one kind (external religion) he was commanded to impart to his people, another (the spiritual doctrine) he was left free to communicate or not, and the last (concerning the mysteries of the Godhead) he was forbidden to divulge. Some, however, learn it by mystical revelation (K I. 99, 10 foll.).

[5] K I. 97, 15 foll. According to Jílí, the Gospel was revealed to Jesus in Syriac, and its opening words are *Bismi 'l-ab wa 'l-umm wa 'l-ibn*, "In the name of the Father and the Mother and the Son" (K I. 105, 15 foll.).

[6] Kor. 5, 116.

[7] Musil, *Arabia Petraea*, III. 91.

While Jesus spoke the Truth allegorically, the Christians have taken his words literally[1]. Polytheists as they are, God after punishing them for their error will pardon them because of the inward sincerity of their belief, for "they acted in accordance with the knowledge which He bestowed upon them: therefore blame them not, since their polytheism was essentially belief in One God (*kána shirkuhum 'ayna 'l-tawḥíd*)[2]." It is this sentence and others of like tenor that the editor would erase, and we can understand his indignation, though Jílí is simply applying to a special case the monistic doctrine which has been explained already. Of all non-Islamic religious communities he holds that the Christians are nearest to God, for while they worship Him in Jesus, Mary, and the Holy Ghost, they assert the indivisibility of the Divine nature and that God is prior to His existence in the created body of Christ. Thus they recognise the two complementary sides of true belief concerning God, namely that from the one point of view (*tanzíh*) He is above all likeness and that from the other (*tashbíh*) He reveals Himself in the forms of His creatures[3]. But, in addition to the grave error of anthropomorphism (*tajsím*), they are at fault in restricting the Divine self-manifestation to these three. God said, "I breathed My Spirit into Adam[4]," and here the name "Adam" signifies every human individual[5]. The contemplation of those who behold God in Man is the most perfect in the world. Something of this vision the Christians possess, and their doctrine about Jesus will lead them at last, "when the Thing

[1] "The Christians supposed that the Father was the Spirit (*al-Rúḥ*), the Mother Mary, and the Son Jesus; then they said 'God is the Third of Three,' not knowing that 'the Father' signifies the Name Allah, and that 'the Mother' signifies the *Ummu 'l-Kitáb* ('the Mother of the Book,' an expression generally understood as meaning the fundamental part of the Koran), *i.e.*, the ground of the Essence, and that 'the Son' signifies the Book, which is Absolute Being because it is a derivative and product of the aforesaid ground" (K I. 105, 17 foll.).

[2] K I. 106, 2.

[3] K II. 105, 16 foll.

[4] Koran, 15, 29. Jílí declares that the entire Gospel is contained in this verse, and that the Moslems alone have fulfilled the true doctrine of the Gospel, which is "the manifestation of the Creator (*al-Ḥaqq*) in the creatures (*al-khalq*)."

[5] K I. 107, 1 foll.

shall be discovered as it really is[1]," to the knowledge that mankind are like mirrors set face to face, each of which contains what is in all; and so they will behold God in themselves and declare Him to be absolutely One[2].

Jílí concludes his work with a mystical interpretation of Islam, "the crown of religions[3]." Much of what he says has no interest except for specialists, *e.g.*, his definitions of technical terms used by Ṣúfís and his explanations of the esoteric meanings which he finds under every detail of Mohammedan ritual. He is careful to guard against antinomianism. Certain Ṣúfí saints claimed to have outdistanced the prophets[4], but Jílí decides in favour of the latter. He admits that saintship—the revelation of the Divine attributes to man—is the essence of prophecy, and that the prophet *quâ* saint is superior to the prophet *quâ* prophet. Every prophet has "the prophecy of saintship" (*nubuwwatu 'l-wiláyat*), although some, like Jesus and al-Khaḍir, have nothing more[5]; others, like Moses and Mohammed, have also "the prophecy of institution" (*nubuwwatu 'l-tashrí'*), *i.e.*, they were sent to promulgate and establish a new religious code. The Ṣúfí Shaykhs, whom God brings back from the state of trance (*faná*) in order that they may guide the people to Him, are vicegerents (*khulafá*) of Mohammed and, as such, are invested with "the prophecy of saintship" and bound to observe the laws of the last of the institutional prophets, Mohammed, who in both respects is supreme and unique[6]. Jílí must be called a pantheist in so far as he takes "There is no god but Allah" in the sense of "Nothing really exists but the Divine Essence with its creative and creaturely modes of being." These modes are unified in the abstraction of intellect as well as in the mystic's flight to God, but the author of the *Insánu 'l-Kámil* is neither a pure philosopher at any time nor an ecstatic always. "Perception of the Essence," he writes, "consists

[1] At the Resurrection. [2] K II. 105, 20 foll. [3] K II. 106, 4 foll.

[4] K I. 105, 6 foll. Jílí cites an assertion of the superiority of the saints by his ancestor, 'Abdu 'l-Qádir al-Jílání.

[5] On the other hand, Ibnu 'l-'Arabí says that the Jews believed in Jesus until he, as an apostle, reformed the Mosaic law (*Fuṣúṣ*, 205).

[6] K II. 109, 5 foll. Cf. *Fuṣúṣ*, 34 foll., 203 foll.

in thy knowing that thou art He and that He is thou, and that this is not identification or incarnation, and that the slave is a slave and the Lord a Lord, and that the slave does not become a Lord nor the Lord become a slave[1]." Even the Perfect Man is *a* reality (*ḥaqq*), not *the* Reality (*al-Ḥaqq*) which displays itself in the mirror of his consciousness as God and Man[2].

[1] K I. 29, 16 foll.

[2] K I. 26, 5 from foot. So the Logos of Philo is θεός, but not ὁ Θεός (Bigg, *Christian Platonists of Alexandria*, 2nd ed., p. 42, note 2). Cf. Ibnu 'l-'Arabí, cited by Massignon, *Kitáb al-Ṭawásín*, p. 184.

APPENDIX I

JÍLÍ'S *'AYNIYYA*

Mention has been made (p. 99, note 2 *supra*) of Jílí's ode entitled *al-Nawádiru 'l-'ayniyya fí 'l-bawádiri 'l-ghaybiyya*. In the *Insánu 'l-Kámil* he cites 36 of its 534 verses (I. 30, 3; 39, 6 fr. foot; 52, 17; 66, 19; and 76, 15) and describes it as a magnificent and unique composition, too sublime to be fully understood. It is, however, little more than a versified summary of matter set forth in the *Insánu 'l-Kámil*, though in some instances the author expresses himself with a freedom and boldness which would hardly be tolerated in a prose treatise. As a poem, apart from its ungraceful style, it suffers from expounding a theory of mystical philosophy and cannot bear comparison with Ibnu 'l-Fáriḍ's *Tá'iyya*—the poetry of pure mysticism. The extracts given below have been copied from a manuscript in the British Museum (Or. 3684; Rieu's Suppl. to the Catalogue of Arabic MSS. No. 245) containing the text together with a commentary by 'Abdu 'l-Ghaní al-Nábulusí.

I (f. 130 *b*)

فديني وإسلامي وتقواي أنّني * لحسنك فانٍ لاتّمارك طائعْ
اذا قيل قُلْ لا قلتُ غيرَ جمالها * وان قيل إلّا قلتُ حُسْنُك شائعْ
أُصلّي اذا صلّي الانام وانّما * صلاتي بأنّي لاعتزازك خاضعْ
أُكبّر في تحريم ذاتك عن سوى * وإسمك تسبيحي اذا انا راكعْ
اقوم اصلّي اي اقوم علي الوفا * بأنّك فردٌ واحد الحُسْن جامعْ
وأُقرأُ من قرآن حسنك آيةً * فذلك قرآني اذا انا خاشعْ
وأسجدُ اي أفْنَي وأفْنَي عن الفَنَي * وأسجدُ أُخْرَي والمتيَّم والعْ
وقلبيَ مذ ابقاهْ حسنك عنده * تحيّاته منكم اليكم تسارعْ
صيامي هو الإمساك عن رؤية السوي * وفطريَ أنّي نحو وجهك أرْجعْ

v. ٢. Instead of "there is no god but Allah" the poet says, "there is nothing but Absolute Beauty (*jamál*) and phenomenal beauty (*ḥusn*)," these being the inward and outward aspects of the Beloved.

2 (f. 139 *b*)

تجلّى حبيبى فى مَرائى جماله * ففى كلّ مرأًى للحبيب طلائعْ
فلمّا تبدّى حسنُهُ متنوّعًا * تسمَّى بأَسمآءٍ فهنّ مَطالعْ
فأَبرز منه فيه آثارَ وصفه * فذلكم الآثارُ ما هو صانعْ
فاوصافه والاسم والأَثر الذى * هو الكون عَيْنُ الذات واللهُ جامعْ
فما ثَمَّ من شىءٍ سوى الله فى الورى * ولا ثمّ مسموعٌ ولا ثمّ سامعْ

* * *

حقائق ذاتٍ فى مراتب حقّه * تُسمَّى بإِسم الخلق والحقّ واسعْ
وفى فيهِ مِنْ رُوحى نَفَخْتُ كفايةٌ * هل الروحُ إلّا عَيْنُهُ يا منازعْ
ونزّهْهُ عن حكم الحلول فما له * سِوًى وإلى توحيده الامرُ راجعْ

* * *

فيا احدىّ الذات فى عين كثرة * ويا واحد الأَشيآء ذاتك شائعْ
تجلّيتَ فى الاشيآء حين خلقتها * فها هى ميطت عنك فيها البراقعْ
قطعتَ الورى من ذات نفسك قطعةً * ولم تك موصولًا ولا فَصْلَ قاطعْ
ولكنّما احكام رُتْبتك اقتست * أُلوهيّةً للضدّ فيها التجامعْ
فأنت الوَرا حقًّا وأَنت أَمامنا * وانّك ما يعلو وما هو واضعْ
وما الخلق فى التمثال الّا كثلجةٍ * وأنت بها المآء الذى هو نابعْ
فما الثلج فى تحقيقنا غير مائه * وغيران فى حكم دَعَتْه الشرائعْ
ولكن بذوب الثلج يرفع حكمه * ويوضع حكم المآء والأَمْرُ واقعْ

vv. ٦—٧. The individualisations of the Divine Essence are named "the creatures of God," but in reality they are no other than the Essence itself.

v. ١١. K (I. 76, 16): من ذات حسنك.

v. ١٣. The MS. and K read الورى.

3 (f. 146 *b*)

وكن ناظرًا فى القلب صورةَ حسنه * على هيئة المنقوش تظهرُ طالعْ
فقد جآء فى نصّ الحديث تخلّقوا * بأَخْلاقه ما للحقيقة مانعْ
فها هو سمعٌ بل لسانٌ يدٌ لنا * به هكذا بالنقل أَخْبَرَ شارعْ
فعمَّ قُوانا والجوارحَ كونُهُ * لسانًا وسمعًا ثمّ رجْلًا تسارعْ
ولسنا سوى تلك الجوارح والقُوَى * هو الكلّ منّا ما لقولىَ دافعْ
ويكفيك ما قد جآء فى الخلق أنّه * على صورة الرحمن آدمُ واقعْ
ولو لم يكن فى وجه آدم نورُهُ * لما سجد الأَمْلاكُ وهى خواضعْ
ولو شاهدتْ عينٌ لإبليس وَصْفَهُ * على آدمٍ لم يَعْصِ وهو مُطاوعْ
ولكن جرى المقدور فهو على عَمًى * عن العَيْن اذ حالت هناك موانعْ
فلا تك من إبليس فى شبه ستْره * ودعْ قَيْدَهُ العقلىَّ فالعقل رادعْ
وغُصْ فى بحار الاتّحاد منزَّهًا * عن المزج بالاغيار ان انت شاجعْ

* * *

فلا تك محجوبًا برؤية حسنه * عن الذات أنت الذات أنت المَجامعْ
فعَيْنُك شاهدْها بمَحْتَدِ اصلها * فانّ عليها للجمال لوامعْ
أَنيّتك اللائى هى القصد والمُنَى * بها الامرُ مرموزٌ وحسنك بارعْ
ونفسك تحوى بالحقيقة كلّ ما * أَشَرْتُ بحدّ القول ما انا خادعْ
تَهَنَّ بها وٱعرفْ حقيقتها فما * كعرفانها شىءٌ لذاتك نافعْ
فحقّقْ وكن حقًّا فأنت حقيقة * بحقّك والمخلوقُ بالذات جامعْ
ووحّدْهُ فى الاشيآء فهو منزَّهٌ * وخلفَ حجاب الكون للنور ساطعْ
ولا تطلبنْ فيه الدليل فانّه * ورآء كتاب العقل تلك الوقائعْ
ولكن بايمان وحسن تتبّعٍ * اذا قمتَ جاءتك الامور توابعْ

v. ١٦. The MS. reads تهزّ for تهنّ.

v. ٢٠. The rhyme in this poem is *muqayyad*. Even Jílí could not have written توابعُ here, or وقائعُ (4, *v.* ٢٢). He neglects the rule that in this form of *Ṭawíl* the third foot of the second hemistich should be ⏑ – ⏑ (not ⏑ – –).

4 (f. 156 *a*)

وها انا ذا أُنبئك عن سُبُل الهُدَى * وأُفصحُ عمّا قد حَوَتْهُ المشارعْ
اقصُّ حديثًا تمّ لى من بدايتى * لنَحْوِ انتهآءٍ علمُهُ لك نافعْ
برزتُ من النور الإلٰهىّ لمعةً * بحكمة ترتيب قضتها البدائعْ
الى سقف عرش الله فى أُفُق العلا * ومنه الى الكرسىّ جئتُ أُسارعْ
الى القلم الاعلى ولى منه برزةٌ * الى اللوح لوحِ الأَمْرِ والحقُّ واسعْ
الى الهَبَأ السامى وقَبْلُ مكرَّمًا * نزلتُ الهَيولَى وهو للخلق جامعْ
هناك تلقّتْنى العناصر حكمةً * ومنها أُحلّتْنى حُلاها الطبائعْ

* * *

فهذا نزول الجسم من عند ربّه * وللروح تنزيلٌ مَجازىْ متابعْ
وذلك أنّ الروح فى المركز الذى * لها هو روح الحقّ فافهمْ أَسامعْ
وليس لها فيه هبوطٌ مُنزِّلٌ * وليس لها فيه صعودٌ مُرافعْ
ولكنّ فى تعييننا بمخصَّصٍ * تنزّه عن حكم بأن هو شائعْ
وذلك للارواح خَلْقٌ حقيقةً * وذلك تنزيلٌ لها وقواطعْ
ففى المَثَل المفروض منه ترتّبت * مراتبُهُ حتى بدا متناوعْ
فيبرز فى حكم المرآة للورى * تجلّيه والمقدور اذذاك طالعْ
فتنويعها ذاك التجلّى هو الذى * نسمّيه روحًا وهو بالنفخ واقعْ
وإلّا فلا إسمٌ له غير ربّنا * وليس له الّا الصفات مواضعْ
تنزّه ربّى عن حلول بقدسه * وحاشاه ما بالاتّحاد مواقعْ

* * *

v. ١. المشارع, variant الاضالع.

v. ٦. MS. وقيل مكرما. Cf. p. 123 *supra*.

v. ٨ foll. The terms "ascent" and "descent" are improperly applied to the spirit, which has its being in God (فيه in *v.* ١٠ means فى الحقّ). In order to distinguish it from God, we say that it is particularised and individualised, *i.e.* created; and we give the name of "spirit" to this individualisation, by means of which God displays Himself as in a mirror.

v. ١٤. تجلّيه is a correction of the MS. reading على.

وانّ نزول الجسم للخلق فى الثرى * سواءٌ ولكن بعد ذاك تناوعْ
فمن سبقت للّه فيه عنايةٌ * فغيرَ مُكوثٍ فى التراب يسارعْ
ومن ابعدتْه السابقات فانّه * له بين نَبْتٍ والتراب تراجعْ
فقد يك عُشْبًا ثمّ ترعاه دابّةٌ * ويشزب اذ يفنى ويخضرُّ ضارعْ
على قدر تكرار التردّد بُعْدُهُ * ليَنْسى عهودًا بالحِمَى ووقائعْ
وعند مرور النفس فى كلّ منزل * سينقش فيها منه طبعًا طبائعْ
فتظهر نفسُ المرء كاملةَ البها * ومن نسخة الأَكوان فيها خلائعْ
لتذكر بالمشهود غايةَ امرها * فيرجع للاوطان من هو راجعْ

5 (f. 163 *b*)

رأيتُ قيامى راجعًا نحو ربّه * فقهقر منّى للحبيب مَراجعْ
فعاينتُ انّى كنتُ فى العلم ثابتًا * وللحقّ علمُ الحقّ فى الحكم تابعْ
وبالعلم فالمعلوم ايضًا فمُلْحَقٌ * وليس لهذا الحكم فى العقل رادعْ
فحينئذٍ حقّقتُ انّىَ نفحةٌ * من الطيب طيبِ الله فى الخلق ضائعْ
وما النشرُ غير المِسك فأفهمْ اشارتى * ويُغنيك فى التصريح للسرّ ذائعْ

* * *

وسلّمتُ نفسى حين اسلمتُ للقضا * وما لىَ معْ هذا الحبيب تنازعْ
فطورًا ترانى فى المساجد عاكفًا * وانّىَ طورًا فى الكنائس راتعْ
ارانىَ كالآلات وهو محرّكى * انا قلمٌ وإقتدارٌ أَصابعْ
ولستُ بجَبْرىّ ولكن مشاهد * فعالَ مريد ما له من يدافعْ
فآونةً يقضى علىّ بطاعة * وحينًا بما عنه نهتْنا الشرائعْ
لذاك ترانى كنتُ أَتْرُكُ امره * وآتى الذى ينهاهُ والجفنُ دامعْ
ولى نكتةٌ غرّا هنا سأقولها * وحُقّ لها أن ترعويها المسامعْ
هى الفرق ما بين الولىّ وفاسقٍ * تنبّهْ لها فالامر فيه فظائعْ
وما هو الّا انّه قبل وَقعِهِ * يخبّر قلبى بالذى هو واقعْ

v. ٢١. MS. يشرب.

v. ١٢ foll. Cf. p. 126 *supra*.

5, *v.* ٢ foll. Cf. p. 151 *infra*.

فأجنى الذى يقضيه فىّ مرادُها * وعينى له قبل الفعال تطالعْ
وكنت ارى منها الارادة قبل ما * ارى الفعل منّى والاسيرُ مطاوعْ
فآتى الذى تهواهُ منّى ومهجتى * لذلك فى نار حَوَتْها الاضالعْ
وان كنتُ فى حكم الشريعة عاصيًا * فانّىَ فى حكم الحقيقة طائعْ

6 (f. 170 *b*)

انا الحقُّ والتحقيق جامعُ خَلْقه * انا الذاتُ والوصف الذى هو تابعْ
فأحوى بذاتىِ ما علمتُ حقيقةً * ونورىَ فيما قد اضآء فلامعْ
ويسمع تسبيحَ الصوامت مسمعى * وانّى لأسرار الصدور أُطالعْ
وأعلمُ ما قد كان فى زمن مضى * وحالًا وأدرى ما اراهُ مضارعْ

* * *

وأنظرُ تحقيقًا بعينى محقّقًا * قصورَ جنان الخلد وهى قلائعْ
وأُتقنُ علمًا بالاحاطة جملةً * لأوراق اشجار هناك ايانعْ
وكلّ طباق فى الجحيم عرفتُها * وأعرفُ اهليها ومن ثمّ واقعْ
وأنواع تعذيب هناك علمتُها * وأهوالها طرًّا وهنّ فظائعْ
وأملاكها حقًّا عرفتُ ولم يكن * علىّ بخافٍ ما له انا صانعْ
وكلّ عذاب ثمّ ذقتُ ولم اقل * أُخَشّى وانّى للمقامَيْن جامعْ
وكلّ نعيم انّنى لمنعَّمٌ * به وهو لى مِلْكٌ وما ثمّ رادعْ

* * *

وأُفنى اذا شئتُ الانام بلمحة * وأُحيى بلفظٍ من حَوَتْهُ البلاقعْ
وأجمع ذرّات الجسوم من الثرى * وأُنشى كما كانت وانّىَ بادعْ

* * *

وانّى على هذا عن الكلّ فارغٌ * وليس به لى همّةٌ وتنازعْ
ووصفىَ حقًّا فوق ما قد وصفتُهُ * وحاشاىَ من حَصْرٍ وما لىَ قاطعْ
وانّى على مقدار فهمك واصفٌ * وإلّا فلى من بعد ذاك بدائعْ
وثَمّ امورٌ ليس يمكن كَشْفُها * بها قلّدتْنى عِقْدَهنّ الشرائعْ
قفوتُ بها آثار أحْمَدَ تابعًا * فأعْجَبْ لمتبوع وما هو تابعْ
نبىّ له فوق المكانة رتبةٌ * ومن عَيْنه للناهلين منابعْ

APPENDIX II

SOME NOTES ON THE *FUṢÚṢU 'L-ḤIKAM*[1]

I have already referred to the work of Ibnu 'l-'Arabí, bearing a title which may be rendered "The Bezels of Divine Wisdom," and have pointed out that its subject-matter coincides, to a large extent, with that of the *Insánu 'l-Kámil*, while both writers are not only inspired by the same mystical philosophy but use similar methods in order to develop their ideas[2]. The following notes, inadequate as they are, will at least show the magnitude of Jílí's debt to his predecessor, besides making clearer some fundamental principles which in the *Insánu 'l-Kámil* are assumed rather than expounded. The *Fuṣúṣ* purports to be a treatise on the nature of God as manifested through prophecy, each of its 27 chapters being attached to the logos (*kalima*) of a prophet typifying a particular Divine attribute. Since God does not reveal Himself completely except in Man, the first chapter treats of Adam as the microcosm, the Perfect Man, the absolute mirror of Divinity. Often Ibnu 'l-'Arabí takes a text of the Koran and elicits his doctrine from it in a fashion well known to students of Philo and Origen. The theories set forth in the *Fuṣúṣ* are difficult to understand and even more difficult to explain. Many years ago I translated the greater part of the work, with the commentary by 'Abdu 'l-Razzáq al-Káshání, for my own use, but the author's language is so technical, figurative, and involved that a literal reproduction would convey very little. On the other hand, if we reject his terminology, we shall find it impossible to form any precise notion of his ideas. By collecting and arranging illustrative passages and by availing myself of the commentator's aid I may, perhaps, throw some light on a peculiarly recondite phase of mystical scholasticism.

[1] The edition used is that published at Cairo in A.H. 1321.

[2] See p. 88.

The Divine Essence, which is all that exists, may be regarded from two aspects: (*a*) as a pure, simple, attributeless essence; (*b*) as an essence endowed with attributes. God, considered absolutely, is beyond relation and therefore beyond knowledge—the Neoplatonic One, inconceivable and ineffable. From this point of view God, in a sense, is not God. "Some philosophers and Abú Ḥámid (al-Ghazálí) have asserted that God is known without reference to the universe, but they are mistaken. An eternal Essence is known, but it is not known to be a god, *i.e.*, an object of worship (*iláh*), until the *ma'lúh* (the logical complement of *iláh*) is known[1]." Here we are introduced to a dialectic which dominates the *Fuṣúṣ*. While God is independent of created beings in respect of His essence, He requires them in respect of His divinity[2]. His existence is absolute, theirs is relative, *i.e.*, it is Real Being limited and individualised by appearing as a relation of Reality. Hence all things are attributes of God. As such, they are ultimately identical with God, apart from whom they are nothing[3]. Regarded externally, they depend on the universals of which they are the particulars. Thus, a "living" person is not judged to be "living" unless he have in him the universal "life" which, though as a universal it exists only in the mind, has an external existence in so far as it is attached to phenomena. Universals, being mental concepts, imply a subject and an object. As the universal, knowledge, necessarily predicates of any one endowed with it that he is "knowing," so the person endowed therewith necessarily predicates of the knowledge that it is originated in relation to himself, eternal

[1] *Fuṣúṣ*, 74.

[2] This mode of thought leads Ibnu 'l-'Arabí to indulge in daring paradoxes, *e.g.*, "He praises me (by manifesting my perfections and creating me in His form), and I praise Him (by manifesting His perfections and obeying Him). How can He be independent when I help and aid Him? (because the Divine attributes derive the possibility of manifestation from their correlates). For that cause God brought me into existence, and I know Him and bring Him into existence (in my knowledge and contemplation of Him)." *Fuṣúṣ*, 78.

[3] God is the *'ayn* (identity) of the attributes, in the sense that they are not superadded to His Essence but are relations of the Essence as subject to itself as object (*Fuṣúṣ*, 226). The universe is the objectified sum of these relations.

in relation to God[1]. The Divine Essence, in knowing itself, knows all things in itself and distinguishes them from itself as objects of its knowledge. The difference, of course, does not impair the essential unity of knowledge, knower, and known, but is none the less inherent in the nature of things, *i.e.*, in Reality as manifested to us. "Triplicity (*tathlíth*) is the foundation of becoming[2]." God is single (*fard*), but according to Ibnu 'l-'Arabí the first single (odd) number is 3, not 1. "One" is the object of numeration, whence all numbers from 2 upwards are derived. Creation depends on knowledge and therefore involves *tathlíth*. That which is brought into existence is a correlate[3], which already exists ideally and contains in itself the potentiality of existing objectively, inasmuch as it must correspond with the knowledge and will of God concerning it; otherwise, it would not exist either potentially or actually[4]. The essences (*a'yán*) of things are eternally known to God and "give" His knowledge to Him in virtue of their being that which He knows of them. His creative Word (*Kun*, "Be!") actualises their existence, but properly they bring themselves into existence, because He only wills what they have it in them to become. From the proposition that "knowledge is a relation depending on the object known (*al-'ilm nisbat^{un} tábi'at^{un} li 'l-ma'lúm*), and the object known is thou and all appertaining to thee[5]," Ibnu 'l-'Arabí infers that human actions are logically self-determined[6]. The fate of every individual is his *'ayn thábita* or essential character as it exists from eternity in the Divine knowledge. Men receive of good and evil just what the necessity of their natures demands. The verse, "Had God willed, He would have guided you all aright" (Koran, 6, 150), means that God could not will the impossible. His wisdom requires that the infinite diversity of His attributes should be matched by infinitely diverse capacities in the objects wherein these attributes are displayed[7].

[1] *Fuṣúṣ*, 16 fol. [2] *Ibid.* 142.

[3] *Múјad* (the thing brought into existence) implies *múјid* (one who brings it into existence).

[4] *Fuṣúṣ*, 139 foll. [5] *Ibid.* 76.

[6] *Ibid.* 77. The determining "self" is really an individualisation (*ḥaqíqa*) of God. [7] *Ibid.* 75–6.

Mystics see that God is One and All, and One in All.

Sublimity (*'uluww*) belongs to God alone. The essences (*a'yán*) of things are in themselves non-existent, deriving what existence they possess from God, who is the real substance (*'ayn*) of all that exists. Plurality consists of relations (*nisab*), which are non-existent things. There is really nothing except the Essence, and this is sublime (transcendent) for itself, not in relation to anything, but we predicate of the One Substance a relative sublimity (transcendence) in respect of the modes of being attributed to it: hence we say that God is (*huwa*) and is not (*lá huwa*). Kharráz[1], who is a mode of God and one of His tongues, declared that God is not known save by His uniting all opposites in the attribution of them to him (Kharráz)[2]: He is the First, the Last, the Outward, the Inward; He is the substance of what is manifested and the substance of what remains latent at the time of manifestation; none sees Him but Himself, and none is hidden from Him, since He is manifested to Himself and hidden from Himself; and He is the person named Abú Sa'íd al-Kharráz and all the other names of originated things. The inward says "No" when the outward says "I," and the outward says "No" when the inward says "I," and so in the case of every contrary, but the speaker is One, and He is substantially identical with the hearer....The Substance is One, although its modes are different. None can be ignorant of this, for every man knows it of himself[3], and Man is the image of God.

Thus things became confused and numbers appeared, by means of the One, in certain degrees[4]. The One brought number into being, and number analysed the One, and the relation of number was produced by the object of numeration....He that knows this knows that the Creator who is declared to be incomparable (*munazzah*) is the creatures which are compared (*mushabbah*) with Him—by reason of His manifesting Himself in their forms—albeit the creatures have been distinguished from the Creator. The

[1] Abú Sa'íd al-Kharráz (ob. A.D. 890) was a well-known Ṣúfí of Baghdád. See *Kashf al-Maḥjúb*, translation, p. 241 foll.

[2] The mystic cannot know God unless he is illuminated by all the Divine attributes, so that he becomes a *ḥaqq*. See p. 128.

[3] Every individual is conscious of having different faculties and qualities.

[4] One in the first degree is one, in the second ten, in the third a hundred, in the fourth a thousand, and each of these degrees comprises simple and complex numbers, just as species comprise individuals and genera species.

Creator is the creature, and the creature is the Creator: all this proceeds from One Essence; nay, He is the One Essence and the many (individualised) essences....Who is Nature and Who is all that is manifested from her[1]? We did not see her diminished by that which was manifested from her, or increased by the not-being of aught manifested that was other than she. That which was manifested is not other than she, and she is not identical with what was manifested, because the forms differ in respect of the predication concerning them: this is cold and dry, and this is hot and dry: they are united by dryness but separated by cold and heat. Nay, the Essence is (in reality) Nature. The world of Nature is many forms in One Mirror; nay, One Form in diverse mirrors[2]. Bewilderment arises from the difference of view, but those who perceive the truth of what I have stated are not bewildered[3].

We do not find in the *Fuṣúṣ* any systematic scheme of Plotinian emanation or process of self-propulsive thought such as Jílí ascribes to the Absolute[4]. Ibnu 'l-'Arabí indicates the relation of the One to the Many by means of metaphors, *e.g.*, *tajallí* (self-unveiling), *fayḍ* (overflowing), *takhallul* (permeation)[5], and *ta'thír* (producing an effect or impression)[6]. Contingent Being resembles a shadow cast by a figure (Real Being), falling on a place (the forms of phenomena), and made visible by a light (the Divine Name *al-Ẓáhir*, "the Outward"). The universe is imaginary if we deem it external to God and self-subsistent; it is real only as an aspect of the Real[7]. It is "the breath of the Merciful" (*nafasu 'l-Raḥmán*). God exhales, as it were, the essences and forms of things which are contained potentially in His nature, and unites the active and passive elements in one medium of self-expression, just as words and letters are united in the breath of man[8].

[1] Real Being, when limited by a universal individualisation, is Nature, from which are manifested secondary and tertiary individualisations, *viz.*, natural bodies of various kinds.

[2] Nature may be regarded either as all the particular forms in which Reality reveals itself or as the universal form of Reality revealing itself in all particular forms.

[3] *Fuṣúṣ*, 63 foll.

[4] See p. 94.

[5] *Fuṣúṣ*, 72 fol.

[6] *Ibid.* 230 fol.

[7] *Ibid.* 113 foll.

[8] *Ibid.* 182.

Phenomena are perpetually changing and being created anew[1], while God remains as He ever was, is, and shall be. The whole infinite series of individualisations is in fact one eternal and everlasting *tajallí* which never repeats itself. Ibnu 'l-'Arabí observes that his doctrine agrees superficially with that of the Ash'arite atomists, who held the universe to be homogeneous in substance but dissimilar in quality. On the other hand, he points out that instead of identifying the substance with God, and the sum of those forms and relations which they call "accidents," with the universe, the Ash'arites postulate certain monads: these, although by definition they are composed of accidents, are regarded (he says) as having an independent existence, as *a* reality (*ḥaqq*) but not essentially *the* Reality (*al-Ḥaqq*)[2]. To our minds the atoms, which have extension neither in space nor in time, seem insubstantial enough. But Ibnu 'l-'Arabí will brook no *secundum quid*, not even one that only endures for a moment. God is both the spirit and the form of the universe. We must not say that the universe is a form of which He is the spirit[3].

What has been said in the foregoing essay regarding the nature and function of Man was first put forth by Ibnu 'l-'Arabí. A few quotations will make this clear.

When God willed in respect of His Beautiful Names (attributes), which are beyond enumeration, that their essences (*a'yán*)—or if you wish, you may say "His essence (*'aynuhu*)"—should be seen, He caused them to be seen in a microcosmic being (*kawn jámi'*) which, inasmuch as it is endowed with existence[4], contains the whole object of vision, and through which the inmost consciousness (*sirr*) of God becomes manifested to Him. This He did, because the vision that consists in a thing's seeing itself by means of itself is not like its vision of itself in something else that serves as a

[1] But there is no moment of not-being between the successive acts of creation (*Fuṣúṣ*, 196 fol.). The author compares this with the Ash'arite *tajdídu 'l-a'ráḍ*.

[2] *Fuṣúṣ*, 153 foll., 239. Cf. Macdonald, *Development of Muslim Theology*, p. 201 foll.

[3] *Fuṣúṣ*, 46, 132. The attributes are really latent in the Essence and identical with it. Cf. p. 90 *supra*.

[4] *I.e.*, relative existence, wherein Absolute Being is reflected.

mirror for it: therefore God appears to Himself in a form given by the place in which He is seen (*i.e.*, the mirror), and He would not appear thus (objectively) without the existence of this place and His epiphany to Himself therein. God had already brought the universe into being with an existence resembling that of a fashioned soulless body, and it was like an unpolished mirror[1]. Now, it belongs to the Divine decree (of creation) that He did not fashion any place but such as must of necessity receive a Divine soul, which God has described as having been breathed into it; and this denotes the acquisition by that fashioned form of capacity to receive the emanation (*fayḍ*), *i.e.*, the perpetual self-manifestation (*tajallí*) which has never ceased and never shall. It remains to speak of the recipient (of the emanation). The recipient proceeds from naught but His most holy emanation, for the whole affair (of existence) begins and ends with Him: to Him it shall return, even as from Him it began[2].

The Divine will (to display His attributes) entailed the polishing of the mirror of the universe. Adam (the human essence) was the very polishing of that mirror and the soul of that form, and the angels are some of the faculties of that form, *viz.*, the form of the universe which the Ṣúfís in their technical language describe as the Great Man, for the angels in relation to it are as the spiritual and corporeal faculties in the human organism[3]....The aforesaid microcosmic being is named a Man (*insán*) and a Vicegerent (*khalífa*). He is named a Man on account of the universality of his

[1] The world of things was brought into existence before the creation of Man, in so far as every Divine attribute (universal) logically implies the existence of its corresponding particular, which is the Essence individualised by that relation, whereas Man alone is the Essence individualised by all relations together. Since the universe could not manifest the unity of Being until Man appeared in it, it was like an unpolished mirror or a body without a soul.

[2] The "most holy emanation" (*al-fayḍu 'l-aqdas*) is the eternal manifestation of the Essence to itself. This emanation is received by the essences of things (*al-a'yánu 'l-thábita*) in the plane of unity-in-plurality (*wáḥidiyya*), *i.e.*, in the Divine knowledge where no distinctions exist. From one point of view, God is never revealed except to Himself; from another, He is revealed to "recipient" modes of Himself, to each in accordance with its "capacity."

[3] I have omitted a few lines here, to the effect that Man unites all aspects of God—the oneness of the Essence, the plurality of the Divine attributes, and the world of Nature. This truth, the author adds, cannot be apprehended save by mystical perception.

organism and because he comprises all realities[1]. Moreover, he stands to God as the pupil (*insán*), which is the instrument of vision, to the eye; and for this reason he is named a Man. By means of him God beheld His creatures and had mercy on them[2]. He is Man, the originated (in his body), the eternal (in his spirit); the organism everlasting (in his essence), the Word that divides and unites. The universe was completed by his existence, for he is to the universe what the bezel is to the seal—the bezel whereon is graven the signature that the King seals on his treasuries[3]. Therefore He named him a Vicegerent, because he guards the creatures (of God) just as the King guards his treasuries by sealing them; and so long as the King's seal remains on them, none dares to open them save by his leave. God made him His Vicegerent in the guardianship of the universe, and it continues to be guarded whilst this PERFECT MAN is there. Dost not thou see that when he shall depart (to the next world) and his seal shall be removed from the treasury of this world, there shall no more remain in it that which God stored therein, but the treasure shall go forth, and every type shall return to its (ideal) antitype, and all existence shall be transferred to the next world and sealed on the treasury of the next world for ever and ever[4]?

This was the knowledge of Seth, and it is his knowledge that replenishes every spirit that discourses on such a theme except the spirit of the Seal (the Perfect Man), to whom replenishment comes from God alone, not from any spirit; nay, his spirit replenishes all other spirits. And though he does not apprehend that of himself during the time of his manifestation in the body, yet in respect of his real nature and rank he knows it all essentially, just as he is ignorant thereof in respect of his being compounded of elements. He is the knowing one and the ignorant, for as the Origin (God) is capable of endowment with contrary attributes—the Majestical, the Beautiful, the Inward, the Outward, the First, the Last—so is he capable thereof, since he is identical (*'ayn*) with God, not other

[1] *I.e.*, the etymolcgical explanation of the name *insán* is that Man *yu'nis* or *yu'ánis* (knows or is familiar with) all things: the three Arabic words are derived from the same root.

[2] By bringing them into existence. Cf. p. 98 *supra*.

[3] Man's heart (*qalb*) bears the impression of the Greatest Name of God (*i.e.*, the Essence) together with all the other Divine Names.

[4] *Fuṣúṣ*, 8 foll.

than He[1]. Therefore he knows and knows not, perceives and perceives not, beholds and beholds not[2].

Mohammed is the Logos who unites the Essence, the Attributes, and the Names in his single nature (*fardiyya*)[3].

His wisdom is singular (*fardiyya*), because he is the most perfect being in the human species: therefore existence was begun and ended with him, for he was a prophet whilst Adam was water and clay[4].

We have seen whither these principles lead when applied in the sphere of positive religion[5]. Ibnu 'l-'Arabí's doctrine that knowledge is sequent to the object known[6] enables him formally to assert men's individual responsibility for their actions.

Fate (*Qaḍá*)," he says, "is the decree of God concerning things, which is conditioned by His knowledge of them; and His knowledge of them depends on what they give Him of their essential nature. Determination (*Qadar*) is the temporal limitation of a thing's essential nature. Whatsoever Fate decrees concerning a thing is decreed (not by an external agent, but) by means of the thing itself. This is the essence of the mystery of Determination (*sirru 'l-Qadar*)[7]."

In other words, God's knowledge of His essence is His knowledge of all individual souls: the soul as a mode of Divine being determines its own destiny. Every one's portion in this world is that which God knows he will receive, and which is all that he is capable of receiving. God Himself cannot alter it[8]. The true believer here and now was a true believer when his soul existed only as an idea in God, the infidel of to-day has been an infidel from eternity. Hence God says in the Koran (50, 28): "I am not unjust to My servants," *i.e.*, "I did not ordain the unbelief which dooms them to misery and

[1] Man is Absolute Being limited by individualisation (*ta'ayyun*). This limitation, however, is negative and unreal: it consists in failure to receive all individualisations, to be endowed with all attributes, to be named with all names. In so far as Man is a reality (*ḥaqq*) he is not a human creature (*khalq*).

[2] *Fuṣúṣ*, 39 fol.

[3] "Single" is equivalent to "threefold." Cf. p. 151 *supra*.

[4] *Fuṣúṣ*, 267.

[5] P. 130 foll.

[6] See p. 151 *supra*.

[7] *Fuṣúṣ*, 161.

[8] Jílí denies this. See p. 102.

then demand of them what lay not in their power to perform. ...If there be injustice, *they* are the unjust[1]." "Therefore do not praise any one but yourself or blame any one but yourself. All that remains to God is praise for having given you existence, for that (existence) is His, not yours[2]."

Ibnu 'l-'Arabí makes the same distinction as Ḥalláj[3] between the Divine uncreated will (*mashí'a*), which decrees nothing that does not come to pass, and the mediate command (*amr*), which is the religious law (*shar'*) and is often disobeyed. God decrees the establishment of the law, but not the practice of what is enjoined by the law. "Sin" is disobedience to the law: it cannot be disobedience to the Divine will.

In reality the Divine will decrees only the coming into existence of the act itself and is not directed towards the agent in whom the act is manifested. That the act should not occur is impossible, but in the individual who is its *locus* (*i.e.*, the particular agent) it is sometimes named "obedience to the Divine command" and sometimes "disobedience to the Divine command," and is followed by praise or blame accordingly[4].

Thus, although the sinner violates God's law, the act named "sin" by us is necessitated by the Divine nature, which reveals itself in acts of various quality corresponding with the variety of its attributes. Reward and punishment in the future life may be regarded as effects of obedience or disobedience, *i.e.*, Divine manifestations determined by the state of the individual soul, but it is a more profound view that God Himself feels the pleasure and the pain[5].

[1] *Fuṣúṣ*, 159.
[2] *Ibid.* 77.
[3] See p. 54, note 5.
[4] *Fuṣúṣ*, 206 fol. Cf. 108–9.
[5] *Ibid.* 105–6. Job's prayer that God might relieve his pain is justified on the ground that in praying God to remove it he really removed it from God, inasmuch as man is the outward form of God. Such prayer does not evince a want of submission to the Divine decree (*qaḍá*), but dissatisfaction with the thing decreed (*al-maqḍí bihi*), which—as explained above—is decreed by means of the individual soul, *i.e.*, a particular mode of God, not the absolute God (*ibid.* 218–9). All particular modes, together with the effects attached to them, are (as such) relations devoid of reality. "Effect (*athar*) belongs to the non-existent" (*ibid.* 224). This distinction appears in

The finite God of religion is contrasted with the infinite God of mysticism in many passages, *e.g.*:

The believer praises the God who is in his form of belief and with whom he has connected himself. He praises none but himself, for his God is made by himself, and to praise the work is to praise the maker of it: its excellence or imperfection belongs to its maker. For this reason he blames the beliefs of others, which he would not do, if he were just. Beyond doubt, the worshipper of this particular God shows ignorance when he criticises others on account of their beliefs. If he understood the saying of Junayd, "The colour of the water is the colour of the vessel containing it[1]," he would not interfere with the beliefs of others, but would perceive God in every form and in every belief. He has opinion, not knowledge: therefore God said, "I am in My servant's opinion of Me," *i.e.*, "I do not manifest Myself to him save in the form of his belief." God is absolute or restricted, as He pleases; and the God of religious belief is subject to limitations, for He is the God who is contained in the heart of His servant. But the absolute God is not contained by any thing, for He is the being of all things and the being of Himself, and a thing is not said either to contain itself or not to contain itself[2].

It may be noted that while Ibnu 'l-'Arabí admits the immutability of the Koranic revelation, he claims for Moslem saints the right to modify by abrogation or addition the religious code that is based on *ijtihád*, *i.e.*, on non-Prophetic authority, and to put aside any *ḥadíth* in which their inner light detects a flaw[3].

Like Jílí, he is confident that all souls will be saved at last, and argues it in his own scholastic way:

Every one whom Mercy remembers is blessed, and there is

a verse by Jalálu'ddin Rúmi, which has puzzled Mr Whinfield: گفتمش این کفر مقضی نی قضاست "I said to him, 'Infidelity is the thing decreed, not the decree'" (*Masnavi-i Ma'navi*, tr. and abridged by E. H. Whinfield, 2nd ed., p. 125).

[1] *I.e.*, God is revealed in different forms of belief according to the capacity of the believer. The mystic alone sees that He is One in all forms, for the mystic's heart (*qalb*) is all-receptive: it assumes whatever form God reveals Himself in, as wax takes the impression of the seal (*Fuṣúṣ*, 145).

[2] *Fuṣúṣ*, 282. Cf. 135.

[3] *Ibid.* 205.

nothing that Mercy has not remembered. Mercy's remembrance (*dhikr*) of things is identical with her bringing them into existence[1]: therefore every existent thing is an object of mercy. Do not let thy perception of what I say be hindered by the doctrine of everlasting punishment. Know, first, that Mercy's bringing into existence comprises all, so that the pains of Hell were brought into existence by Mercy. Then, secondly, Mercy has an effect in two ways: (1) an essential effect, which is her bringing into existence every *'ayn* (individual idea) without regard to purpose or absence of purpose, or to what is congruous or incongruous, for she was beholding every *'ayn* as it existed in the knowledge of God before its actual existence, and therefore she saw the reality (*ḥaqq*), created in men's beliefs, as a potentially existent *'ayn*, and showed mercy to it by bringing it into existence (in their beliefs). Accordingly, we have said that the reality created in men's beliefs was the first object of mercy, after mercy was shown by bringing into existence the individual believers. (2) An effect produced by asking (*su'ál*): those who are veiled from the truth ask God[2] to have mercy upon them in their belief, but the mystics ask God that Mercy may subsist in them[3], and they ask for mercy in God's name, saying, "O God, have mercy upon us!" That which has mercy upon them is the subsistence of Mercy in them[4].

The remainder of this passage, though one can readily see its drift, is too abstruse and technical to bear translation. Ibnu 'l-'Arabí agrees with Jílí that the damned, even if they remain in Hell-fire, ultimately cease to suffer pain[5]. Religious intolerance appeals as little to the pantheist who says "All is God" as to the freethinking pessimist who cries out that all is vanity; but here Ibnu 'l-'Arabí feels more deeply and pleads more earnestly than Ma'arrí. What God created in His own

[1] Cf. p. 98 fol.

[2] *I.e.*, the finite Lord (*rabb*) who stands in a special and different relation to every object of lordship (*marbúb*). Cf. *Fuṣúṣ*, 95.

[3] *I.e.*, the true mystic prays that he may be "illumined" with the Divine attribute of Mercy so as to become a *ráḥim* (ἐλεῶν), which necessarily involves a *marḥúm* (ἐλεούμενος), and to know himself as a mode of the absolute God who is in reality both the *ráḥim* and the *marḥúm*.

[4] *Fuṣúṣ*, 225.

[5] *Ibid.* 212. Cf. 100. They may experience a positive pleasure like that of the inhabitants of Paradise (*ibid.* 137).

image let none take upon himself to destroy except by God's command. Men are not blameworthy in their real nature: their actions are praised or blamed, but all action belongs to God. As regards those who legally deserve death—infidels and idolaters—God rebuked David for slaying them, and when he said, "For Thy sake, O Lord," God answered and said, "Yea, but are not they My servants?" It is right to be indignant on God's behalf, yet "compassion towards His servants has the greater claim[1]." Love is the highest form in which God is worshipped[2]. Ibnu 'l-'Arabí anticipates Wordsworth[3] in a reasoned tribute to the heavenly influence of children.

The child affects the father's disposition, so that he descends from his authority and plays with him and prattles to him and brings his mind down to the child's, for unconsciously he is under his sway; then he becomes engrossed with educating and protecting his child and with seeking what is good for him and amusing him, that he may not be unhappy. All this is the work of the child upon the father and is owing to the power of his state, for the child was with God a short while ago (*ḥadíthu 'ahd[in] bi-rabbihi*) since he is newly come into the world, whereas the father is further away; and one that is further from God is subject to one that is nearer to Him[4].

1 *Ibid.* 209 fol.

2 *Ibid.* 245. Elsewhere (272) he remarks that God is never seen immaterially and that the vision of Him in women is the most perfect of all.

3 "Heaven lies about us in our infancy."

4 *Fuṣúṣ*, 250.

CHAPTER III

THE ODES OF IBNU 'L-FÁRIḌ[1]

Pensando al bel ch' età non cangia o verno.
MICHAEL ANGELO.

ONE of the deepest differences between Arabs and Persians shows itself in the extent and character of the mystical poetry of each people. As regards Persia, the names of Saná'í, 'Aṭṭár, Jalálu'ddín Rúmí, Sa'dí, Hafiz, and Jámí are witnesses enough. Whether quantity or quality be considered, the best part of medieval Persian poetry is either genuinely mystical in spirit or is so saturated with mystical ideas that it will never be more than half understood by those who read it literally. When we turn to Arabic poetry of the period subsequent to the rise and development of Ṣúfism, what do we find? No lack of poets, certainly, though few of them reach the first rank and their output is scanty compared with the opulent genius of their Persian contemporaries. But from Mutanabbí and Ma'arrí down to the bards unknown in Europe who flourished long after the Baghdád Caliphate had fallen, it is

[1] I have used the following editions and commentaries:

(*a*) *Díwán* of Ibnu 'l-Fáriḍ, ed. by Rushayyid b. Ghálib al-Daḥdáḥ (Marseilles, 1853). This contains the minor poems, with a grammatical commentary by Ḥasan al-Búríní as well as extracts from the mystical commentary of 'Abdu 'l-Ghaní al-Nábulusí.

(*b*) The *Tá'iyyatu 'l-kubrá*, with the commentary of 'Abdu 'l-Razzáq al-Káshání bearing the title *Kashfu 'l-wujúhi 'l-ghurr li-ma'ání naẓmi 'l-durr* (Cairo, A.H. 1319).

(*c*) The *Tá'iyyatu 'l-kubrá*, with the commentary of al-Nábulusí entitled *Kashfu 'l-sirri 'l-ghámiḍ fí sharḥi Díwán Ibni 'l-Fáriḍ* (MS. in the British Museum, Add. 7564–5 Rich.). The commentary on the *Tá'iyya* begins at f. 176 of the first volume.

(*d*) The *Tá'iyyatu 'l-kubrá*, ed. with a German verse-translation by Hammer-Purgstall (Vienna, 1854).

Concerning the Italian translation of the *Tá'iyyatu 'l-kubrá* by Sac. Ignazio Di Matteo (Rome, 1917) and the valuable notice of it by Prof. Nallino which appeared in *Rivista degli studi orientali*, vol. VIII (Rome, 1919), some remarks will be found in the preface to this volume.

The abbreviations *Díwán*, K. and N. refer to (*a*), (*b*) and (*c*) respectively.

remarkable how seldom they possess the note (as Newman would say) of mysticism. The main reason, I think, lies in racial endowment. The Arab has no such passion for an ultimate principle of unity as has always distinguished the Persians and Indians[1]. He shares with other Semitic peoples an incapacity for harmonising and unifying the particular facts of experience: he discerns the trees very clearly, but not the wood. Like his art, in which "we everywhere find a delicate sense for detail, but nowhere large apprehension of a great and united whole[2]," his poetry, intensely subjective in feeling and therefore lyrical in form, presents only a series of brilliant impressions, full of life and colour, yet essentially fragments and moments of life, not fused into the substance of universal thought by an imagination soaring above place and time. While nature keeps Arabian poetry within definite bounds, convention deprives the Arabic-writing poet, who is not necessarily an Arab, of the verse-form that is most suitable for continuous narrative or exposition—the allegorical, romantic, or didactic *mathnawí*—and leaves him no choice but to fall back upon prose if he cannot make the *qaṣída* or the *ghazal* answer his purpose. Both these types of verse are associated with love: the *ghazal* is a love-lyric, and the *qaṣída*, though its proper motive is praise, usually begins "with the mention of women and the constantly shifted habitations of the wandering tribesmen seeking pasture throughout the Winter and Spring; the poet must tell of his love and its troubles, and, if he likes, may describe the beauty of his mistress[3]." Thus the models of Arabic mystical poetry are the secular odes and songs of which this passion is the theme; and the imitation is often so close that unless we have some clue to the writer's intention, it may not be possible to know whether his beloved is human or

[1] Even Zoroastrianism does not exclude the monistic principle. It seems to be uncertain whether Ormuzd and Ahriman stood in direct and equal antagonism to each other, or whether Añra Mainyu (Ahriman), the evil spirit, and Spenta Mainyu, the good spirit, were conceived as opposite emanations of One (Ormuzd) who is above them both. In any case, the struggle between Ormuzd and Ahriman ends with the complete destruction of the latter.

[2] Nöldeke, *Sketches from Eastern History*, tr. by J. S. Black, p. 20.

[3] Sir Charles Lyall, *Ancient Arabian Poetry*, p. xix.

divine—indeed, the question whether he himself always knows is one which students of Oriental mysticism cannot regard as impertinent.

Ibnu 'l-'Arabí, a great theosophist rather than a great poet, deserves to be mentioned amongst the few Arabs who have excelled in this ambiguous style[1]; but its supreme master is Sharafu'ddín 'Umar Ibnu 'l-Fáriḍ, a native of Cairo, who was born seventeen years after Ibnu 'l-'Arabí and died five years before him (A.D. 1182–1235)[2]. The two seem never to have met. The description of Ibnu 'l-'Arabí as Ibnu 'l-Fáriḍ's teacher (*ustádh*) rests upon a far-fetched interpretation of the verse,

> O camel-driver crossing the wilderness with thy howdahs,
> Kindly halt beside the hills of Ṭayyi'!

Here N. detects an allusion to Ibnu 'l-'Arabí, who belonged to the Ṭayyi' tribe[3].

It rarely happens that the outward lives of mystics are eventful. The poet's chief biographer—his grandson, 'Alí—has much to say about his personal beauty, his ecstatic temperament, his generosity and unselfishness, his seclusion from the world, and the veneration in which he was held by all[4]. As his name declares, he was the son of a notary (*fáriḍ*). In his youth he practised religious austerities on Mt Muqaṭṭam near Cairo, returning at intervals to attend the law-courts with his father and study theology. One day he encountered a saint in the guise of an old greengrocer, who told him that the hour of his illumination was at hand, but that he must go to the Ḥijáz to receive it. Accordingly Ibnu 'l-Fáriḍ set out for Mecca, where the promise was fulfilled. Many of his odes celebrate the hills and valleys in the neighbourhood of the

[1] The present writer has edited and translated a collection of mystical odes by Ibnu 'l-'Arabí, entitled *Tarjumán al-Ashwáq*, in the Oriental Translation Fund, New Series, vol. XX (London, 1911).

[2] The date of his birth is usually given as A.D. 1181, but see Nallino, *op. cit.*, p. 1, note 3.

[3] *Díwán*, p. 4, l. 13 foll. and p. 75, l. 1 foll.

[4] The Life of Ibnu 'l-Fáriḍ by his grandson has been printed as an introduction to the *Díwán* (pp. 3–24). A shorter notice, extracted from my MS. of the *Shadharátu 'l-dhahab*, was published in the *JRAS.* for 1906, pp. 800–806. See also Ibn Khallikán, No. 511 (De Slane's translation, vol. II, p. 388 foll.).

Holy City, scenes endeared by the visions and ecstasies which they recalled to his mind. After fifteen years' absence from Egypt he heard the voice of the saint, who was then on his deathbed, bidding him return to Cairo, in order to pray over him and bury him. Ibnu 'l-Fáriḍ obeyed, and having performed this pious duty settled in Cairo for the rest of his life, lodging (it is said) in the mosque al-Azhar, as his father had done. The biographer 'Alí, whose mother was a daughter of Ibnu 'l-Fáriḍ, mentions two sons of the poet, Kamálu'ddín Muḥammad and 'Abdu 'l-Raḥmán, who were invested with the *khirqa*[1] by the famous Ṣúfí, Shihábu'ddín Abú Ḥafṣ 'Umar al-Suhrawardí on the occasion of his meeting with Ibnu 'l-Fáriḍ at Mecca in A.D. 1231.

The *Díwán*, first edited by the aforesaid 'Alí from a manuscript in the author's handwriting, is a thin volume comprising about twenty *qaṣídas* and *qiṭ'as* together with some quatrains (*rubá'iyyát*) and enigmas (*algház*). The longest ode, the *Naẓmu 'l-sulúk* or "the Mystic's Progress," generally known as the *Tá'iyyatu 'l-kubrá*[2], has been omitted from the Marseilles edition, which is otherwise complete. Owing to its expository and descriptive character this poem stands apart from the purely lyrical odes, and I have treated it as an independent work. The Wine Ode (*Khamriyya*) and several other pieces have been published with a French prose translation in the *Anthologie arabe* of Grangeret de Lagrange (Paris, 1828), and a few more will be found in De Sacy's *Chrestomathie arabe*. Italy possesses a prose rendering of the minor poems by P. Valerga (Firenze, 1874). There is nothing in English except some fragments which hardly amount to a hundred lines in all[3]. I hope to persuade my readers that the *Díwán* of Ibnu 'l-Fáriḍ, though it will not please every

[1] See p. 22 *supra*.

[2] *I.e.* the Greater Ode rhyming in *t*. It is so named in order to distinguish it from the *Tá'iyyatu 'l-ṣughrá*, *i.e.* the Lesser Ode rhyming in *t* (*Díwán*, p. 142 foll.).

[3] See Professor Browne's *Literary History of Persia*, vol. II, p. 504; my *Literary History of the Arabs*, p. 397 fol., and *The Don and the Dervish*, pp. 105–9. A Latin version of one entire ode (*Díwán*, p. 306 foll.) is given by Sir William Jones in his *Poeseos Asiaticae commentarii* (*Works*, ed. by Lord Teignmouth, vol. VI, p. 74).

taste, is too curious and exquisite to be left on one side by those who take an interest in Oriental poetry.

Concerning the subtle quality of his thought no less than of his style, it would be hard to better what a French critic wrote ninety years ago:

L'intelligence parfaite de ses productions ne peut être que le fruit d'une étude longue et approfondie de la poésie arabe. Deux causes principales les rendent d'un difficile accès. La première, c'est qu'il arrive souvent à ce poëte de quintessencier le sentiment; et alors ses idées sont si subtiles, si déliées, et, pour ainsi dire, si impalpables, qu'elles échappent presque aux poursuites du lecteur le plus attentif: souvent même elles disparoissent dès qu'on les touche pour les transporter dans une autre langue. On voit qu'il a pris plaisir, par un choix de pensées extraordinaires, et par la singularité des tours, à mettre à l'épreuve la sagacité de ceux qui étudient ses ouvrages. Au reste, les lettrés de l'Orient pensent qu'un poëte est sans génie et sans invention, ou bien qu'il compte peu sur leur intelligence, quand il n'a pas soin de leur ménager des occasions fréquentes de faire briller cette pénétration qui sait découvrir les sens les plus cachés. Il faut donc que le poëte arabe, si'l veut obtenir les suffrages et l'admiration des connoisseurs, n'oublie pas de porter quelquefois à l'excès le raffinement et la subtilité dans ses compositions, d'aiguiser ses pensées, et de les envelopper de telle sorte dans les expressions, qu'elles se présentent au lecteur comme des énigmes, qu'elles réveillent son attention, piquent sa curiosité, et mettent en jeu toutes les facultés de son esprit. Or, il faut convenir qu' Omar ben-Fâredh n'a point manqué à ce devoir prescrit aux poëtes arabes, et qu'il n'a point voulu que ses lecteurs lui reprochassent de leur avoir enlevé les occasions de montrer leur sagacité[1].

This describes very well a general and obvious feature of Ibnu 'l-Fáriḍ's style, a feature which is entirely absent both from pre-Islamic and early Islamic poetry, although since the time of Mutanabbí, who first brought it into prominence, it has maintained itself, not merely as a local or temporary fashion but with all the force of a fixed and almost universally accepted tradition. While Ibnu 'l-Fáriḍ has nothing in common

[1] Grangeret de Lagrange, *Anthologie arabe*, p. 118.

with the *imitatorum seruum pecus*, he neither attempted nor desired to swim against the stream; and it is probable that only his mysticism saved him from the worst excesses of metaphysical wit. In him, as in Meleager and Petrarch, "the religion of love is reduced to a theology; no subtlety, no fluctuation of fancy or passion is left unregistered[1]." If his verse abounds in fantastic conceits, if much of it is enigmatic to the last degree, the conceits and enigmas are not, as a rule, rhetorical ornaments or intellectual conjuring tricks, but like tendrils springing from a hidden root are vitally connected with the moods of feeling which they delineate. It may be difficult to believe, what is related on the testimony of his most intimate friends, that he used to dictate his poems at the moment when he came out of a deep ecstatic trance, during which "he would now stand, now sit, now repose on his side, now lie on his back, wrapped like a dead man; and thus would he pass ten consecutive days, more or less, neither eating nor drinking nor speaking nor stirring." His style and diction resemble the choicest and finest jewel-work of a fastidious artist rather than the first-fruits of divine inspiration. Yet I am not inclined to doubt the statement that his poetry was composed in an abnormal manner[2]. The history of mysticism records numerous instances of the kind. Blake said that he was drunk with intellectual vision whenever he took a pencil or graver in his hand. "St Catherine of Siena," we are told, "dictated her great Dialogue to her secretaries whilst in the state of ecstasy[3]." "When Jalálu'ddín Rúmí was drowned in the ocean of Love he used to take hold of a pillar in his house and set himself turning round it. Meanwhile he versified and dictated, and people wrote down the verses[4]." Since the form of such automatic composition will largely depend on materials stored within the mystic's brain, and on the literary models with which he is familiar, we need not be surprised if his visions and revelations sometimes find spontaneous utterance in an elaborately artificial style. The

[1] J. W. Mackail, *Select Epigrams from the Greek Anthology*, p. 34.
[2] Preface to the *Díwán*, p. 11, l. 20.
[3] Evelyn Underhill, *Mysticism*, p. 352.
[4] Introd. to *Selected Poems from the Dīvāni Shamsi Tabrīz*, p. XL.

intense passion and glowing rapture of Ibnu 'l-Fáriḍ's poetry are in keeping with this account of the way in which it was produced[1]. That he may have written it while not under the influence of ecstasy, I can conceive[2]; but that he wrote it in cold blood, for the sake of those who might enjoy sharpening their wits upon it, seems to me incredible.

The double character of Islamic mystical poetry makes it attractive to many who are out of touch with pure mysticism. Ibnu 'l-Fáriḍ would not be so popular in the East if he were understood entirely in a spiritual sense. The fact that parts of the *Díwán* cannot be reasonably understood in any other sense would not, perhaps, compel us to regard the whole as spiritual, unless that view of its meaning were supported by the poet's life, the verdict of his biographers and commentators, and the agreement of Moslem critical opinion; but as things are, we can declare, with Nábulusí, that "in every erotic description, whether the subject thereof be male or female, and in all imagery of gardens, flowers, rivers, birds and the like he refers to the Divine Reality manifested in phenomena, and not to those phenomena themselves[3]." This Reality, *i.e.* God (or, in some places, Mohammed conceived as the Logos) is the Beloved whom the poet addresses and celebrates under many names—now as one of the heroines of Arabian Minnesong, now as a gazelle or a driver of camels or an archer shooting deadly glances from his eye; most frequently as plain He or She. The Odes retain the form, conventions, topics, and images of ordinary love-poetry: their

[1] Of course these remarks do not apply to many passages in the *Tá'iyyatu 'l-kubrá*, which in respect of its didactic purpose bears the same relation to the minor odes as the *Masnaví* of Jalálu'ddín Rúmí to his *Díwán*.

[2] Prof. Nallino (*op. cit* p. 17) points out that at a later period the Odes were often chanted in the musical concerts of the Ṣúfís and suggests that they were composed for this purpose.

[3] *Díwán*, p. 52, l. 8 foll. Búríní (*ibid.* p. 202, 12 foll.) asserts that Ibnu 'l-Fáriḍ's poetry is not invariably mystical. The two verses which he cites might bear an allegorical sense as easily as many of a similar kind in the Song of Solomon; and, in any case, they are extracted from *rubá'ís*. The fact that Ibnu 'l-Fáriḍ is known to have written one amatorious epigram (*Díwán*, p. 549, 9 fol. Ibn Khallikán, De Slane's translation, vol. II, p. 389), and that he may have written others, proves nothing against those who find mysticism in every line of the Odes.

inner meaning hardly ever obtrudes itself, although its presence is everywhere suggested by a strange exaltation of feeling, fine-drawn phantasies in which (as the same French critic remarks) the poet is rapt "au-delà des bornes de la droite raison," mysterious obscurities of diction and subtle harmonies of sound. If Ibnu 'l-Fáriḍ had followed the example of Ibnu 'l-'Arabí and written a commentary on his own poems, it might have added considerably to our knowledge of his mystical beliefs, but I am not sure that it would have had much greater interpretative value than the work of his commentators, who profess to explain the esoteric meaning of every verse in the Odes. While such analysis may be useful within certain limits, we should recognise how little it is capable of revealing. An eminent scholar came to Ibnu 'l-Fáriḍ and asked permission to write a commentary on his masterpiece, the *Naẓmu 'l-Sulúk*. "In how many volumes?" "Two." The poet smiled. "Had I wished," said he, "I could have written two volumes of commentary on every verse of it[1]." The more interpreters, the more interpretations, as those who have given time and labour to the study of mysticism well know. Poetry of this kind suggests more than it says, and means all that it may suggest.

We cannot do without the commentators, however, and they will help us a good deal if we learn to use them discreetly. When they handle their text like philologists and try to fasten precise mystical significations upon individual words and phrases, the process is as fatal to poetry as the result is likely to be far from truth. Against this, they have the immense advantage of being Ṣúfís, that is to say, of knowing through tradition and their own experience what Europeans can only acquire by study and perceive by sympathy. They are the poet's fellow-citizens in the ideal world from which he drew his inspiration; they have dreamed his dreams and travelled on his path towards his goal; they do not miss the main drift of his allegory even though they err in some of the details.

Any one who has read the *Díwán* of Ibnu 'l-Fáriḍ in

[1] Preface to the *Díwán*, p. 11, l. 1 foll.

Arabic will admit that while a complete rendering into English verse would be a quixotic enterprise, some entire odes and not a few passages in others are suitable for that form of translation. Therefore, instead of confining myself to prose, I have sought here and there to capture the shadows at least of things that no prose version can reproduce.

Má bayna ḍáli 'l-munḥaná wa-ẓilálihi
ḍalla 'l-mutayyamu wa-'htadá bi-ḍalálihi[1].

Where lote-trees o'er the valley cast their shade
The frenzied lover strayed.
Alone with thoughts confusing
Which love put in his brain,
He lost and in his losing
Found the way again:
Lo, on yon gorge's southern slope
The vision long-desired, that far seemed from his hope.
This is 'Aqíq[2], my friend!
Halt! here to pass were strange.
Feign rapture, if thou be
Not rapt indeed, and let thine eye range free:
Mine, with tears overflowing, cannot range.
Ask the Gazelle that couches in this valley,
Knows he my heart, its passion and distress?
Delighting with his beauty's pride to dally,
He recks not of my love's abasedness.
My dead self be his ransom! 'Tis no giving:
I am all his, dead or living!
Think you he knows that I his absence love
Even as I loved his presence? that I move
Nightly his image to my waking eye?—
A phantasy within a phantasy[3].
So let me ne'er have savour
Of peace from counsellors, as I never bent
A listening ear towards their argument!
By his sweet grace and favour,

[1] *Díwán*, p. 263 foll. Prof. Browne has given a translation of this ode in his *Literary History of Persia*, vol. II, p. 504.

[2] A valley with fountains and date-palms in the neighbourhood of Medina.

[3] The dream-form (*khayál*) of the Beloved in the poet's fancy (*khayál*).

I vow my heart tired not, when he did tire,
Of love-desire.
Woe's me, 'Udhayb's fair water might I win
And with its coldness quench the flames within!
But since my longing durst
Not soil that noble stream,
Ah! how I thirst
For its mirage agleam!

The following ode, though characteristically subtle, presents no special difficulties:

Tih dalál^{an} *fa-anta ahl*^{un} *li-dháká*
wa-taḥakkam fa-'l-ḥusnu qad a'ṭáká[1].

Feign coy disdain, for well art thou entitled;
And domineer, for Beauty hath given thee power.
Thine is the word: then will whatso thou willest,
Since over me Beauty hath made thee ruler.
If in death I shall be with thee united,
Hasten it on, so may I be thy ransom!
And try, in all ways thou deem'st good, my passion,
For where thy pleasure is, my choice attends it.
Whate'er betide, thou to myself art nearer
Than I, since but for thee I had not existed.
Not of thy peers am I: enough of glory,
That loving thee I bow in lowly worship.
And though I claim not—'twere too high relation—
Favour with thee, and thou in truth my Master,
Yet me sufficeth to be thought to love thee
And counted by my folk amongst thy slain ones.
Yea, in this tribe thou own'st a dead man, living
Through thee, who found it sweet to die for love's sake;
A slave and chattel who never pined for freedom
Nor, hadst thou left, would let thee leave him lonely;
Whom beauty veiled by awe doth so enravish,
He feels delicious even that veil of torment,
When thou, brought nigh to him by hope's assurance,
Art borne afar by fear of sundering darkness.
Now, by his ready advance when thee he visits,

[1] *Díwán*, p. 230 foll.

By his alarmed retreat when thou affright'st him,
I swear mine heart is melted: oh, allow it
To crave thee whilst it hath of hope a remnant;
Or bid sleep (yet, methinks, 'twill disobey thee,
Obedient else) pass o'er mine eyelids lightly;
For in a dream, perchance, will rise before me
Thy phantom and reveal to me a mystery.
But if thou wilt not stir my life's last embers
With the hand of hope, and thy All needs must naught me[1],
And if Love's law not even a fitful slumber
Lets trespass on my lids, and bans our meeting,
Spare me an eye, that some day, ere I perish,
Haply I may behold those who beheld thee[2]!
Alas, how far is that desire! Nay, never
Mine eyelashes durst kiss the earth thou tread'st on,
For had my messenger brought a word of kindness
From thee, and life were mine, I would cry, "Take it!"
Enough of blood hath welled from these chapped eyelids:
Ah, have I not yet shown what shall content thee?
Guard safe against thine hate a man afflicted,
Who loved thee fondly ere he knew what love was!
Grant that uncivil flyting tongues forbade him
To go near thee: by whom wast thou forbidden?
Grant that thy beauty moved him to such passion,
Yet who moved thee to part from him? Who, think'st thou?
Who, think'st thou, gave the sentence thou should'st scorn him?
Who gave the sentence thou should'st love another?
By my heart-brokenness and humiliation,
By my most bitter need, by thine abundance,
Leave me not to the forces that betrayed me
Of mine own strength: to thee I turn in weakness.
Thou didst ill use me when I had some patience:
Now for its loss God help thee to console me!
Scorn upon scorn! It may be thou wilt pity
My plaint, if but to hear me say, "It may be."
The mischief-makers shamed thee with my parting

[1] Literally, "if thy everlastingness (*baqá*) demands my passing-away (*faná*)."

[2] According to N. the words "those who beheld thee" refer to the Light of Mohammed, which emanated from the Light of God.

And gave out that thy love I had forgotten.
I loved not with *their* hearts, that I should ever
Forget thee—God forfend!—so let them babble!
Thee how should I forget? At every lightning
That flashes, lo, mine eye starts up to meet thee.
If 'neath the light of thy *lithám*[1] thou smilest
Or breathest soft—and on the wind thy news comes—
Glad is my soul when clear dawn of thy side-teeth
Breaks on my sight, and keenly blows thy fragrance.
Within thy borders all do love thee, natheless
My single worth buys all within thy borders[2].
There dwells in thee a notion that endeared thee
To mind's eye, fixed my gaze on thy perfections.
The lords of beauty thou in grace and goodness
Excellest so, they hunger for thy notion.
Beneath my flag the lovers shall be gathered
To Judgment, as beneath thine all the fair ones.
From thee dire sickness never turned me: wherefore
Turn'st thou from me, then, O disdainful charmer?
Thou art present with me in thine absence from me,
And in thy cruelty I feel a kindness.
Taught by Desire to wake through night's long hours,
Mine eye hath won to see thee while it sleeps not.
O happy, happy night in which thy vision
I hunted after with my net of waking!
The full moon, being thy copy, represented
To my unslumbering eye thy face's image[3];
And in such alien form thine apparition
Cooled mine eye's fever: I saw thee, none other.
Thus Abraham of old, the Friend of Allah,
Upturned his eye, what time he scanned the heavens[4].

[1] A veil covering the lower part of the face.

[2] "Within thy borders": literally "within thy preserve (*ḥimd*)." The Divine Essence is preserved (made inaccessible) by the spiritual and sensible forms in which it veils itself. As the Bedouin poet brags about himself in order to assert the dignity of his tribe, so when the Mohammedan saints boast of the unique endowments which God has bestowed upon them, it is not self-glorification, but thanksgiving to Him "from whom all blessings flow."

[3] Real Being is manifested in phenomena, just as the light of the sun is reflected by the moon.

[4] See Kor. 6, 76 foll. "And when the night overshadowed him, he saw a

Now is the pitchy gloom for us made dazzling,
Since thou thy splendour gav'st me for my guidance;
And when thou from mine eye in outward seeming
Art gone, I cast it inward, there to find thee.
Of Badr are they with whom by night thou faredst—
Nay, not of Badr: they journeyed in thy daylight[1].
That men do borrow radiance from mine outward,
'Tis not strange, when mine inward is thy dwelling.
Ever since thou to kiss thy mouth didst call me,
Musk lingers wheresoe'er my name is spoken,
And the rich air teems in every place of meeting
With spice—a metaphor of thine aroma.
The beauty of all things seen tempted me, saying,
"Enjoy me," but I said, "I aim beyond thee.
Beguile not me, thyself by my Beloved
Distraught, in whom thou seem'st but an idea[2].
Averted, over men's souls he is mighty[3];
Unveiled, he makes the ascetics be his vowed slaves.
For his sake I exchanged my truth for error,
My right for wrong, my modesty for ill-fame[4].
My heart confessed his love One: then my turning
To thee were dualism, a creed I like not."

star, and he said, This is my Lord; but when it set, he said, I like not gods which set. And when he saw the moon rising, he said, This is my Lord; but when he saw it set, he said, Verily, if my Lord direct me not, I shall become one of the people who go astray" (Sale's translation).

[1] In this verse there is an untranslatable play on the double meaning of Badr, which signifies (1) a place between Mecca and Medina where the Prophet won his memorable victory over the Meccan idolaters in A.D. 624; (2) a full moon. Thus the *ahlu Badr* are to Moslems more than what οἱ μαραθωνομάχαι were to the Greeks of Plato's time, while the phrase also suggests the perfect illumination reserved for adepts in mysticism. Irish politics of forty years ago would provide an exact parallel, if the Moonlighters were regarded as national heroes and saints. The poet says that the men of Badr, *i.e.*, the noble company of mystics, journey not so much in the light which phenomena derive from Reality as in the light of Reality itself.

[2] Material beauty is not worthy to be loved except in so far as it is one of the ideas (attributes and manifestations) of Absolute Beauty.

[3] When God withdraws Himself (from the inward eye of the mystic), He still lays His commands on the soul, so that it performs its predestined good and evil works.

[4] Divine Love sweeps away the conventional standards of truth and right and honour.

Beauty itself is mad with passion for him—
O friend that chid'st me, may I lack thy friendship!
Hadst thou his beauty seen—ne'er shalt thou see it—
That me enthralled, it surely had enthralled thee.
At a glimpse of him my wakefulness I pardon,
And "This for that" I say to my aching eyeballs.

After reading a little of Ibnu 'l-Fáriḍ's poetry, one can take a general view of the whole. All his odes are variations on a single theme, and the variations themselves have a certain interior uniformity. Not only do the same "leitmotifs" recur again and again, but the same metaphors, conceits and paradoxes are continually reappearing in new dress. Although translators must regret this monotony, which *they* cannot make other than tedious, I think most of them would agree that the poet has triumphed over it by means of the delicacy of his art, the beauty of his diction, and the "linkèd sweetness" of his versification—powerful spells to enchant those who read him in his own language. The *Díwán* is a miracle of literary accomplishment, yet the form would be cold and empty without the spirit which it enshrines. Like Sidney, Ibnu 'l-Fáriḍ looked into his heart before he wrote. His verse is charged with the fire and energy of his inmost feelings.

Where eyes encounter souls in battle-fray,
I am the murdered man whom 'twas no crime to slay.
At the first look, ere love in me arose,
To that all-glorious beauty I was vowed.
God bless a racked heart crying,
And lids that passion will not let me close,
And ribs worn thin,
Their crookedness wellnigh to straightness shaped
By the glow within,
And seas of tears whence I had never 'scaped
But for the fire of sighing!
How sweet are maladies which hide
Me from myself, my loyal proofs to Love!
Though after woeful eve came woeful dawn,
It could not move
Once to despair my spirit: I never cried

To Agony, "Begone!"
I yearn to every heart that passion shook,
And every tongue that love made voluble,
And every deaf ear stopped against rebuke,
And every lid not dropped in slumbers dull.
Out on a love that hath no melting eyes!
Out on a flame from which no rapture flies[1]!

In exquisite contrast with this high-wrought prelude is another passage of the same ode, describing the mystic's vision of the Divine beauty revealing itself in all things beautiful.

Though he be gone, mine every limb beholds him
In every charm and grace and loveliness:
In music of the lute and flowing reed
Mingled in consort with melodious airs;
And in green hollows where in cool of eve
Gazelles roam browsing, or at break of morn;
And where the gathered clouds let fall their rain
Upon a flowery carpet woven of blooms;
And where at dawn with softly-trailing skirts
The zephyr brings to me his balm most sweet;
And when in kisses from the flagon's mouth
I suck wine-dew beneath a pleasant shade[2].

Here the Moslem commentator, startled for a moment out of his lucubrations on syntax and rhetoric, pauses to pay a tribute of admiration to the poet, a tribute which is the more noteworthy because in these six verses Ibnu 'l-Fáriḍ comes as near as he ever does to the modern European conception of what poetry should be. Unadorned simplicity is the antithesis of his style. For our taste, he has far too much of the gift of

[1] *Díwán*, p. 331 foll.

[2] *Ibid.* p. 347, l. 6 foll. Cf. Shelley, *Epipsychidion*:

In solitudes
Her voice came to me through the whispering woods,
And from the fountains, and the odours deep
Of flowers...
And from the breezes whether low or loud,
And from the rain of every passing cloud,
And from the singing of the summer birds,
And from all sounds, all silence.

Holofernes: he plays with sound and sense alike, though in the daintiest and subtlest fashion imaginable. Concerning his verbal euphuism a treatise might be written. One verse—an extreme instance, no doubt—will serve as a sample of many:

Amá laki 'an ṣadd^{in} amálaki 'an ṣad^{in}
li-ẓalmiki ẓulm^{an} minki mayl^{un} li-'aṭfati

Hast thou no desire to withdraw from a resistance that has caused thee to turn away, with wrong on thy part, from one who thirsts for the water of thy teeth[1]?

His extravagant flights of fancy are generally accompanied by an equal exaltation of feeling and sustained by the fiery element in which they move; at times, however, they sink into something very like the "sweet smoke of rhetoric," *e.g.*,

I sowed roses on his cheek by looking (at him): mine eye has the right to gather that which it planted.
But if he refuses, then his (teeth white as) camomile will be my amends: 'tis no bad bargain when one is given pearls instead of flowers[2].

They said, "Thy tears flowed red." I answered, "They flowed from causes which are small in comparison with the greatness of my desire:
I slaughtered sleep on my eyelids to entertain my phantom-guest, and therefore my tears flowed bloody over my cheek[3]."

The following examples are more typical:

Thou stol'st away mine heart when it was whole:
Now at my last gasp give it back in shreds[4]!

O thou who didst treacherously take my heart away, how didst not thou let follow it the rest of me that thou sparedst?
Part of me is made jealous of thee by part of me, and my outward envies my inward because thou art there[5].

[1] *Ibid.* p. 173. It is true, as Prof. Nallino has observed (*op. cit.* p. 16), that some odes are less artificial in style than others.
[2] *Ibid.* p. 467.
[3] *Ibid.* p. 165.
[4] *Ibid.* p. 108.
[5] *Ibid.* p. 278.

I am so wasted by lovesickness that those who come to visit me have lost their way, for how can the visitors see one who hath no shadow[1]?

To affirm that lovers and mystics delight in paradox is only to acknowledge that in states of spiritual enthusiasm we enter a region where the logic of common experience is perceived to be false. This *alta fantasia* moulds the language of the Odes, imposing its own laws and revelling in its power to transcend contradictions which, for the intellect, are final.

When I died of his love, I lived by him, through the wealth of my self-denial and the abundance of my poverty[2].

'Tis Love! Keep thy heart safe. Passion is no light thing, and he that is wasted thereby chose it not when he was sane.
And live fancy-free, for love's joy is sorrow: its beginning a sickness and its end a slaying;
Yet, methinks, death owing to love-desire is a life that my loved one bestows upon me as a boon[3].

If separation be my guerdon from you, and if there be no (real) distance between us, I regard that separation as union.
Repulse is nothing but love, so long as it is not hate; and the hardest thing, excepting only your aversion, is easy to bear.
Delicious to me is the torment which ye inflict; and the injustice which Love ordains that ye do unto me is justice.
And my patience, a patience both without you and with you[4]—its bitterness seems to me everlastingly sweet[5].

Besides the two protagonists, Arabian love-poetry introduces several minor figures, who play a helping or hindering part in the idyll. Ibnu 'l-Fáriḍ, of course, uses them allegorically. One of them is the "watcher" (*raqíb*), who prevents the lover from approaching. The "slanderer" (*wáshí*) represents the logical and intellectual faculty, which cannot pierce beyond the outward forms of things. More important than either of these (to judge by the frequent passages of descrip-

[1] *Díwán*, p. 410. [2] *Ibid.* p. 384. [3] *Ibid.* p. 391 foll.
[4] "Patience without you," *i.e.* in bearing your separation from me; "patience with you," *i.e.* in bearing the pain which you, as the object of my love, cause me to suffer. [5] *Díwán*, p. 402.

tion and dialogue in which he appears), and more dangerous, because of his greater plausibility, is the "blamer" (*lá'im*) or "railer" (*láḥí*), a type of the Devil, suggesting evil and inspiring doubt, of sensual passion, and of all that lures the soul away from Divine contemplation.

And in my silencing him who blamed me on thy account, when it was no time to dispute concerning thee[1], my argument was thy face;

Whereby, after having been my rebuker, he was made my excuser; nay, he became one of my helpers.

And, as I live, my vanquishing in argument a guide whose reproaches would have led me astray is like my greater and lesser pilgrimages[2].

He perceived that my scornful ear was Rajab (deaf) to baseness and false counsel, and that blame of me was al-Muḥarram (forbidden)[3].

Full oft had he desired me to forget thy love and seek another than thee, but how should he change my fixed purpose?

He said, "Mend what remains in thee (of life)." I answered, "Methinks, my mind turns nowhither but towards death."

My refusal refused everything except thwarting a counsellor who would beguile me to show a quality that was never mine[4],

One to whom chiding me on thy account is sweet, as though he deemed my separation (from thee) his manna and my forgetfulness (of thee) his quails[5].

It is a favourite paradox of Ibnu 'l-Fáriḍ that reproof bears a message of love, and that the "railer" deserves to be thanked and praised.

[1] The poet was rapt in contemplation of the Beloved and could not bandy words with his critic.

[2] *I.e.* by convincing my "blamer" of the error of his ways I acquired as much religious merit as by making the pilgrimage to Mecca. It is meritorious to combine the greater pilgrimage (*ḥajj*) with the lesser pilgrimage (*'umra*).

[3] Rajab is the seventh and al-Muḥarram the first month of the Mohammedan year.

[4] *I.e.* inconstancy.

[5] *Díwán*, p. 179 foll. The last verse alludes to the manna and quails which dropped from heaven upon the Israelites (Kor. 2, 54). In the original there is a double word-play: *mann* (separation), *mann* (manna), *salwat* (forgetfulness), *salwá* (quails).

Pass round the name of my Dearest, if only in blaming me—for talk of the Beloved is my wine—
That she may be present to mine ear, though she be far away, as a phantom called up by blame, not by sleep.
For sweet to me is her name in every mould, even if my chiders mingle it with disputation.
Methinks, he that blames me brings to me the glad news of her favour, though I was not hoping to have my greeting returned[1].

But I found thee in one way my benefactor, albeit thou wouldst have hurt me by the scorch of thy rebuke, had I obeyed thee.
Thou didst me a kindness unawares, and if thou wroughtest ill, yet art thou the most righteous of wrong-doers.
The phantom that visits me in the hour of blame[2] brings the Beloved, though he dwell afar, close to the eye of my waking ear.
And thy reproof is, as it were, my Loved One's camels which came to me when my hearing was my sight[3].
Thou tiredst thyself and I was refreshed by thy mention of him, so that I regarded thee as excusing me for my passion.
Marvel, then, at a satirist lauding with the tongue of a thankful complainant those who blame him for his love[4]!

The hyperfantastic strain in Ibnu 'l-Fáriḍ's poetry is surprisingly relieved by a poignant realism, of which there is no trace in the work of his Persian rivals. They have, what he reserves for his great *Tá'iyya*, the power of lifting themselves and their readers with them into the sphere of the infinite and eternal,

All breathing human passion far above.

The Arabic odes, on the contrary, are full of local colour and redolent of the desert; and the whole treatment of the subject is intimately personal. Jalálu'ddín Rúmí writes as

[1] *Díwán*, p. 443 foll.
[2] *I.e.* the image or vision of the Beloved which appears when his name is pronounced by the "blamer."
[3] As camels bring the beloved to the lover's eye, so reproof brings him to the lover's ear.
[4] *Díwán*, p. 275 foll. Cf. p. 346, l. 5, and p. 419, l. 17—p. 420, l. 6.

a God-intoxicated soul, Ibnu 'l-Fáriḍ as a lover absorbed in his own feelings. While the Persian sees a pantheistic vision of one reality in which the individual disappears, the Arab dwells on particular aspects of the relation of that reality to himself.

Some of the finest passages are inspired by the author's recollection of the years which he spent in the Ḥijáz, where (he says) he left his heart behind when his body returned to Egypt[1].

Give aid, my brother dear, and sing me the tale of them that alighted in the water-courses—if thou wilt keep a brother's faith with me—
And recall it to mine ears; for the spirit yearns for tidings, if the loved ones be afar.
When the anguish of pain settles on my soul, the aroma of the fresh herbs of the Ḥijáz is my balm.
Shall I be debarred from the sweetness of going down to the waters in its land, and turned aside from it, when my very life is in its sandhills,
And its dwellings are my desire, yea, and its springtide is my joy and averts from me the most bitter distress,
And its mountains are to me a vernal abode, and its sands a pasture, and its daytime shadows are my (cool) shades of eve,
And its earth is my fragrant spice, and its water a full well for my thirst, and in its soil are my riches,
And its ravines are to me a garden, and its tents a shield, and on its rocks my heart is untroubled[2]?
May the rain bless those haunts and hills, and may showers following each other moisten those homes of bounty,
And shed abundance on the shrines of pilgrimage and the pebbles at al-Miná, and plenteously bedew the halting-places of the jaded camels!
And may God preserve my dear companions there with whom I whiled away the night with tales of lovers' meetings!
And may He preserve the nights at al-Khayf that were but as a dream that passed in the wakefulness of a light sleep!

[1] *Ibid.* p. 370, l. 11.

[2] The Arabic word for rocks (*ṣafá*) is also the name of a peak near Mecca, and this may be its meaning here.

Ah me for that time and all that was in that goodly place, when the spies were off their guard!—

Days when I blithely pastured in the fields of Desire and tripped in flowing skirts of Ease[1].

How wonderful is Time, which lays benefits on a man and proves him by taking the gift as spoil!

O would that our bygone pleasure might return once more! Then would I freely give my life.

Alas, vain is the endeavour, and cut are the strands of the cord of desire, and loosed is the knot of my hope.

'Tis torture enough that I pass the night in frenzy, with my longing before me and Fate behind me[2].

From many such passages I select one that is characteristic, because it illustrates Ibnu 'l-Fáriḍ's habit of seeking his imagery in Nature, as seen by Bedouins[3], and also his sense of the poetic value of proper names.

O that I knew whether Sulaymá is dwelling in the valley of the demesne, where the bondsman of love is crazed!

Hath thunder crashed with bursting showers at La'la', and hath rain gushing from the clouds flooded it?

And shall I come down to the waters of al-'Udhayb and Ḥájir openly, when the mystery of night is declared by dawn?

And are there green dunes in the camping-place at al-Wa'sá? and will the joy that passed there ever return?

And, O ye dear folk at al-Naqá, is there in the hills of Najd any one that relates from me, to show forth what my ribs enclose[4]?

And on the sand-slope of Sal' do they ask news of a rapt lover at Káẓima and say, "How is Passion dealing with him?"

And are the blossoms being culled from the myrtle-boughs, and in the Ḥijáz are there mimosas with ripe berries?

And the tamarisks at the bend of the vale, are they fruitful, and are the eyes of despiteful Time asleep to them?

And are there fair women at 'Álij looking shyly with large eyes, as I knew them once, or is it a vain thing?

[1] Reading with the commentator *ḥayá* instead of *ḥibá*.

[2] *Díwán*, p. 297 foll.

[3] This is quite different, of course, from the pictorial treatment of desert life and scenery which we find in the pre-Islamic odes.

[4] Reading فيُوضِح.

And did the gazelles of the Two Meadows remain there a little while after us, or did something not let them stay?

And will girls at al-Ghuwayr show me where dwells my Nu'm in spring?—how pleasant are those dwelling-places!

And is the shade of yon willow east of Ḍárij still spread wide?—for my tears have watered it.

And is Shi'b 'Ámir prospering since we departed, and will it one day bring the lovers together?

* * * * * *

Perchance when my dear comrades at Mecca think of Sulaymá, they will feel the flame cooled of that which their bosoms hide,

And perchance the sweet nights that are vanished will come again to us, that a hoping man may win his desire,

And a sorrowing one rejoice and a lovelorn one revive and a longing one be made happy and a listening one thrill with delight[1].

It needs but a slight acquaintance with Ibnu 'l-Fáriḍ to discover that he fully possesses a gift which the Arabs have always prized in their rulers no less than in their poets and orators—the power of terse, striking, and energetic expression. He depicts the lover wasted by suffering,

> Hidden from his visitors, appearing only
> As a crease in garments after their unfolding[2].

An exceeding great love hath hewn my bones, and my body is vanished, all but the two least parts of me[3].

I felt such passion for you that if the strengths of all who love had borne half the burden thereof, they would have tired.

My bones were hewn by a desire twice as great as that of my eyelids for my sleep or of my weakness for my strength[4].

Any one of the Odes will furnish examples of this Arabian eloquence which has its roots deep in the structure of the language and defies all attempts to transplant it.

In his famous Wine Ode (*Khamriyya*) Ibnu 'l-Fáriḍ develops a symbolism which elsewhere he only uses incidentally. His sparing use of it may perhaps be attributed to

[1] *Díwán*, pp. 429–441. [2] *Ibid.* p. 6.

[3] *Ibid.* p. 70. "The two least parts" are the heart and the tongue.

[4] *Ibid.* p. 160, l. 24 foll.

his respect for the Mohammedan religious law, just as the antinomian bias of some Persian mystics seems to express itself in the freedom of their bacchanalian imagery. According to Ibnu 'l-Fáriḍ's custom, the symbolism is precise and circumstantial, so that its interpretation is far more baffling than in Persian odes of the same kind, where large and simple ideas carry the reader easily along. I hope that the literal translation given below, together with the notes accompanying it, will make the meaning tolerably clear, though we may doubt whether the poet would always have accepted the interpretation given by his commentator, 'Abdu 'l-Ghaní al-Nábulusí, who not only explains too much but brings in philosophical theories that belong to Ibnu 'l-'Arabí rather than to Ibnu 'l-Fáriḍ. Into this question, however, I need not enter now.

Sharibná 'alá dhikhri 'l-ḥabíbi mudámat^{an}
sakirná bihá min qabli an yukhlaqa 'l-karmu[1].

(1) In memory of the Beloved we quaffed a vintage that made us drunk before the creation of the vine[2].

(2) Its cup the full-moon; itself a sun which a new moon causes to circle. When it is mingled (with water), how many stars appear[3]!

(3) But for its perfume, I should not have found the way to its taverns; and but for its resplendence, the imagination would not have pictured it[4].

[1] *Díwán*, p. 472 foll.

[2] The soul was intoxicated with the wine of Divine Love (*i.e.* was rapt in contemplation of God) during its pre-existence in the eternal knowledge of God before the body was created.

[3] The full-moon is the Perfect Man, *i.e.* the gnostic or saint in whom God reveals Himself completely and who is, as it were, filled with Divine Love. The new moon is the gnostic veiled by his individuality, so that he manifests only a part of the Divine Light, not the whole; he causes the wine of Love to circle, *i.e.* he displays and makes known to others the Names and Attributes of God. When the wine is watered, *i.e.* when pure contemplation is blended with the element of religion, the seeker of God obtains spiritual direction and is like a traveller guided by the stars in his night-journey.

[4] N.'s commentary on this verse is characteristically recondite. He interprets "its perfume" as the sphere of the Primal Intelligence, whence emanate all created things; "its taverns" as the Divine Names and Attributes; "its resplendence" as the human intellect, which is a flash of the Primal Intelligence. Divine Love, being of the essence of God, has no form except in the imagination.

(4) Time hath preserved of it but a breath: it is unseen as a thing hidden in the bosom of the mind[1].

(5) If it be mentioned amongst the tribe, the tribesmen become intoxicated without incurring disgrace or committing sin[2].

(6) It oozed up from the inmost depths of the jars (and vanished), and in reality nothing was left of it but a name[3].

(7) If it ever come into the mind of a man, joy will abide with him and grief will journey away.

(8) And had the boon-companions beheld the sealing of its vessel, that sealing would have inebriated them without (their having tasted) the wine[4];

(9) And had they sprinkled with it the earth of a dead man's grave, his spirit would have returned to him, and his body would have risen;

(10) And had they laid down in the shadow of the wall where its vine grows a man sick unto death, his malady would have departed from him;

(11) And had they brought to its taverns one palsied, he would have walked; and at the mention of its flavour the dumb would speak;

(12) And had the breath of its aroma floated through the East, and were there in the West one that had lost the sense of smell, he would have regained it;

(13) And had the palm of one touching its cup been stained red thereby, he would not have gone astray at night, the lodestar being in his hand;

(14) And had it been unveiled in secret (as a bride) to one blind from birth, he would have become seeing; and at the sound of its (decanting into the) strainer the deaf would hear;

(15) And had a party of camel-riders set out for the soil that bore it, and were there amongst them one bitten by a snake, the venom would not have harmed him;

[1] "Time," *i.e.* the world of change. The second hemistich may be rendered literally: "'Tis as though its occultation were a concealment in the breasts of (human) minds."

[2] "The tribesmen," *i.e.* mystics capable of receiving illumination.

[3] This verse describes the gradual fading of ecstasy from the heart of the mystic.

[4] I need not trouble my readers with the detailed allegorical analysis to which the commentator subjects this and the next nine verses. They explain themselves, if taken as a fanciful description of the miracles wrought by Divine Love.

(16) And had the sorcerer inscribed the letters of its name on the brow of one smitten with madness, the writing would have cured him;

(17) And had its name been blazoned on the banner of the host, that blazon would have intoxicated those beneath the banner.

(18) It corrects the natures of the boon-companions, so that those who lack resolution are led by it to the path of resolution,

(19) And he whose hand was a stranger to munificence shows himself generous, and he who had no forbearance forbears in the hour of wrath.

(20) Had the dullest-witted man in the tribe kissed its *fidám*, his kissing it would have endued him with the real inwardness of the wine's qualities[1].

(21) They say to me, "Describe it, for thou art acquainted with its description." Ay, well do I know its attributes:

(22) Pure, but not as water; subtle, but not as air; luminous, but not as fire; spirit, but not (joined to) body.

(23) The (Divine) discourse concerning it was eternally prior to all existing things (in the knowledge of God), where is no form nor any external trace[2];

(24) And there through it all things came into being because of a (Divine) providence whereby it was veiled from every one that lacketh understanding.

(25) And my spirit was enamoured of it in such wise that they (my spirit and the wine) were mingled together and made one, not as a body pervades a body[3].

(26) There is a wine without a vine, when Adam is a father to me; there is a vine without a wine, when its mother is a mother to me[4].

[1] The *fidám* is a strainer placed over the mouth of the bottle, so that the wine may run clear.

[2] *Vv.* 23–30 are wanting in the commentary of Búríní and may have been inserted in the poem by a copyist. See Nallino, *op. cit.* p. 31, note 1. Divine Love, as the eternal source of all created things, is logically prior to them, although it does not precede them in time, which itself is created.

[3] Inasmuch as real being belongs to God alone, mystical union cannot be likened to the permeation of one body by another, as when water is absorbed by a sponge.

[4] This enigmatic verse refers to Being under its two aspects. Wine signifies pure being, vine phenomenal being. In so far as man is related to the Divine Spirit (here identified with Adam, whom God "created in His own

(27) The (essential) subtlety of the vessels (forms) depends in truth on the subtlety of the realities; and by means of the vessels the realities increase[1]

(28) After division has occurred, so that, while the whole is one, our spirits are a wine and our bodies a vine.

(29) Before it is no "before" and after it is no "after"; it is the "before" of every "after" by the necessity of its nature[2].

(30) Its grapes were pressed in the winepress ere Time began, and it was an orphan although the epoch of our father (Adam) came after it[3].

(31) Such are the beauties that lead its praisers to laud it, and beautiful is their prose and verse in its honour.

(32) And he that knows it not thrills at the mention of it, like the lover of Nu'm when her name is spoken.

(33) They said, "Thou hast drunk the draught of sin." Nay, I have only drunk what, in my judgment, 'twere the greatest sin to renounce.

(34) Health to the people of the Christian monastery! How often were they intoxicated by it without having drunk thereof! Still, they aspired[4].

image"), he is pure reality; but in so far as he belongs to Nature, he is unreal. "Its mother" is the mother of wine, *i.e.* the vine, which is a symbol for the material world.

[1] The "vessels" are the phenomenal forms by which real being is manifested. They are "subtle," *i.e.* spiritual, because every such form is the veil of a reality. These realities "increase," *i.e.* appear as the Many, by means of the forms which our senses perceive.

[2] Absolute Being or God or Divine Love—all these terms are the same in essence—is not conditioned by time.

[3] *I.e.* it was an orphan before the beginning of fatherhood. This, I think, is merely a paradox indicating the timeless nature of reality. The word "orphanhood" (*yutm*) may allude to Mohammed (cf. note on the *Tá'iyya*, *vv.* 288–9). In this case the meaning will be that Mohammed (as the Logos) existed before the creation of Adam. According to N., Absolute Being is made an "orphan" by the passing-away (*faná*) of the spirit in man. Universal Spirit or Reason, the first emanation, may be said to "die" when its essence (the human spirit) is mystically re-united with the Absolute; and its "death" leaves the Absolute, *i.e.* the phenomenal world regarded as the other self of the Absolute, "an orphan in the bosom of its mother Nature."

[4] Moslems associate with Christianity the beverage forbidden by their own religion. When their poets describe a wine-party, the scene is often laid in the neighbourhood of a Christian monastery (*dayr*). Ibnu 'l-Fáriḍ says that the Christians became intoxicated without having drunk, *i.e.* their doctrine that God reveals Himself in Christ is only a glimpse of the truth,

(35) In me, ere I was born, it stirred a transport that abides with me for ever, though my bones decay.

(36) Take it pure! but if thou wish to temper it, the worst wrong is thy turning aside from the water of the Beloved's teeth[1].

(37) Seek it in the tavern, and there to the accompaniment of tuneful notes bid it display itself, for by means of music it is made a prize[2].

(38) Wine never dwelt with Care in any place, even as Sorrow never dwelt with Song;

(39) And, though thy intoxication with it have but the life of a moment, thou wilt regard Time as a slave obedient to thy command.

(40) Joyless in this world is he that lives sober, and he that dies not drunk will miss the path of wisdom.

(41) Let him weep for himself—he whose life is wasted without part or lot in wine!

The *Khamriyya* forms a link between the love-lyrics and the great Ode in which Ibnu 'l-Fáriḍ describes his own mystical experience and puts it forth (excepting, however, the highest stage of all) as a doctrine for others. This Ode, the author's masterpiece, bears a plain and appropriate title, *Naẓmu 'l-sulúk*, "The Poem of the Mystic's Progress"; the meaning of the name *al-Tá'iyyatu 'l-kubrá*, by which it is commonly known, has been explained above[3]. The *Tá'iyya*, with its 760 verses, is nearly as long as all the minor poems together, if we leave the quatrains and enigmas out of reckoning. It was edited in 1854 by Joseph von Hammer and may be studied in the fully vocalised text which he copied from an excellent manuscript in his possession. To transcribe

which is fully realised by Moslem saints, that God reveals Himself in every atom of existence. Cf. the *Tá'iyya*, *v*. 730 foll. and p. 140 *supra*.

[1] *I.e.* seek to contemplate the Divine Essence alone, or if you must seek anything besides, let it be the first and highest manifestation of that Essence, namely, the Spirit or Light of Mohammed, which is figuratively called "the water of the Beloved's teeth."

[2] The Ṣúfís have always known the value of music as a means of inducing ecstasy. Cf. *The Mystics of Islam*, p. 63 foll.; D. B. Macdonald, *Emotional Religion in Islam as affected by Music and Singing* in the *Journal of the Royal Asiatic Society*, 1901, pp. 195 foll. and 748 foll., and 1902, p. 1 foll.

[3] P. 165, note 2.

is one thing, to translate is another; and as "translation" of a literary work usually implies that some attempt has been made to understand it, I prefer to say that Von Hammer rendered the poem into German rhymed verse by a method peculiar to himself, which appears to have consisted in picking out two or three words in each couplet and filling the void with any ideas that might strike his fancy. Perhaps, in a sense, the *Tá'iyya* is untranslatable, and certainly it offers very slight encouragement to the translator whose aim may be defined as "artistic reproduction." On the other hand, it seemed to me that a literal prose version with explanatory notes would at least enable the reader to follow the course of the poem and become acquainted with its meaning, while any one who ventured on the Arabic text would profit by the labours of a fellow-student and would not be so likely to lose heart,

> Voyaging through strange seas of thought, alone.

Though formally an ode (*qaṣída*), the *Tá'iyya* is addressed to a disciple, so that its prevailing tone is didactic and descriptive, the exposition being only now and then interrupted by strains of pure lyric enthusiasm. Not that the poem is deficient either in beauty or in power; much, if not most of it, combines these qualities, and in the following version I have tried to preserve some traces of them. Ibnu 'l-Fáriḍ is here illustrating the doctrine that phenomena are merely the illusory medium through which the soul acts in the world. For this purpose he compares the soul to the showman of the shadow-lantern who throws his puppets on a screen, keeping himself out of sight while he manipulates them[1]. The passage beginning

> And so it comes that now thou laugh'st in glee

describes the various scenes and incidents of the shadow-play and the emotions aroused in the spectators.

> Lo, from behind the veil mysterious
> The forms of things are shown in every guise

[1] See *v.* 679 of the prose translation *infra*.

Of manifold appearance; and in them
An all-wise providence hath joined what stands
Opposed in nature: mute they utter speech,
Inert they move and void of splendour shine[1].
And so it comes that now thou laugh'st in glee,
Then weep'st anon, like mother o'er dead child,
And mournest, if they sigh, for pleasure lost,
And tremblest, if they sing, with music's joy.
Birds warbling on the boughs delight thine ear,
The while their sweet notes sadden thee within;
Thou wonderest at their voices and their words—
Expressive unintelligible tongues!
On land the camels cross the wilderness,
At sea the ships run swiftly through the deep;
And thou behold'st two armies—one on land,
On sea another—multitudes of men,
Clad, for their bravery, in iron mail
And fenced about with points of sword and spear.
The land-troops march on horseback or on foot,
Bold cavaliers and stubborn infantry;
The warriors of the sea some mount on deck,
Some climb the masts like lances straight and tall.
Here in assault they smite with gleaming swords,
There thrust with tough brown shafts of quivering spears;
Part drowned with fire of arrows shot in showers,
Part burned with floods of steel that pierce like flames[2];
These rushing onward, offering their lives,
Those reeling broken 'neath the shame of rout;
And catapults thou seest hurling stones
Against strong fortresses and citadels,
To ruin them. And apparitions strange
Of naked viewless spirits thou mayst espy[3],

[1] "The forms of things," *i.e.* the puppets, typify phenomena, which in themselves are lifeless and passive: all their life and activity is the effect of the manifestation in them of the actions and attributes of Reality.

[2] The Greek fire to which Von Hammer finds an allusion here is, I think, an *ignis fatuus*.

[3] The genies (*Jinn*) are described as ethereal creatures, endowed with speech, transparent (so that they are normally invisible), and capable of assuming various shapes.

That wear no friendly shape of humankind,
For genies love not men.
And in the stream
The fisher casts his net and draws forth fish;
And craftily the fowler sets a snare
That hungry birds may fall in it for corn.
And ravening monsters wreck the ships at sea,
And lions in the jungle rend their prey,
And in the air some birds, and in the wilds
Some animals, hunt others. And thou seest
Many a form besides, whose names I pass,
Putting my trust in samples choice, tho' few.

Regard now what is this that lingers not
Before thine eye and in a moment fades.
All thou beholdest is the act of one
In solitude, but closely veiled is he.
Let him but lift the screen, no doubt remains:
The forms are vanished, he alone is all;
And thou, illumined, knowest that by his light
Thou find'st his actions in the senses' night[1].

Ibnu 'l-Fáriḍ more often reminds us of Dante than of Lucretius, but these verses may be compared with a passage in the *De rerum natura* (2, 323 foll.) where the author illustrates "the perpetual motion of the atoms going on beneath an appearance of absolute rest" by a picture "taken from the pomp of human affairs and the gay pageantry of armies":

Praeterea magnae legiones cum loca cursu
camporum complent belli simulacra cientes,
fulgor ibi ad caelum se tollit totaque circum
aere renidescit tellus supterque uirum ui
excitur pedibus sonitus clamoreque montes
icti reiectant uoces ad sidera mundi
et circumuolitant equites mediosque repente
tramittunt ualido quatientes impete campos.

[1] *Tá'iyya, vv.* 680–706.

"The truth and fulness of life in this passage are immediately perceived, but the element of sublimity is added by the thought in the two lines with which the passage concludes, which reduces the whole of this moving and sounding pageant to stillness and silence—

> et tamen est quidam locus altis montibus unde
> stare uidentur et in campis consistere fulgor[1]."

A similar and perhaps even more striking effect is produced when Ibnu 'l-Fáriḍ, after having brought before his readers the spectacle of restless life and strife which fills the world, at once transforms it into a vision of eternal order and harmony—

وكُلُّ ٱلّذى شاهدتَهُ فِعْلُ واحدٍ

All thou beholdest is the act of One.

In reading the *Tá'iyya* it is a rare pleasure to meet with even ten or twenty consecutive lines like these, which require no commentary to interpret them. Yet the poem, as a whole, is not unduly cryptic in expression. Those who blame a writer for obscurity ought to ask themselves whether his meaning could have been given more clearly; and if so, whether he can allege good and sufficient reasons for his default. On these counts I think Ibnu 'l-Fáriḍ will secure an acquittal, if we remember that he was bound by the poetic forms and fashions of his day. The obscurity does not lie in his style so much as in the nature of his subject.

How little may a heart communicate in the form of thought, or a tongue utter in the mould of speech[2]!

[1] W. Y. Sellar, *The Roman poets of the Republic*, p. 403. I give Munro's translation: "Again when mighty legions fill with their movements all parts of the plains, waging the mimicry of war, the glitter then lifts itself up to the sky, and the whole earth round gleams with brass, and beneath a noise is raised by the mighty trampling of men, and the mountains stricken by the shouting re-echo the voices to the stars of heaven, and horsemen fly about and suddenly wheeling scour across the middle of the plains, shaking them with the vehemence of their charge. And yet there is some place on the high hills, seen from which they appear to stand still and to rest on the plains as a bright spot."

[2] *Tá'iyya*, *v*. 489.

While his symbolism may have served him at times as a mask when plain speaking would have been dangerous[1], he generally uses it as the only possible means of imparting mystical truth; and in his own circle, no doubt, it was understood readily enough. We, on the other hand, must begin by learning it and end with recognising that no intellectual effort will bring us to the stage whence an initiated Mohammedan sets out.

What makes the interpretation of the poem especially uncertain is that the author's account of his religious and mystical experience is psychological in character and throws but a faint light on his theological position. Was he really a pantheist, or was he an orthodox mystic whose feeling of oneness with God expressed itself in the language of pantheism? Does the *Tá'iyya* reflect the doctrines of Ibnu 'l-'Arabí, as its commentators believe? Although such questions cannot be ignored by any one who attempts to translate or explain the poem, they are not easy to answer definitely. I have followed Káshání in the main; nevertheless I regard his interpretation as representing a point of view which is alien to Ibnu 'l-Fáriḍ. Logically, the mystical doctrine of *ittiḥád* (*Einswerden*) leads to the pantheistic monism of Ibnu 'l-'Arabí; but those who find in the *Tá'iyya* a poetical version of that system are confusing mysticism with philosophy. In some passages, however, we meet with philosophical ideas[2] and may draw inferences from them. While they do not appear to me to support the view that Ibnu 'l-Fáriḍ was a follower of Ibnu 'l-'Arabí, they imply pantheism and monism on the plane of speculative thought, where commentators and theologians

[1] *Tá'iyya*, *vv*. 395–6.

[2] *E.g.* emanation (*fayḍ*) in *vv*. 403–5. The spiritual and sensible worlds derive their life from Universal Spirit and Universal Soul (*v*. 405; cf. *v*. 492). In *v*. 455 the Ḥallájian terms, *láhút* (divinity) and *násút* (humanity) are used in the same way as by Ibnu 'l-'Arabí, to denote the inward and outward aspects of the Being with whom the "unified" mystic is one (cf. Massignon, *Kitáb al-Ṭawásín*, p. 139). Allusions to the pre-existence of the soul occur in *vv*. 41, 157–8, 428, 670 and 759. Unlike Jílí, Ibnu 'l-Fáriḍ shows no sign of acquaintance with Ibnu 'l-'Arabí's philosophical terminology or, so far as I have observed, of being directly influenced by him in any considerable degree.

(not poets and mystics) are accustomed to dwell. I consider, therefore, that K.'s interpretation, false as it is to the spirit of the poem, places it in a medium intelligible to us and conveys its meaning in a relatively adequate form. And my readers will see at once how the mystical content of the *Tá'iyya* as well as its philosophical implications are illustrated by the foregoing essay on the *Insánu 'l-Kámil.*

Was Ibnu 'l-Fáriḍ consciously a pantheist? I do not think so. But in the permanent unitive state which he describes himself as having attained, he cannot speak otherwise than pantheistically: he is so merged in the Oneness that he identifies himself now with Mohammed (the Islamic Logos), now with God, whose attributes he assumes and makes his own.

Many of these passages are such as no medieval religion but Islam would have tolerated, and we cannot wonder that he was charged with heresy. His opponents accused him of holding the doctrine of incarnation (*ḥulúl*) and of pretending to be the *Quṭb*. He disavows *ḥulúl* and shows how it differs from his own doctrine (*vv.* 277 foll.). As regards the *Quṭb*, the most explicit reference occurs in *vv.* 500–1:

Therefore 'tis upon me the heavens turn, and marvel thou at their *Quṭb* (Pole) which encompasses them, howbeit the Pole is a central point.

And there was no *Quṭb* before me, whom I should succeed after having passed three grades (of sanctity), although the *Awtád* rise to the rank of *Quṭb* from the rank of *Badal*.

Here is another suspected verse (313):

And my spirit is a spirit to all the spirits (of created beings); and whatsoever thou seest of beauty in the universe flows from the bounty of my nature.

Evidently the poet declares himself to be one with the spiritual *Quṭb* (the Logos), whom in *v.* 501 he distinguishes from the terrestrial *Quṭb* (the head of the Ṣúfí hierarchy). The latter presides over the visible world. On his death he is succeeded by one of the three saints known as *Awtád*, who are next to him in dignity and have themselves risen from the ranks of the forty *Abdál* or *Budalá*[1]. The dominion of the spiritual *Quṭb*, the real Pole (*al-Quṭbu 'l-ḥaqíqí*), extends over the created things of both the visible and invisible worlds. He has neither predecessor nor successor, for he is the Spirit of Mohammed, *i.e.*, the essence of Man and the final cause of creation[2]. Ibnu 'l-Fáriḍ, then, does not profess this heretical doctrine (*quṭbiyya, quṭbániyya*) in the sense which Ṣúfís ordinarily assign to it. His "Poleship" is not the temporal vicegerency delegated by Mohammed to the supreme saint of every age, but a pure consciousness of being one with the Spirit, who as the perfect image of God encompasses all things with his knowledge, power and glory.

My translation covers three-fourths of the poem[3]. The omitted passages are generally unimportant, but I have given a summary whenever I thought it would be of use.

Argument

The poem, addressed to a real or imaginary disciple, sets forth in due order the phases of mystical experience through which the writer passed before attaining to oneness with God, and describes the nature of that abiding oneness so far as it can be indicated by words.

In the opening verses (1–7) Ibnu 'l-Fáriḍ recalls a time when his love of God was still imperfect and unfixed, so that the "intoxication" of ecstasy would be followed by the "sobriety" of a relapse into selfhood.

He tells (8–83) how he sought the favour of the Belóved and related to her his sufferings, not by way of complaint—

[1] K. on *v.* 501. Cf. *Kashf al-Maḥjúb*, transl., p. 214. Concerning the *Quṭb* and the subordinate members of the Ṣúfí hierarchy see Blochet, *Études sur l'ésotérisme musulman* in the *Journal asiatique*, vol. 20 (1902), p. 49 foll.; Haneberg, *Ali Abulhasan Schadeli* in *ZDMG.*, vol. 7, p. 21 foll.; Flügel, *Scha'rânî und sein Werk über die muhammadanische Glaubenslehre*, *ibid.* vol. 20, p. 37 foll.

[2] Cf. pp. 87 and 103 foll.

[3] 574 verses out of a total of 761. The following verses have not been translated: 111–114, 117–119, 122–125, 141–143, 164–167, 175–193, 195–196, 265–276, 334–393, 503–505, 515–520, 549–574, 580–588, 602–613, 622–626, 632–636, 750–758.

for suffering is the law of love—but in the hope of relieving them; how he said that he was enraptured by her beauty, that he would never change, that he cared for nothing but her and for her sake had abandoned all.

The Beloved answers (84–102), accusing him of insincerity and presumption. He is not really in love with her, but only with himself. If he would love her in truth, he must die to self.

In reply he protests that this death is his dearest wish and prays the Beloved to grant it, whatever pain it may cost (103–116). Then, addressing the disciple, he describes his dying to self and its effects: how it has brought him great glory, though he is despised by his neighbours and regarded as a madman; and how it has caused his love to be hidden even from himself, his faculties to be jealous of one another, and his identity to be lost, so that in worshipping he feels that he is the object of worship (117–154). He proceeds to explain the mystery of his love, saying that he loved before the creation but was separated from his Beloved in this world, and that by casting-off his self-existence he has found her to be his own real self. There was no thought of merit in his sacrifice, so she accepted it (155–174). He exhorts the disciple to follow the *via purgativa*, by which mystics are prepared for the highest things, and describes how he himself disciplined his soul (175–203).

The poet now begins to explain the origin and nature of his *ittiḥád* or oneness with the Beloved. As it is hard for the mind to conceive that two may be one, he points to the analogous case of a woman possessed by a spirit. He urges the disciple to get rid of the illusion of dualism, and the mystery will then become clear to him. He says that this was the way by which he himself attained to his present state (204–238).

He bids the disciple mark that all beauty is absolute. Every fair earthly form is in reality a manifestation of the Beloved (239–264).

He then explains why, notwithstanding his exalted degree, he strictly fulfils the duties of the religious law and occupies himself with voluntary works of devotion. Antinomianism would be consistent with belief in incarnation (*ḥulúl*); but he does not hold that doctrine. His own doctrine is supported by the Koran and the Apostolic Traditions (265–285).

He calls on the disciple to follow him in the path of love, but warns him that he must not aspire to the supreme grade of *ittiḥád*, which is now described as being beyond love (286–333).

After a hymn of praise to the Beloved (336–387), he resumes the description of his oneness. His spirit and soul, which formerly drew him up and down between them, are in reality one with the Beloved, *i.e.*, they are identified with Universal Spirit and Universal Soul, whence all forms of spiritual and sensible life are fed. The image of the Beloved that he receives through sensation agrees with the image of her in his spiritual consciousness; and this is a proof that he is one with her. He says that she is presented to him by all that he sees, hears, tastes and touches. He describes particularly his listening to music: at that time he beholds her with his whole being and is riven asunder by the struggle of his spirit to escape from the body; then dancing soothes him, and, as it were, rocks him to sleep (388–440).

Continuing, he declares that the state which he has now reached is higher than "union" (*wiṣál*). He gained it through casting aside every vestige of self-regard. It was he who imposed the laws of religion on himself and was sent as an apostle to himself before any prophet appeared in the world. His overruling influence is exerted throughout heaven and earth. He is beyond all relations: place, time, and number are gone; he has no rival or opposite; he is the object of his own worship. No change of state can now befall him: the alternation of "intoxication" and "sobriety" has been superseded by a permanent consciousness in which past and future are the same. He is the Pole (*Quṭb*) on which the universe revolves (441–501).

He mentions, as a strange effect of his love, that he sought his Beloved in himself until he found that he was seeking himself, so that in being united with himself he embraced his own essence (502–532). Speaking in the person of God, he says that his attributes, names, and actions cannot be known except through himself, and that he cannot be known through them. As the names of his external attributes, *e.g.*, sight and hearing, which are really faculties of the soul, are derived from his organs of sensation, so the names of his inward attributes are ultimately derived from his (the Divine) essence. By means of the names God manifests Himself in creation. Their qualities and the benefits which they confer on the body and the soul are described at some length (533–574).

He is so entirely one, he says, that all his faculties are interfused and each part has become absorbed in the whole. Hence he acts universally and infinitely. This is the explanation of the miracles wrought by the prophets. Mohammed, the last of the prophets, not only summed up in himself all the marvellous powers of his predecessors but is the source from which these powers were bestowed on the prophets before him and the Moslem saints after him. Ibnu 'l-Fáriḍ, making himself one with the spirit of Mohammed, claims to be the father of Adam, the final cause of creation, and the origin of life: all creatures obey his will, speak his word, see with his sight; he is hidden in everything sensible, intellectual, and spiritual (575–650).

He forbids the disciple to believe in metempsychosis, pointing out that what appears in different forms is really the same, *e.g.*, Abú Zayd (the hero of Ḥarírí's fiction) in all his disguises, the image in a mirror, the echo, the phantom seen in dream, and the figures shown by a shadow-lantern. He describes the various scenes of the shadow-play—all of them the work of a single person behind a screen—and likens the soul to the showman, the body to the screen, and the figures to the objects perceived in sensation. When the bodily screen is removed, the soul becomes unified (651–730).

He says that faith and infidelity are not essentially different. The One God is adored in every form of worship—by Moslems, Christians, Jews, Zoroastrians, even by idolaters; those who go astray from Him are none the less seeking Him: it is He that guides and misguides them, according as they are destined for salvation or perdition. All is determined by the Divine will and is the effect of the Divine nature. This the soul knows from itself (731–749).

He declares that he is not to be blamed for having revealed the mysteries imparted to him, and concludes with the assertion that none living or dead has attained to such a height as he (750–761).

Saqatní ḥumayya 'l-ḥubbi ráḥatu muqlatí
wa-ka'sí muḥayyá man 'ani 'l-ḥusni jallati

(1) The hand of mine eye gave me love's strong wine to drink, when my cup was the face of Her that transcendeth beauty,

(2) And in my drunkenness, by means of a glance I caused my comrades to fancy that it was the quaffing of *their* wine that gladdened my inmost soul,

(3) Although mine eyes made me independent of my cup, and my inebriation was derived from her qualities, not from my wine;

(4) Therefore in the tavern of my intoxication was the hour of my thanksgiving to youths through whom my love was completely hidden notwithstanding my celebrity (as a lover).

(5) And when my sobriety was ended, I sought union with her, and no restraint of fear affected me in my boldness towards her,

(1) *I.e.* "my love arose from contemplation of Divine Beauty, which transcends phenomenal beauty" (*ḥusn*). Cf. p. 90, note 1.

(2) "In order to disguise my love and to guard myself against reproach, I let my comrades, *i.e.* the worshippers of material beauty, suppose that my love was of the same kind as theirs."

(3) "But in fact my vision of Divine Beauty took away all desire to behold the form in which material beauty is contained, like wine in a cup." So K. rightly explains the verse, regarding *al-ḥadaq* (properly, "the blacks of the eyes") as equivalent to *ḥadaqí*, "my eyes." N., however, understands by *al-ḥadaq* "the darkness of phenomenal being" and by *qadaḥí* ("my cup") the Divine Essence (cf. verse 1). According to his interpretation, the poet means to say that whereas he formerly saw only the Divine Reality, and not phenomena, he had now reached the higher stage of seeing phenomena in their true relation to that Reality—a relation symbolised by his description of them as the black of the all-encompassing Divine eye.

(4) "I render thanks to the votaries of vulgar love"—the "youths" are the "comrades" of verse 2—"because my being confused with them enables me to hide my love from the ignorant, though its real nature is well-known to mystics." N. gives an unsuitable explanation, *viz.* "In my ecstasy I praised the illustrious theosophists who taught me the mysteries of Divine Love, which are hidden from the vulgar."

(5) The intoxication of ecstasy is associated with unreserve (*basṭ*); restraint (*qabḍ*) is characteristic of the return to consciousness (sobriety).

(6) And in the privacy of bridal unveiling, when no continuance of self-regard was beside me as a watcher, I declared to her that which I felt,

(7) And I said—my state bearing witness to my ardent love, and my finding her (in my heart) effacing me, whilst my losing her brings me back to myself—

(8) "Bestow on me the glance of one who turns for a moment, ere Love makes pass away what remains in me (of self-existence) to see thee by.

(9) And if thou forbid that I see thee, favour mine hearing with, 'Thou shalt not (see me)': this word was sweet to another before me;

(10) For, because of my drunkenness, I have need of a recovery (from drunkenness) which, but for passion, would not break my heart.

(11) Had the mountains felt what I suffer, and were Sinai amongst them, they would have been razed to the earth ere the revelation—

(6) Prof. Nallino (*op. cit.* p. 68) proposes to take *baqá* as an accusative of duration, but this seems to me unnecessary. The poet likens the continuance of self-regard—*ḥaẓẓ* = *ḥaẓẓu 'l-nafs* (see Glossary to the *Kitáb al-Luma'*)—to the watcher (*raqíb*) who prevents the lover from gaining access to the beloved.

(7) The illuminated mystic suffers an effacement (*maḥw*) of his human attributes. The restoration (*ithbát*) of these attributes coincides with the occultation of the Divine light in his heart.

(8) "Let me behold thee, ere my rapture makes me one with thee, so that I can no more behold thee."

(9) "If thou wilt not grant me vision, at least let me hear thee deny it to me, as thou didst once deny it to Moses (Kor. 7, 139)."

(10) "Inasmuch as I desire vision, which cannot be attained in the state of drunkenness (entire loss of self-consciousness), I have need of a return to sobriety; yet sobriety brings with it repentance (*tawba*)—as Moses, on coming out of his swoon, cried, 'Glory to thee! I turn to thee with repentance' (Kor. 7, 140)—and a renewal of the anguish of love" (described in the following verses). The "recovery" which the poet desires is not the heart-breaking relapse into normal consciousness after ecstasy, but the state of *abnormal* consciousness and clairvoyance (technically known as "the second sobriety" or "the second separation") which is characteristic of the unitive life at its highest level. Cf. notes on *vv.* 213–4, 233–5, 479.

(11) This verse alludes to the same passage of the Koran: "And when Moses came at our appointed time and his Lord spake unto him, Moses said, 'O Lord! let me see, that I may behold thee.' God answered, 'Thou shalt not see me, but look towards the mountain: if it stand firm in its place, then shalt thou see me.' But when his Lord revealed himself to the mountain, he razed it to the earth, and Moses fell in a swoon."

(12) A passion that only tears betrayed, and an inward ardency that increased the burning heats whose maladies brought me to ruin.

(13) The Flood of Noah is like my tears, when I lament, and the blazing of Abraham's fire is like my bosom's glow.

(14) But for my sighs, I should be drowned by my tears; and but for my tears, I should be burned by my sighs.

(15) That (grief) which Jacob uttered is the least of my sorrow, and all the woe of Job is but a part of my affliction;

(16) And the last sufferings of those who loved unto death are but a part of what I suffered in the beginning of my tribulation.

(17) Had the ear of my guide heard my moaning caused by pains of love-sickness which wasted my body,

(18) My grief would have called to his memory the bitter distress of travellers left behind, when the camels are reined (and ready for the journey).

(19) Anguish hath sorely oppressed and naughted me, and emaciation hath laid bare the secret of my true being;

(20) And in complaining of my leanness I made him who spied upon me my confidant, acquainting him with the sum of my inmost feelings and with the particulars of my way (in love).

(21) I appeared to him as an idea, while my body was in such case that he saw it not, because of the woeful burning of love that consumed it;

(22) And though my tongue spake not, the hidden conceptions of my soul revealed to his ear the mystery of that which my soul had concealed from him,

(13) Abraham, having broken his people's idols, was cast into a burning fire, which by the command of God became cold and did him no harm (Kor. 21, 52 foll.).

(17) K. explains that the "guide" is the person who reproaches the lover and tries to induce him to forget his beloved. According to N., the "guide" is "the perfect spiritual director."

(20) The spy (*muráqib*) apparently signifies here the judgment or estimative faculty (*wahm*). Cf. verse 137. "My way of love" is K.'s rendering of *sírati*. N. defines it more explicitly as "my outward state," *i.e.*, acts of worship and devotion, asceticism, piety and thanksgiving.

(21) Or, reading *waṣfan* for *ma'nan*, "I appeared to him only in virtue of my external attributes, such as my acts of devotion" (N.).

(22) N. says: "This is the practice of the Naqshbandís at the present day. Whilst engaged in silent meditation, they converse spiritually and understand each other though no word is uttered."

(23) And his ear became for my thought a mind, so that my thought was moving in his ear, which thereby stood him in stead of ocular vision;

(24) And he gave news of me to those in the tribe, setting forth my inward state, for he knew me well.

(25) 'Twas as though the Recording Angels had come down to his heart to inspire him with knowledge of what was written in my book (the book of my experience).

(26) He would not have known what I was covering and what was the guarded secret that my bosom hid,

(27) But the drawing aside of the bodily veil disclosed the secret, which it had screened from him, of my inmost soul.

(28) And I should have been invisible to him in respect of my secret unless my groans arising from the weakness of emaciation had divulged it,

(29) So that I was made visible by a malady that hid me from him: there is no strange thing but Love brings it to pass.

(30) A sore anguish o'erwhelmed me, at whose stroke the suggestions of my soul—suggestions that betrayed me, like tears—vanished into nothingness.

(31) If hateful death had sought me, it would not have known where I was, since I was concealed by concealing my love for thee (or 'by thy love's concealing me').

(32) Betwixt yearning and longing I passed away, whilst thou didst either avert thyself in repulse or display thyself in presence.

(33) And were my heart sent back to me from thy court, to redeem my passing-away, it would not desire the abode of my exile.

(24) "The tribe," *i.e.* my Ṣúfí brethren.

(29) "A malady that hid me from him": cf. verse 21.

(30–33) In these verses the poet describes the passing-away (*faná*) of the phenomenal self in the rapture of love. "Like tears": cf. verse 12.

(32) His ecstasy was the result of successive states of Divine manifestation (*tajallí*) and occultation (*tawallí*). Instead of "presence" (*ḥaḍra*) N. reads "favour" (*ḥuẓwa*).

(33) According to K., "the abode of my exile" means this phenomenal existence by which the heart is separated from God. N., taking *li-faná'i* in the sense of *ilá faná'i*, paraphrases the verse as follows: "If my heart were sent back from the sphere of thy most beautiful Names (the Divine Attributes) to the original state of non-existence in which I was before I manifested the light of thy real Being, which is the sphere of the most beautiful Names, it would not desire the home of my exile (*i.e.* my original non-existence)." The poet (he says) describes this original state as "exile,"

(34) That whereof I declare unto thee a part is (only) the frontispiece of my state: 'tis beyond my power to express what lies underneath;

(35) And, being unable, I refrain from (speaking of) many matters; they shall not be recounted by my speech, and even if I told them, they would be few.

(36) My cure drew nigh unto death; nay, passion decreed that it should die, since the cooling of my thirst finds the heat of my burning drought (still remaining).

(37) And my heart is more threadbare than the garments of my endurance; nay, my selfhood is linked with my pleasure in respect of its being reduced to naught.

(38) Had God revealed me to my visitors (as I really am), and had they ascertained from the Tablet how much of me Love had allowed to survive,

(39) Their eyes would not have beheld anything of me except a spirit pervading the garments of a dead man.

(40) And ever since my tracks were obliterated and I wandered distraught, I had vain imaginings about my existence, but my thought could not lay hold upon it.

(41) And after this, my feelings (of love) for thee became self-

because, if he returned to it, it would seem strange to him after his long absence—a very forced interpretation, I think.

(35) "Few," *i.e.* in comparison with the whole. Another rendering is "they would be little," *i.e.* less than they are in reality, but this does not preserve the natural antithesis of *kathirat*[in] and *qallat*.

(36) "My cure was on the point of death" (K.) or "became incurable" (N.), *i.e.* I could not possibly be cured, because the presence of the beloved, which relieves pain, also kindles in me a fiercer flame of love.

(37) "My *faná* is so complete that not only do I feel no pleasure but my very selfhood (*dhát*) has vanished."

(38) The "visitors" are the sick man's friends who come to see how he is. On the Guarded Tablet (*al-Lawḥu 'l-maḥfúẓ*) are inscribed the archetypes of all things past, present and future.

(39) "Eyes," *oculi cordis*. "The garments of a dead man": K. says, "*i.e.* the members of my body, which are the vesture of my dead soul (*nafs*)." The word for "garments" (*athwáb* or *thiyáb*) sometimes has this meaning in non-mystical Arabic poetry. Ibnu 'l-Fáriḍ indicates that Love has left in him nothing except what is immortal and incorruptible, namely, his spirit (*rúḥ*), which belongs to the Unseen World.

(40) "Since my passing-away (*faná*) my thought searches in vain after my lost self."

(41) "My love of God is not a property of my perishable self (*nafs*), but of my spirit (*rúḥ*); otherwise the *rúḥ* would be dependent on the *nafs*, which

subsistent (independent of my phenomenal being): my proof is the fact that my spirit existed before my mortal frame.

(42) I told how I fared in my love of thee, not because impatience made me weary of my sufferings, but in order to assuage my grief.

(43) 'Tis good to show fortitude towards enemies, but in the presence of loved ones aught save weakness is unseemly.

(44) The excellence of my patience keeps me from complaining, though if I complained to my enemies of what I feel, they would do away with my complaint.

(45) And the issue of my patience in loving thee is praiseworthy if I endure the sorrows thou layest on me; but if I endure to be separated from thee, it is not praiseworthy.

(46) Whatever woe befalls me is a favour, inasmuch as my purpose holds firm against breaking my vows;

(47) So for every pain in love, when it arises from thee, I give thanks instead of complaining.

(48) Ay, and if the agonies of passion do me despite, yet are they reckoned in love as a kindness;

(49) And my unhappiness, nay, my tribulation is a bounty when wrought by thee, and my raiment of hardship worn for thy sake is the most ample of felicities.

(50) My ancient fealty to thee caused me to regard the worst of slaves, who were bestowed on me (by thee), as the best of treasures.

(51) One of them a railer and one a slanderer: the former leads

is not the case, for it existed before the creation of the body." Cf. the Tradition, "God created the spirits two thousand years before the bodies." According to N., the poet associates his love with his original state of non-existence, *i.e.* when he existed only in the eternal knowledge of God. This verse explains why love continues after the passing-away (*faná*) of the lover.

(46) The clause, "inasmuch as, etc." conveys an intimation that it is only to the *constant* lover that afflictions are favours in disguise.

(49) K. says: "He rejects the word 'unhappiness' (*shaqá*) and substitutes 'tribulation' (*balá*), because the sufferings of love are not an unhappiness, but a trial and probation, which is a mark of regard (*iltifát*) on the part of the Beloved towards the lover and is therefore the very essence of happiness."

(50) "My ancient fealty": see note on verse 69. "The best of treasures," because they were the predestined means by which my love was tried.

(51) This verse is variously read. I translate *li-'izzat^in* in the first hemistich and *li-ghayrati* in the second. According to K., the "railer" is

me astray because of vainglory, while the latter talks foolishness about me because of jealousy.

(52) I oppose that one in his blame, from fear (of God), and I ally myself with this one in his meanness, from caution.

(53) And my face was not turned from thy path by dread of that which I encountered, nor by any harm that smote me therein,

(54) Although in bearing what hath befallen me on account of thee I have no patience that tends to praise of me or to the lauding of my love;

(55) But thy beauty, which calls to thee (every heart), ordained that I should endure all that I have told and all the sequel of my tale to its farthest length.

(56) It was only because thou appearedst to mine eye with the most perfect qualities, surpassing (mortal) loveliness;

(57) And thou madest my tribulation an ornament to me and gavest it a free hand over me, and coming from thee it was the most glorious of distinctions;

(58) For when one is snared by Beauty, methinks his soul (even) from the most delicious life is (gladly) rendered up to death.

(59) A soul that thinks to meet with no suffering in love, when it addresses itself to love, is spurned.

the Devil, who in the guise of a candid friend seeks to draw the pilgrim into the path of sensuality, while the "slanderer" is the Angel, who exhorts him to piety and other-worldliness, thereby diverting him from his love of the Divine Essence. Cf. the passage in the Koran (2, 28), where the angels, being jealous of Adam, maligned him and said to God, "Wilt Thou place on the earth (as Thy vicegerent) one who will do evil there?" See also note on verse 400.

(52) "I resist the Devil because I should be separated from God, if I were to succumb to his wiles; but not the Angel, because I am afraid of letting him know my real aspiration." The Angel is described as "mean," for he attributes the love and wrath of God to secondary causes, such as obedience and disobedience—he thinks, *e.g.*, that Adam's sin was the cause of his incurring the Divine anger—whereas in truth God's love and wrath are eternal and uncaused. The poet, though professing to agree with the Angel, keeps to himself the higher knowledge to which none but mystics can attain, who love God not as the Lord of Paradise, but as the Essence of all that exists.

(55–57) "Thy beauty called me to union with thee, and since union with thee requires complete detachment from the phenomenal self—a result which cannot be secured without much suffering—thou didst cause my suffering to appear to me in the form of thy beauty."

(58) "Death," *i.e. faná*.

(60) No spirit that was given repose ever gained love, nor did any soul that desired a tranquil life ever win devotion.

(61) Tranquillity! how far is it from the life of a lover! The garden of Eden is compassed about with terrors.

(62) Mine is a noble soul—a soul that would not forget thee even though thou shouldst offer it, on condition of forgetting thee, what is beyond its wishes;

(63) A soul that would not let go the true love I bear, even though it were removed far (from thee) by scorn and absence and hatred and the cutting off of hope.

(64) I have no way of departing from my Way in love, and if ever I shall turn aside from it, I shall abandon my religion;

(65) And had a thought of fondness towards any one save thee come into my mind unawares, I should have pronounced myself a heretic.

(66) 'Tis for thee to give judgment in my case. Do as thou wilt, for my feeling towards thee was ever desire, not aversion.

(67) I swear by the firm pact of love between us, which was not alloyed with any imagination of annulment—and 'tis the best of oaths—

(68) And by thy taking the covenant of troth in a place where I did not appear in such a form that my soul was clothed in the shadow of my clay,

(69) And by the primal pledge that never was changed since I

(61) "The garden of Eden, etc.": this sentence is borrowed from a Tradition of the Prophet—"Paradise is encompassed with things disliked, and Hell with things desired," *i.e.* Paradise is reached only by passing through painful experiences.

(62) "A noble soul": literally, "the soul of a free man." Freedom (*ḥurriyya*), as a mystical term, denotes emancipation from the bondage of creatureliness.

(69) K. identifies "the primal pledge" with "the covenant of troth" mentioned in the preceding verse. This refers to a passage of the Koran (7, 171) where it is written that God, having drawn forth from the loins of Adam all the future generations of mankind, said to them, "Am not I your Lord?" and received the answer, "Yea," which (according to the Ṣúfí interpretation) sealed the covenant of mutual love between God and His creatures. "The succeeding bond," into which they entered after their souls had been joined to their bodies, is the bond of Islam contracted through the mediation of the prophets. N. most unreasonably explains "the primal pledge" as the pledge given by Mohammed's vicegerents and companions to accept his religion, and "the succeeding bond" as the solemn vow made by Ibnu 'l-Fáriḍ to his spiritual directors that he would be steadfast in the Mohammedan faith.

plighted it, and by the succeeding bond that was too solemn for any frailty to loose,

(70) And by the rising of thy radiant countenance, whose splendour caused all the full moons to become invisible,

(71) And by the attribute of perfection in thee, from which the fairest and shapeliest form in creation drew support,

(72) And by the quality of thy majesty with which my torment is pleasant to me and my being slain is sweet;

(73) And by the mystery of thy beauty, whereby all loveliness in the world is manifested and fulfilled;

(74) And by thy comeliness which captivates the mind and which guided me to a love wherein my abasement for thy glory's sake was comely;

(75) And by an idea in thee beyond comeliness—an idea which I beheld through itself, too subtle to be apprehended by the eye of perception:

(76) Verily, thou art the desire of my heart, and the end of my search, and the goal of my aim, and my choice and my chosen.

(77) I disrobed myself of modesty and deprecation, clothing myself in shamelessness, rejoicing in my disrobing and in my robe;

(78) And 'tis my duty to cast off modesty for thy sake, even though my folk shrink from approaching me; and shamelessness is my law.

(79) And no folk of mine are they, so long as they find fault with my recklessness and show hatred and deem it right to abuse me for thy sake.

(70) As the moon is hidden by its nearness to the sun on the last night of the lunar month, so the Divine attributes are eclipsed by the splendour of the Essence which reveals them.

(71–73) In these verses the poet describes the three main aspects, in one or other of which all the Divine attributes, except those that are purely essential, may be regarded: *viz.* perfection (*kamál*), majesty (*jalál*), and beauty (*jamál*). "The fairest and shapeliest form" is the Perfect Man (*al-insánu 'l-kámil*), who was created in God's image. "Fulfilled," *i.e.* through the love that Divine beauty inspires.

(75) "An idea in thee beyond comeliness" (*ḥusn*), *i.e.* Absolute Beauty (*jamál*).

(77) K. omits this verse, which is certainly spurious (see Nallino, *op. cit.* p. 56). Having translated it, I let it stand, as its removal would alter the numeration of the verses from this point to the end of the poem.

(79) "They who find fault, etc." *i.e.* the exoteric Ṣúfís, who devote themselves to asceticism and religious works and dislike mystical enthusiasm.

(80) My fellows in the religion of love are those who love; and they have approved my ignominy and thought well of my disgrace.

(81) Let who will be wroth, save only thee: there is no harm (in their anger), when the noble of my kin are pleased with me.

(82) If the ascetics are fascinated by some of the beauties that are thine, everything in thee is the source of my fascination.

(83) And I never was bewildered until I chose love of thee as a religion. Woe is me for my bewilderment, had it not been on account of thee!"

(84) She said, "Another's love thou hast sought and hast taken the wrong path, forsaking in thy blindness the highway unto me.

(85) And the imposture of a soul that cherished vain desires beguiled thee so that thou saidst what thou saidst, putting on thereby the shame of falsehood,

(86) And didst covet the most precious of boons with a soul that crossed its bound and trespassed.

(87) How wilt thou win my love, which is the best of affections, by means of pretence, which is the worst of qualities?

(88) Where is Suhá to a man blind from birth who in his

(80) The commentators say that Ibnu 'l-Fáriḍ alludes here to the school of Ṣúfís who are known as the Malámatís, because they deliberately acted in such a way as to incur blame (*malámat*). See *Kashf al-Maḥjúb* (translation), pp. 62–9.

(81) According to K., the words "when the noble of my kin, etc." are a half-verse composed by another poet and inserted by Ibnu 'l-Fáriḍ as a quotation (*taḍmín*).

(82) While ascetics love God for His mercy and for the blessings which He bestows on them now and hereafter, true mystics love Him for all His attributes, since they behold the beauty of His essence in all His manifestations—in His wrath and vengeance no less than in His mercy and forgiveness.

(83) Bewilderment (*ḥayra*) when caused by letting the eye wander in different directions, is pernicious; but praiseworthy, when it is the result of gazing concentratedly on the beauty of the Beloved. The latter is characteristic of one who has lost himself in Divine contemplation. "O Lord, increase my bewilderment!" was a famous Ṣúfí's prayer.

(86) "The most precious of boons," *i.e.* Divine Love. "Crossed its bound," because the appetitive soul (*nafs*) has no object beyond its own gratification.

(88) To win Divine Love by false pretences is as impossible as to be blind and see the star Suhá, which is so small and obscure that only the keenest sight can descry it.

confusion has forgotten what he seeks? Nay, thy vain hopes have duped thee,

(89) So that thou stoodest in a position to which thy rank was inferior, on a foot that overstepped not its own province,

(90) And soughtest a thing towards which how many stretched out their necks and were beheaded!

(91) Thou didst come to tents which are not entered by their back parts and whose doors are closed against the knocking of one like thee;

(92) And thou didst lay (as an offering) before thy converse (with me) mere tinsel, aiming thereby at a glory whose ends are hard to reach;

(93) And thou camest to woo my pure love with a shining face, not letting thine honour be lost in this world or in the next;

(94) But hadst thou been with me as the *kasra* below the dot of the letter *b*, thou wouldst have been raised to a rank that thine own effort did not gain for thee,

(95) Where thou wouldst see that what thou didst (formerly) regard is not worth a thought, and that what thou didst provide is no (sufficient) provision.

(96) To those who are rightly guided the straight road unto me is plain, but all men are made blind by their desires.

(89) "On a foot, etc." *i.e.* relying on thy lower self (*nafs*), which never transcends the sphere of its selfish interests.

(91) Cf. Kor. 2, 185: "It is not righteousness that ye should come into houses (tents) by the back parts thereof." The back parts of the House of Love, through which none can enter it, are egoism and self-conceit; the door that lets in those worthy of admission is self-abandonment (*faná*).

(92) "Instead of being ready to sacrifice thy existence as an individual in the hope of attaining unto me, thou broughtest me nothing but thine own acts and words and feelings."

(93) The true lover has no regard for his name and fame. Cf. the Tradition, "Spiritual poverty is blackness of the face in both worlds."

(94) "As the *kasra*, etc." *i.e.* having no independent existence, but subsisting only through God. *Kasra* is the vowel *i*, which is always written under the consonant that it belongs to. The letter *b* (ب) denotes the form of phenomenal being, just as the letter *a* (ا) denotes the form of Real Being; while the dot of the *b* symbolises contingency as opposed to absoluteness. Hence the mystical saying, "Existence was manifested by means of *b*, and the worshipper was distinguished from the Worshipped by means of the dot."

(96) "The straight road," *i.e.* selflessness (*faná*).

(97) It is time that I reveal (the nature of) thy love, and who it is that hath wasted thee, by a denial of thy claim to love me.

(98) Thou art sworn to love, but to love of self: amongst my proofs (of this) is the fact that thou sufferest one of thy attributes to remain in existence.

(99) For thou lov'st me not, so long as thou hast not passed away in me; and thou hast not passed away, so long as my form is not seen within thee.

(100) Cease, then, pretending to love, and call thy heart to something else, and drive thy error from thee by that (state) which (is the best).

(101) And shun the quarter of union: 'tis far off, and was never reached (in life), and lo, thou art living. If thou art sincere, die!

(102) Such is Love: if thou diest not, thou wilt not win thy will of the Beloved in aught. Then choose death or leave my love alone!"

(103) I said to her, "My spirit is thine: 'tis for thee to take it. How should it be in my power?

(104) I am not one that loathes to die in love—I am always true (to death): my nature refuses aught else.

(105) What should I hope to be said of me except 'Such a one died of love'? Who will ensure me of that (death)?—for it is that I seek.

(106) Ay, it pleaseth me well that my life be ended by longing ere thou art gained, if my claim to love thee shall be found real;

(107) And if I shall not make good such a claim in regard to thee, because it is too high, I am content with my pride in being reputed thy lover;

(98) "One of thy attributes," because an attribute implies a subject in which it inheres; and that subject is thy "self" (*nafs*), one of whose attributes is the desire to enjoy vision and contemplation of God. N. quotes the saying of Abu 'l-Ḥasan al-Shádhilí, "The desire of union with God is one of the things that most effectually separate from God."

(99) Real love is nothing less than *faná*, which is here defined as the appearance of Divine attributes in the lover (K.) or God's unveiling Himself in the mystic's heart (N.).

(100) "That (state) which (is the best)," *i.e.* the complete passing-away (*faná*) of the self (*nafs*). So N., but K. renders "that (quality) which (is the best)," namely, veracity. In this case the meaning will be: "Do not pretend to love, but give thy passion its true name, and let veracity purge thee of thy false pretensions."

(101) "Shun the quarter of union": cf. note on *v.* 98. For the meaning of "union" (*waṣl*) see note on verse 441.

(107) Cf. p. 171, l. 25 foll.

(108) And if I die of anguish without the reputation, thou wilt have done no wrong to a soul that delights in martyrdom;

(109) And if thou wilt spill my blood in vain and I shall not be reckoned a martyr, 'tis grace enough for me that thou shouldst know the cause of my death.

(110) Methinks, my spirit is not worth so much that it should be offered in exchange for union (*wiṣál*) with thee, for it is too threadbare to be prized."

The poet then refers to the warning that he must show his sincerity by dying to self. Does the Beloved *threaten* him with death?

(115) "To me thy menace is a promise, and its fulfilment is the wish of an affianced lover who stands firm against the blows of all calamity except absence (from thee).

(116) I have come to hope that which others fear: succour therewith a dead man's spirit that is prepared for (everlasting) life!"

By passing-away (*faná*) the mystic wins immortal life in God (*baqá*).

(120) If she lets my blood be shed in love of her, yet hath she established my rank on the heights of glory and eminence.

(121) By my life, though I lose my life in exchange for her love, I am the gainer; and if she wastes away my heart, she will make it whole once more.

But this is an inward glory, which causes him to be scorned by his fellow-men.

(126) 'Tis as though I had never been honoured amongst them but they had always despised me both in easy fortune and in hard.

(127) Had they asked me "Whom dost thou love?" and had I declared her name, they would have said, "He speaks a parable," or "A touch of madness hath smitten him."

(128) Yet, had abasement for her sake been impossible, my passion had not been sweet to me; and but for love, my glory had not been in abasement.

(129) Because of her, I am endowed with the understanding of one crazed, the health of one shattered by disease, and the glory of ignominy.

The following lines, curiously subtle in their psychology and phrasing, represent the "self" (*nafs*) as desiring Divine Love, but keeping its desire beyond the reach of mental perception.

(130) My soul secretly imparted its desire for her love to my heart alone, where the intellect was unable to spy upon it;

(131) For I feared that the tale, if it were told, would transport the rest of me, so that the language of my tears would declare my secret.

(132) In order to keep safe that secret, part of me (my soul) was misleading part of me (my intellect), but my falsehood in hiding it was really my speaking the truth.

(133) And when my first (intuitive) thought refused to divulge it to my ribs (my mental faculties), I guarded it also from my reflection,

(134) And I did my utmost to conceal it, so that I forgot it and was caused to forget my concealment of that which my soul confided to my heart.

(135) And if in planting those desires I shall pluck the fruit of suffering, God bless a soul that suffered for its desires,

(136) Since of all love's wishes the sweetest to the soul is that whereby she who caused it to remember and forget them willed it to suffer.

(137) She set, to guard her, one taken from myself who should watch against me the amorous approach of my spiritual thoughts;

(138) And if they, unperceived by the mind, steal into my heart without hindrance, I cast down mine eyes in reverent awe.

(130) The *nafs* cannot love God purely and disinterestedly: therefore the poet does not say that it loves, but only that it desires to love. It communicates this desire to the *sirr*—the organ of mystical contemplation, Eckhart's "ground of the soul"—but withholds it from the intellect (*'aql*).

(132) "My falsehood, etc."—*i.e.* concealment is one of the signs of true love.

(134) The words "I was caused to forget" indicate the higher stage of unconsciousness that is produced in the mystic by an act of the Divine will, when his own will has entirely ceased.

(138) *Wahm*, here rendered by "mind," is properly the faculty of judgment, which by its activity prevents the thought of God (*khâṭiru 'l-ḥaqq*), residing in the ground of the soul (*sirr*), from penetrating into the heart (*qalb*). For this reason it is depicted in the preceding verse as a "watcher" (*murâqib*).

(139) Mine eye is turned back if I seek but one glance, and if my hand be stretched forth to take freely (its will of her), it is restrained.

(140) Thus in every limb of me is an advance prompted by hope, and in consequence of the awe born of veneration a retreat prompted by fear.

The poet now attempts to describe the mystical union of the lover with the Beloved.

(144) 'Tis my being crazed with love of her that makes me jealous of her; but when I recognise my worth (to be naught), I disown my jealousy,

(145) And my spirit is rapt in ecstatic joy (towards her), though I do not acquit my soul of conceiving a desire.

(146) Mine ear sees her, far though she be from the eye, in the form of blame which visits me in my hours of waking,

(147) And when she is mentioned, mine eye deems mine ear lucky, and the part of me that remains (in consciousness) envies the part that she has caused to pass away.

(148) In reality I led my Imám (leader in prayer), and all mankind were behind me. Wheresoever I faced, there was my (true) direction.

(149) Whilst I prayed, mine eye was seeing her in front of me, but my heart was beholding me in front of all my Imáms.

(150) And no wonder that in conducting the prayer the Imám faced towards me, since in my heart dwelt she who is the *qibla* of my *qibla*,

(151) And that towards me had faced all the six directions with their whole contents of piety and greater and lesser pilgrimage.

(144–5) Jealousy involves duality, and not until it is denied can the spirit (*rúḥ*) attain to oneness with God. Complete spiritual oneness is incompatible with the desire of the soul (*nafs*) for vision.

(146) Cf. p. 180.

(148) The following lines describe a unitive state in which the mystic, by losing his apparent individuality, realises his essential oneness with the One whom he loves and worships.

(150) "My *qibla*" is the point to which Moslems face when they pray, *i.e.* the Ka'ba, which (like every other created thing) turns in worship towards the Being who endues it with existence.

(151) "The six directions" are above, below, before, behind, right and left.

(152) To her I address my prayers at the Maqám, and behold in them that she prayed to me.

(153) Both of us are a single worshipper who, in respect of the united state, bows himself to his essence in every act of bowing.

(154) None prayed to me but myself nor did I pray to any one but myself in the performance of every genuflexion.

(155) How long shall I keep to the veil? Lo, I have rent it! 'Twas in my bond of allegiance that I should loose the loops of the curtains.

(156) I was given my fealty to her before she had appeared to me at the taking of the covenant, on a day when no day was, in my primal state.

(157) I gained my fealty to her neither by hearing nor by sight nor by acquisition nor by the attraction of my nature,

(158) But I was enamoured of her in the world of command, where is no manifestation, and my intoxication was prior to my appearance (in the created world).

(159) The attributes dividing us which were not subsistent *there* (in the world of command) Love caused to pass away *here* (in the created world), and they vanished;

(160) And I found that which I cast off going out of me unto me and again coming from me with an increase,

(152) The Maqám Ibráhím, *i.e.* the standing-place of Abraham, is a rock situated to the east of the Ka'ba.

(153) In mystical union the unity of Being is revealed: worshipper and Worshipped are distinguished only as aspects of one reality.

(156) Those who interpret this verse according to the doctrine of Ibnu 'l-'Arabí take the meaning to be "I was pledged to love God before the creation of Time when all things, though not yet objectified in material forms, existed as objects of knowledge in the Divine essence." God did not become manifest to His creatures until at the word "Be!" they issued forth from the Divine essence (which from this point of view is named "the world of command") into the world of creation. It is by no means certain, however, that Ibnu 'l-Fáriḍ regarded the human spirit as *eternally* pre-existent. Cf. Nallino, *op. cit.* p. 535 foll. "The covenant" refers to the pledge taken by every soul, before its earthly existence, to love God for evermore. See note on verse 69.

(158) "The world of command" is the invisible or intelligible world.

(159) Divine Love enables the mystic to rid himself of the attributes of self which hinder him from attaining to union with God.

(160) The complement and consummation of death to self (*faná*) is everlasting life in God (*baqá*). In this life the lost attributes are restored, but "with an increase," *i.e.* they have been "deified" and display themselves in the eternal process of Divine manifestation, "going out of me," *i.e.* from the undifferentiated Unity, "unto me," *i.e.* to Unity in plurality, and again re-

(161) And in my contemplation (of the Divine essence) I beheld myself endowed with the attributes by which I was veiled from myself during my occultation,

(162) And I saw that I was indubitably she whom I loved, and that for this reason my self had referred me to myself.

(163) My self had been distraught with love for itself unawares, though in my contemplation it was not ignorant of the truth of the matter.

Continuing Ibnu 'l-Fáriḍ shows that the railer and the slanderer (who symbolise respectively the sensual and intellectual attributes of the self) are in reality one with the Lover-Beloved. He next explains more fully what he meant when he spoke of the passing-away (*faná*) of these attributes (*v.* 159), and describes the successive stages by which his self (*nafs*) was gradually stripped bare of all the affections that stood between him and a purely disinterested love.

(168) I sought to approach her by sacrificing my self, reckoning upon her as my recompense and not hoping for any (other) reward from her; and she drew me nigh.

(169) I offered readily what was mine (of promised bliss) in the world to come and what she might peradventure give to me (of her grace),

(170) And with entire disinterestedness I put behind me any regard for that (self-sacrifice), for I was not willing that my self should be my beast of burden.

(171) I sought her with poverty, but since the attribute of poverty enriched me I threw away both my poverty and my wealth.

turning "from me," *i.e.* from the One in the Many to the One who remains when the Many have passed away.

(161) "In my contemplation," *i.e.* in the state of *baqá* after *faná*. "During my occultation," *i.e.* in the state preceding *faná*, when the mystic is veiled by his phenomenal attributes from his real self.

(162) Cf. the Tradition, "He who knows himself knows his Lord."

(163) So long as the "self" is attached to its desires, it is blind to its real nature, which is only revealed to it when God is the sole object of contemplation.

(170) *I.e.* "I was unwilling to attain my goal by means of anything directly or indirectly connected with self." The commentator quotes the Tradition, "Honour the animals which ye offer in sacrifice, for they will carry you across the Bridge of Ṣiráṭ (into Paradise)."

(171) He who is truly poor (in the mystical sense) does not regard himself as possessing anything whatever—not even poverty.

(172) My throwing away my poverty and riches assured to me the merit of my quest: therefore I discarded my merit,

(173) And in my discarding it my own welfare appeared: my reward was she who rewarded me, nothing else.

(174) And through her, not through myself, I began to guide unto her those who by themselves had lost the right ways; and 'twas she that (really) guided them.

The following verses (175–196) show the poet as a director of souls, preaching unselfishness, poverty, humility, and repentance; exhorting his disciple to lose no time and to beware of saying "To-morrow I will work"; bidding him shun vainglory and ambition; pointing out that the true gnostic is silent inasmuch as the mysteries revealed to him are incommunicable. All self-activity, all self-consciousness, must be renounced.

(194) Be sight (not a seer) and look; be hearing (not a hearer) and retain (what is heard); be a tongue (not a speaker) and speak, for the way of union (with the Beloved) is the best.

The detachment or isolation (*tafríd*) of the soul from all desires and affections costs bitter pain.

(197) Formerly my soul was reproachful: when I obeyed her, she disobeyed me, or if I disobeyed her, she was obedient to me.

(198) Therefore I brought her to that of which (even) a part was harder than death and I fatigued her that she might give me rest,

(199) So that she came to endure whatever burden I laid upon her, and if I lightened it she grieved.

(200) And I loaded her with tasks, nay, I took care that she should load herself with them, until I grew fond of my tribulation.

(172–3) It is not enough to regard one's self as possessing nothing: the thought that such a state of mind is meritorious must be eliminated.

(194) In the unitive state (*jam'*) it is God that sees, hears, and speaks through the mystic, who has become His organ of sight, hearing, and speech.

(197) The epithet "reproachful" (*lawwáma*) is applied to the soul whilst it is still engaged in the struggle with the passions; after these have been vanquished, it is called "calm" (*muṭma'inna*). During the former condition the soul is disobedient (sinful) if its desires are complied with, and obedient (virtuous) if they are thwarted.

(201) And in correcting her I deprived her of every pleasure by removing her from her habits, and she became calm.

(202) No terror remained before her but I confronted it, so long as I beheld that my soul therein was not yet purged,

(203) And every stage that I traversed in my progress was an *'ubúdiyya* which I fulfilled through *'ubúda*.

When the soul is completely denuded of affections it is made one with God. In the first verse of the following passage the feminine pronoun, which has hitherto referred to the soul either as reproaching itself for its actions and desires or as being in passionless calm, undergoes a change of meaning, so that "she," who stood for an individual, now denotes the Universal Self.

(204) Until then I had been enamoured of her, but when I renounced my desire, she desired me for herself and loved me,

(205) And I became a beloved, nay, one loving himself: this is not like what I said before, that my soul is my beloved.

(206) Through her I went forth from myself to her and came not back to myself: one like me does not hold the doctrine of return.

(207) And in generous pride I detached my soul from my going forth, and consented not that she should consort with me again,

(208) And I was made absent from (unconscious of) the detachment of my soul, so that in my presence (union with God) I was not pushed (disturbed) by showing any attribute (of individuality).

(203) Both *'ubúdiyya* and *'ubúda* (which literally signify the relation of a slave to his master) are phases of mystical devotion. In *'ubúdiyya* the mystic is concerned with the *means* of drawing nigh to God, *e.g.* with asceticism, quietism, and the like; in *'ubúda*, which is the fulfilment and consummation of *'ubúdiyya*, he rises above egoism and loses himself in the will of his Lord.

(204–5) In ceasing to will for himself the mystic becomes an object of the Divine will, *i.e.* a beloved, and that which loves him is no other than his real self. The words "my soul (self) is my beloved" refer to verse 98 ("Thou art sworn to love, but to love of self"), in which the mystic is described as loving himself, because he still clings to his individuality.

(206–8) Separation from the self, *i.e.* union with God, is brought about by Divine grace, not by any act of the self.

In a passage of high eloquence and beauty the poet endeavours to analyse his experience of the unitive state and reveal the mystery, so far as it can be expressed in a symbolic form.

(209) Lo, I will unfold the beginning of my oneness and will bring it to its end in a lowly descent from my exaltation.

(210) In unveiling herself she unveiled Being to mine eye, and I saw her with my sight in every seen thing.

(211) And when she appeared, I was brought to contemplate that in me that is hidden, and through the displaying of my secret place I found there that I was she;

(212) And my existence vanished in my contemplation and I became separated from the existence of my contemplation—effacing it, not maintaining it.

(213) And in the sobriety following my intoxication I retained the object which, during the effacement of my self-existence, I contemplated in her by whom it was revealed,

(214) So that in the sobriety after self-effacement I was none other than she, and when she unveiled herself my essence became endued with my essence.

(215) When it (my essence) is not called "two," my attributes are hers, and since we are one, her outward aspect is mine.

(216) If she be called, 'tis I who answer, and if I am summoned,

(209) Perfect oneness ultimately involves "a descent from union (*jam'*) to separation (*tafriqa*) and from the Essence to the Attributes, that the saint may repair the disorder of the phenomenal world and instruct those who seek the Truth, yet without losing real union with the Divine Essence; nay, he must unite in himself both union and separation, both Essence and Attributes" (K.). Cf. my *Mystics of Islam*, p. 163, and note on verse 218 *infra*.

(210) The beginning of oneness with God is God's revelation of Himself to the mystic, which causes *faná*, so that he sees the unveiled face of God (*i.e.* Real Being) in the mirror of phenomena.

(212) "I became separated from the existence of my contemplation," *i.e.* "I passed away from (became unconscious of) my contemplation."

(213) The object retained and unceasingly contemplated in the sobriety (mystical clairvoyance) following intoxication (ecstasy) is the inward and real self—the hidden "I" which in the preceding moment of ecstasy was contemplated in God. Cf. note on *vv.* 233–5.

(214) Intoxication or self-effacement is only the beginning of oneness (*ittiḥád*). Perfect oneness is attained in sobriety, when the self, having been restored to consciousness, knows itself as the Divine Essence which reveals itself to itself. This is the state of "abiding after passing-away" (*al-baqá ba'd al-faná*).

(216) Cf. p. 127 *supra*.

she answers the one who calls me, and cries "*Labbayk!*" ("At thy service!").

(217) And if she speak, 'tis I who converse. Likewise, if I tell a story, 'tis she that tells it.

(218) The pronoun of the second person has gone out of use between us, and by its removal I am raised above the sect who separate (the One from the Many).

(219) Now if, through want of judgment, thy understanding allow not the possibility of regarding two as one and decline to affirm it,

(220) I will cause indications of it, which are hidden from thee, to demonstrate it like expressions that are clear to thee;

(221) And, since this is not the time for ambiguity, I will explain it by means of two strange illustrations, one derived from hearing and one from sight,

(222) And I will establish what I say by evidence, showing forth a parable as one who speaks the truth—for Truth is my stay—

(223) The parable of a woman smitten with catalepsy, by whose mouth, whilst she is possessed by a spirit, another—not she—gives news to thee;

(224) And from words uttered on her tongue by a tongue that is not hers the evidences of the signs are shown to be true,

(225) Since it is known as a fact that the utterer of the wondrous sayings which thou heardest is another than she, though in the (material) sense she uttered them.

(218) Literally, "the *ta* (of the 2nd person singular in the past tense of the Arabic verb) has been removed (or 'has become *tu*, the sign of the 1st person singular') between us," *i.e.* "each of us is the 'I' of the other." "The sect who separate" are those who look at things from the aspect of separation (*farq* or *tafriqa* as opposed to union, *jam'*), so that, for example, they view their acts of worship as proceeding from themselves, not as being done by God in them.

(221) The illustration drawn from hearing (oral tradition) is the Prophet's vision of Gabriel in the form of Diḥya (verse 280 foll.), while the parallel analogy from ocular experience is the case of "a woman smitten with catalepsy" (verse 223 foll.).

(223–5) It may be worth while to summarise the commentator's explanation of the argument. *Ittiḥád*, he says, means that Absolute Being overwhelms the being of the individual creature so as entirely to deprive him of the exercise of his faculties: he *appears* to will and act, when he is really the organ through which God wills and acts. To the objection that such a thing is impossible the poet replies by pointing to what occurs in catalepsy; and he makes a woman the subject of his illustration because the

(226) Hadst thou been one, thou wouldst have come to feel intuitively the truth of what I said;

(227) But, didst thou but know it, thou wert devoted to secret polytheism with a soul that strayed from the guidance of the Truth;

(228) And he in whose love the unification of his beloved is not accomplished falls by his polytheism into the fire of separation from his beloved.

(229) Naught save otherness marred this high estate of thine, and if thou wilt efface thyself thy claim to have achieved it will be established indeed.

(230) Thus was I myself for a time, ere the covering was lifted. Having no clairvoyance, I still clave to dualism,

(231) Now losing (myself) and being united (with God) through contemplation, now finding (God) and being sundered (from myself) through ecstasy.

(232) My intellect, through being attached to my presence (with myself), was separating me (from God), while my depriva-

female sex, on account of the weakness of their minds and their general passivity (*infi'ál*), are especially liable to seizures of that kind. Now, the body of a woman suffering from catalepsy is evidently controlled by the *Jinn*: her own personality (*nafs*) is, for the time, defunct (*ma'zúl*): otherwise, how could she foretell future events and speak in a language that she never knew, *e.g.* in Arabic though she be a foreigner, and in a foreign language though she be an Arab? If this relation can exist between a woman and a Jinní, notwithstanding the difference of their forms and qualities and notwithstanding that both of them are helpless contingent beings, surely none will deny that it may exist between the omnipotent Creator and the creature whom He has created in His own image.

(226) Although the possibility of *ittiḥád* can be proved from analogy, knowledge of its real nature depends on the unity (*waḥda*) or simplification (*ifrád*) of the self which is effected by stripping it of attributes and relations. Cf. verse 197 foll. K. renders *munázalat*[an] by "intuition" (contrasted with logical demonstration), but the word may be used here in its ordinary sense, namely, "a permanent state of mystical feeling." See the Glossary to my edition of the *Kitáb al-Luma'*, p. 151.

(227) "Secret polytheism" (*shirk*), *i.e.* latent self-regard which hinders the mystic from becoming entirely one with God.

(229) "Otherness" is equivalent to "polytheism," *i.e.* thinking of one's self as something other than God.

(231–2) These verses can hardly be translated. The language of Islamic mysticism abounds in pairs of correlative terms, *e.g.* "losing" and "finding," "presence" and "absence," "intoxication" and "sobriety," which are not merely artificial antitheses but express the fact that, as has been well said, "the inner life of the Ṣúfí is in large measure a swinging to and fro between opposite poles" (R. Hartmann, *Al-Ḳuschairís Darstellung des Ṣûfîtums*, p. 8). Cf. note on *vv.* 481–2.

tion (of individuality), through the enravishment of my self-existence by my absence (from myself), was uniting me (with God).

(233) I used to think that sobriety was my nadir, and that intoxication was my way of ascent to her (the Beloved), and that my self-effacement was the farthest goal I could reach;

(234) But when I cleared the film from me, I saw myself restored to consciousness, and mine eye was refreshed by the (Divine) Essence;

(235) And at the time of my second separation I was enriched by a recovery from my impoverishment (self-loss) in drunkenness, so that (now) my union (*jam'*) is like my unity (*waḥda*, individuality = *tafriqa*, separation).

(236) Therefore mortify thyself that thou mayst behold in thee and from thee a peace beyond what I have described—a peace born of a feeling of calm.

(233–5) For the expressions used in *v.* 233 cf. Kor. 53, 9 and note on *v.* 729. Here Ibnu 'l-Fáriḍ, writing as an adept, declares that the state of ecstatic rapture, which Ṣúfís call "intoxication" and "self-effacement," is inferior to the subsequent state of conscious clairvoyance, which they describe as "sobriety." Cf. *Kashf al-Maḥjúb*, transl., p. 184 foll. I cannot agree with Prof. Nallino, who thinks (*op. cit.* p. 73) that "sobriety" in *v.* 233 refers to normal and non-mystical consciousness. The meaning of the words "but when I cleared the film from me, etc." is explained by the commentator thus: "Existence (*wujúd*) is a veil (*ḥijáb* = *ghayn*, film) in the beginning of the mystic life, and also in its middle stage, but not in its end. The mystic is veiled in the beginning by the outward aspect of existence (*i.e.* created things) from its inward aspect (*i.e.* God), while in the middle stage (*i.e.* the period of 'intoxication' during which he has no consciousness of phenomena) he is veiled by its inward aspect (God) from its outward aspect (created things). But when he has reached his goal (*i.e.* 'sobriety'), neither do created things veil him from God nor does God veil him from created things, but God reveals Himself to the mystic in both His aspects at once (*i.e.* both as the Creator and as the universe of created things), so that he sees with his bodily eye the beauty of the Divine Essence manifested under the attribute of externality."

The meaning of "separation" (*farq* or *tafriqa*) has been explained in the note on verse 218: it is the state in which the mystic is conscious of himself as an individual. Passing away from himself in the ecstasy of "intoxication," he enters into the state of "union" (*jam'*) in which he is conscious of nothing but God. According to Ibnu 'l-Fáriḍ, the final and supreme degree of "oneness" (*ittiḥád*) consists, not in "intoxication," but in "sobriety," *i.e.* the return to consciousness, "the second separation," when the mystic (who in the former "separation" knew himself as "other than God") knows himself as the subject and object of all action (cf. verses 237–8), and perceives that "union" and "separation" are the same thing seen from different points

(237) After my self-mortification I saw that he who brought me to behold and led me to my (real) self was I; nay, that I was my own example,

(238) And that my standing (at 'Arafát) was a standing before myself; nay, that my turning (towards the Ka'ba) was towards myself. Even so my prayer was to myself and my Ka'ba from myself.

(239) Be not, then, beguiled by thy comeliness, self-conceited, given over to the confusion of folly;

(240) And forsake the error of separation, for union will result in thy finding the right way, the way of those who vied with each other in seeking oneness (*ittiḥád*);

(241) And declare the absoluteness of beauty and be not moved to deem it finite by thy longing for a tinselled gaud;

(242) For the charm of every fair youth or lovely woman is lent to them from Her beauty.

(243) 'Twas She that crazed Qays, the lover of Lubná; ay, and every enamoured man, like Laylá's Majnún or 'Azza's Kuthayyir.

(244) Every one of them passionately desired Her attribute (Absolute Beauty) which She clothed in the form of a beauty that shone forth in a beauty of form.

(245) And this was only because She appeared in phenomena. They supposed that these (phenomena) were other than She, whilst it was She that displayed Herself therein.

(246) She showed Herself by veiling Herself (in them), and She was hidden by the objects in which She was manifested, assuming tints of diverse hue in every appearance.

of view. The interpretation of the concluding words in *v.* 235 is doubtful. Taking *jam'* in a non-mystical sense, we might translate: "My plurality is like my unity."

(237) Self-mortification prepares the mystic for contemplation of God but does not precede it as the cause precedes the effect. In contemplation there is no duality, but only God, who reveals Himself to Himself. The poet describes this state of "union" (*jam'*) symbolically in *vv.* 239–64.

(238) The "standing" on Mt 'Arafát near Mecca is one of the ceremonies observed by the pilgrims.

(240) "Separation" and "union" (*farq* and *jam'*) are used in the technical sense which has been noted (cf. verses 218 and 233–5).

(241) The "tinselled gaud" is beauty regarded as an attribute of phenomena, *i.e.* beauty of form.

(246) The commentator illustrates this doctrine—that phenomena reveal or conceal Absolute Being according to the measure of spiritual

(247) At the first creation She became visible to Adam in the form of Eve before the relation of motherhood,

(248) And he loved Her, that by means of Her he might become a father and that the relation of sonship might be brought into existence through husband and wife.

(249) This was the beginning of the love of the manifestations for one another, when as yet there was no enemy to estrange them with (mutual) hate.

(250) And She ceased not to reveal and conceal Herself for some (divinely ordained) cause in every age according to the appointed times.

(251) She was appearing to Her lovers in every form of disguise in shapes of wondrous beauty,

(252) Now as Lubná, anon as Buthayna, and sometimes She was called 'Azza, who was so dear (to Kuthayyir).

(253) They (fair women) are not other than She; no, and they never were. She hath no partner in Her beauty.

(254) Just as She showed to me Her beauty clad in the forms of others, even so in virtue of oneness (*ittiḥád*)

(255) Did I show myself to Her in every lover enthralled by youth or woman of rare beauty;

(256) For, although they preceded me (in time), they were not other than I in their passion, inasmuch as I was prior to them in the nights of eternity;

insight with which they are regarded—by the following parable (cf. Plato's allegory of the prisoners in the cave in Book VII of the *Republic*). Imagine a house with no aperture except glass windows of various colours and shapes, so that when the sun falls on them, beams of corresponding shape and colour are reflected within. Imagine, further, that in the house are a number of persons who have never gone outside and have never seen the sun but have only been told that it is one simple universal light possessing neither colour nor form. Some, perceiving that the reflected beams resemble the glass in form and colour, will not recognise them as sunbeams. Others will divine the truth, namely, that those beams are the light of the sun endued with form and colour by the medium through which it is seen and preserving its unity unimpaired amidst all variety of appearance.

(249) The "enemy" is Satan, who caused Adam and Eve to eat the forbidden fruit, whereupon God said to them, "Get ye down (from Paradise), the one of you a foe to the other" (Kor. 2, 34).

(256) The commentator quotes the saying of the Prophet, "We are the last and the first," *i.e.* the last in material time, the first in spiritual time. Absolute Being, though logically prior to phenomena, is essentially identical with them.

(257) Nor are they other than I in my passion, but I became visible in them for the sake of clothing myself in every guise,

(258) Now as Qays, anon as Kuthayyir, and sometimes I appeared as Jamíl who loved Buthayna.

(259) In them I displayed myself outwardly and veiled myself inwardly. Marvel, then, at a revelation by means of a mask!

(260) The loved women and their lovers—'tis no infirm judgment—were manifestations in which we (my Beloved and I) displayed our (attributes of) love and beauty.

(261) Every lover, I am he, and She is every lover's beloved, and all (lovers and loved) are but the names of a vesture,

(262) Names of which I was the object in reality, and 'twas I that was made apparent to myself by means of an invisible soul.

(263) I was ever She, and She was ever I, with no difference; nay, my essence loved my essence.

(264) There was nothing in the world except myself beside me, and no thought of beside-ness occurred to my mind.

Having advanced in *ittiḥád* to a point where the "I" is indistinguishable from God, Ibnu 'l-Fárid begins the promised sequel—"a lowly descent from my exaltation" (see *v.* 209). He tells how he returned from the freedom of ecstasy to the bondage of piety, how he occupied himself with works of devotion and ascetic practices. He then makes a solemn declaration that his coming back to the normal life of the mystic was not due to any selfish motive, such as fear of disrepute or hope of honour, but was dictated solely by his anxiety to protect from attack the friends whom he revered. These friends (*awliyá*) were, no doubt, his spiritual masters or other Ṣúfís intimately associated with him. What was the danger which he foresaw and in which he would not have them involved? As the following verses show, it was the charge of heresy in

(259) Absolute Being manifests its attributes through the phenomenal forms which conceal its essence.

(260–4) Love and beauty are aspects of the self-manifestation of the "invisible soul" underlying all phenomena, and since that soul is the One Real Being there can be no essential difference between the lover and the object of his love. The mystic who has attained to "the intoxication of union" (*sukru 'l-jam'*) has no thought of "beside-ness," *i.e.* for him nothing exists beside his unconditioned self, which is God.

respect of a doctrine abominable to all Moslems—the doctrine of incarnation (*ḥulúl*).

(277) If I recant my words, "I am She," or if I say—and far be it from one like me to say it!—that She became incarnate (*ḥallat*) in me, (then I shall deserve to die the death).

(278) I am not referring thee to anything unseen; no, nor to anything absurd which deprives me of my power (to demonstrate its truth).

(279) Since I am stablished on the Name of the Real (God) how should the false tales of error frighten me?

(280) Mark now! Gabriel, the trusted (messenger), came in the shape of Diḥya to our Prophet in the beginning of his prophetic inspiration.

(281) Tell me, was Gabriel Diḥya when he appeared in a human form to the true Guide,

(282) Whose knowledge surpassed that of those beside him inasmuch as he knew unambiguously what it was that he saw?

(283) He saw an angel sent to him with a message, while the others saw a man who was treated with respect as being the Prophet's companion;

(284) And in the truer of the two visions I find a hint that removes my creed far from the doctrine of incarnation.

(285) In the Koran there is mention of "covering" (*labs*), and it cannot be denied, for I have not gone beyond the double authority of the Book and the Apostolic Traditions.

(277) "I am She," *i.e.* the doctrine of *ittiḥád*.

(278) Addressing the reader, Ibnu 'l-Fáriḍ says, "The God to whom I direct you is neither outside of the world and yourself nor within you in the sense of 'incarnate,' which is an absurdity."

(279) "False tales of error," *i.e.* baseless accusations of heresy.

(280) Gabriel, through whom the Koran was revealed to Mohammed, is said to have assumed the shape of Diḥya al-Kalbí, described as a very handsome man, on more than one occasion.

(281–4) As Gabriel was not incarnate in Diḥya, so God is not incarnate in the mystic "united" with Him.

(284–5) *Labs* (the act of covering) is attributed to God in the Koran (cf. 6, 9; 50, 14) and is implied in a group of traditions which record that Mohammed said, "I saw my Lord in such and such a form." For the meaning of the term, see A. J. Wensinck, *The Etymology of the Arabic Djinn* (*Spirits*) in *Verslagen en Mededeelingen der Koninklijke Akademie van Wetenschappen*, Afd. Letterkunde, 5e Reeks, Deel IV (1920), p. 506 foll., who says, "The action of covering is conceived in this way, that the spirit comes upon a man, takes

Ibnu 'l-Fáriḍ, no longer speaking in his own person but as the Logos (Mohammed) or as one merged in the Absolute, of which nothing—not even Love and Oneness—can be predicated, warns his disciple that he must not aim so high: let him fix his eyes on the glory of Love, and he will far excel those who worship God in hope or fear.

(286) I give thee knowledge. If thou desirest its unveiling, come into my way and begin to follow my law,

(287) For the fountain of Ṣaddá springs from a water whose abundant well is with me: therefore tell me not of a mirage in a wilderness!

(288) And take (thy knowledge) from a sea into which I plunged, while those of old stopped on its shore, observing reverence towards me.

(289) The text, "*Meddle not with the substance of the orphan*" (Kor. 6, 153), alludes symbolically to the palm of a hand that was holden when it essayed (to draw water).

(290) And except me none hath gained aught thereof, save only a youth who in constraint or ease never ceased to tread in my footprints.

(291) Stray not darkly, then, from the tracks of my journeying,

its abode in him and overpowers him, so that he is no longer himself but the spirit that is upon or within him." The monistic interpretation of *labs* adopted by Ibnu 'l-Fáriḍ differs essentially from *ḥulúl*. In the former case, God creates the "disguise" of phenomenality in order thereby to manifest Himself to Himself, and nothing exists beside Him; whereas *ḥulúl* (the "infusion" of the Divine element into the human) denotes a relation of immanence comparable to that of spirit and body.

(287) Ṣaddá was proverbial for the sweetness and wholesomeness of its water: cf. the saying, "Water, but not like Ṣaddá." The poet means that his knowledge flows from contemplation of the Divine Essence, so that he need not follow the mirage of intellectual speculation.

(288–9) The "sea" is an emblem of the Beatific Vision which was denied to Moses (Kor. 7, 139) but was granted to Mohammed (Kor. 53, 9). Ibnu 'l-Fáriḍ interprets the text, "*Meddle not with the substance of the orphan*," as an admonition to Moses that he must not encroach upon Mohammed's unique prerogative. When God revealed Himself in glory to Mt Sinai, Moses fell in a swoon; and on recovering his senses he heard a voice saying, "This Vision is not vouchsafed to thee, but to an orphan who shall come after thee." The orphan (*yatím*) is Mohammed (Kor. 93, 6). Cf. *Kashf al-Maḥjúb*, pp. 186 and 381.

(290) The commentator identifies the "youth" with 'Alí b. Abí Ṭálib, the Prophet's cousin and son-in-law. According to the belief of the Ṣúfís, 'Alí received from the Prophet an esoteric doctrine which was communicated to him alone.

and fear the blindness of preferring another to me, and go in my very path;

(292) For the valley of Her friendship, O comrade of sober heart, is in the province of my command and falls under my governance,

(293) And the realm of the high degrees of Love is mine, the realities (thereof) are my army, and all lovers are my people.

(294) Love hath passed away! Lo, I am severed from it as one who deems it a veil. Desire is below mine high estate,

(295) And I have crossed Passion's boundary, for Love is (to me) even as Hate, and the goal that I reached in my ascension to Oneness is become my point of departure.

(296) But do thou be happy with love, for (thereby) thou hast been made a chief over the best of God's creatures who serve Him (by devotion and piety) in every nation.

(297) Win those heights and vaunt thyself above an ascetic who was exalted by works and by a soul that purged itself (of worldly lusts);

(298) And pass beyond one heavily laden (with exoteric knowledge)—who, if his burden were lightened, would be of little weight—one charged with traditional authorities and intellectual wisdom;

(299) And take to thyself through kinship (of love) the heritage of the most sublime gnostic, who made it his care to prefer (above all else) that his aspiration should produce an effect (upon mankind);

(300) And haughtily sweep the clouds with thy skirts—the

(293) "The realities" (*al-ma'ání*) are probably the real content of all expressions that belong to the language of love.

(294–5) To retain consciousness of an attribute is to be limited by it; to pass from it is to escape from limitation and break through to the Absolute, where all contraries are reconciled. In verse 294 some read *fata 'l-ḥubbi*, "O thrall of love," instead of *fani 'l-ḥubbu*.

(296–8) The lover of God is nearer to Him than the ascetic, theologian, or philosopher.

(299) "The most sublime gnostic," *i.e.* Mohammed, from whom the Ṣúfís claim to have inherited not only their knowledge of religion (*'ilm*) but also their mystical knowledge (*ma'rifa*). In the highest degree of gnosis union (*jam'*) is combined with separation (*tafriqa*), so that the mystic while continuing in the unitive state comes down once more to the world of plurality and uses his spiritual powers for the benefit and instruction of his fellow-creatures.

skirts of an impassioned lover which in his union (with the Beloved) trail over the top of the Milky Way!

(301) And traverse the various degrees of oneness and do not join a party that lost their lifetime in (attachment to) something besides.

(302) For its single champion is a host, while all others are but a handful who were vanquished by the most convincing of testimonies.

(303) Therefore make that which it (the term "oneness") signifies thy means of access (to God) and live in it, or else die its captive, and follow a community which attained the primacy therein.

(304) Thou art worthier of this glory than one who strives and exerts himself in hope (of reward) and in fear (of punishment).

(305) 'Tis not marvellous that thou shouldst shake thy sides (boastfully) before him in the sweetest delight and the completest joy,

(306) Since the attributes related to it (to Oneness)—how many a man have they chosen out in obscurity! and its names—how many a one have they raised to renown!

(307) Yet thou, in the degree (of union) to which thou hast attained, art remote from me: the Pleiades have no connexion with the earth.

(308) Thou hast been brought to thy Sinai and hast reached a plane higher than thy soul had ever imagined;

(309) But this is thy limit: stop here, for wert thou to advance a step beyond it, thou wouldst be consumed by a brand of fire.

Leaving his disciple in "the intoxication of union" (*sukru 'l-jam'*), with an emphatic warning not to exceed the measure of his spiritual capacity, Ibnu 'l-Fáriḍ depicts from his own experience the unitive life in its perfect and final development, which is known technically as "the sobriety of union" (*ṣaḥwu 'l-jam'*). Cf. the notes on *vv.* 233–5, 260–4, and 326–7.

(310) My degree is of such a height that a man who has not

(302) An allusion to Kor. 2, 250: "How many a little band hath overcome a great army by the permission of Allah!"

(303) "Or else die its captive," *i.e* "even though you fail to attain to oneness, at least pursue it until you die." *Mu'anndhu* ("its captive") may also mean "pining for it" and is so explained by K.

reached it may still be deemed happy; but the state for which I am deemed happy transcends thy degree.

(311) All men are the sons of Adam, (and I am as they) save that I alone amongst my brethren have attained to the sobriety of union.

(312) My hearing is like that of Kalím (Moses) and my heart is informed (about God) by the most excellent (*aḥmad*) vision of an eye like that of him who is most excellent (Aḥmad = Mohammed).

(313) And my spirit is a spirit to all the spirits (of created beings); and whatsoever thou seest of beauty in the universe flows from the bounty of my nature.

(314) Leave, then, to me (and do not ascribe to any one else) the knowledge with which I alone was endowed before my appearance (in the phenomenal world), while (after my appearance) amongst created beings my friends knew me not (as I really am).

(315) Do not give me the name of "lover" (*muríd*) amongst them (my friends), for even he who is rapt by Her and is called Her "beloved" (*murád*) hath need of my protection;

(316) And let names of honour fall from me and pronounce them not, babbling foolishly, for they are but signs fashioned by one whom I made;

(317) And take back my title of "gnostic," for according to the Koran, if thou approvest people's calling each other names, thou wilt be loathed.

(312) *I.e.* "I hear God with my ear, as Moses did when God said to him 'Thou shalt not see Me' (Kor. 7, 139), and see Him with my eye, as Mohammed saw Him." Moses is called Kalím or Kalímu'llah because God spoke to him (*kallamahu*). As regards Mohammed, cf. *Kashf al-Maḥjúb*, transl., p. 186.

(313 foll.) Here Ibnu 'l-Fáriḍ speaks, as it were, out of the depths of his consciousness of God. According to the commentator, he hints that he is the Quṭb. See p. 194 *supra*.

(314) God created the world in order that He might be known: before the creation He alone knew Himself, and after it His friends (the prophets and saints) did not know Him with His own eternal knowledge of Himself.

(315) See note on *vv.* 204–5 for the distinction between *muríd* and *murád*. Even the latter, as an object of Divine protection, is other than God and therefore not to be identified with the mystic who is wholly one with Him.

(316) A "name of honour" (*kunya*) is one of the class of names which begin with the word *Abú* (father) and are used as a mark of respect to the person addressed. "One whom I made," *i.e.* Man, whose language is meaningless as applied to God.

(317) Cf. Kor. 49, 11. The poet includes the name "gnostic" among *alqáb* (which is here equivalent to "nicknames" or "ill names") because the Absolute suffers a limitation when it is described by any title, however exalted.

(318) The least of my followers—the virgin brides of gnosis were led home to the eye of his heart.

(319) He plucked the fruit of gnosis from a branch of perception that grew by his following me and springs from the root of my nature;

(320) So that, if he is questioned about any (spiritual) matter, he brings forth wondrous sayings which are too sublime for comprehension, nay, too subtle for the mind to conceive.

(321) And amongst them (my friends) do not call me by the epithet of "favourite" (*muqarrab*), which in virtue of my union (with God) I deem to be a sinful severance;

(322) For my meeting is my parting, and my nearness is my being far, and my fondness is my aversion, and my end is my beginning,

(323) Since for Her sake by whom I have disguised myself —and 'tis but myself I mean—I have cast off my name and my style and my name of honour,

(324) And have journeyed beyond where those of old stood still, and where minds perished misled by (the search after intellectual) gains.

(325) I have no attributes, for an attribute is a mark (of substance). Similarly, a name is a sign (of an object). Therefore, if thou wouldst allude to me, use metaphors or epithets.

(326) From "I am She" I mounted to where is no "to," and I perfumed (phenomenal) existence by my returning;

(318–20) The argument is: "Gnostic," a name appropriate to the meanest of my disciples, is a term of abuse in relation to me, who am the source of all gnosis.

(321) *Muqarrab*, literally "one who is brought near (to God)." Ṣúfís often use this term, which is borrowed from the Koran, to describe the highest class of the saints. See *Kitáb al-Luma'*, ch. 43. The *muqarrab* prefers union to separation, whereas in perfect union there are no contraries. Cf. note on *vv.* 294–5.

(323) *I.e.* the name "She," or "Beloved," disguises me, for it really signifies the One Essence, which is my true and eternal self.

(324) The intellect moving in the world of relations and distinctions cannot reach the Absolute.

(326–7) Three stages of Oneness (*ittiḥád*) are distinguished here:

1. "I am She," *i.e.* union (*jam'*) without real separation (*tafriqa*), although the appearance of separation is maintained. This was the stage in which al-Ḥalláj said *Ana 'l-Ḥaqq*, "I am God."

2. "I am I," *i.e.* pure union without any trace of separation (in-

(327) And (I returned) from "I am I" for the sake of an esoteric wisdom and external laws which were instituted that I might call (the people to God).

(328) The goal of my disciple who was rapt to Her (in ecstasy) and the utmost limit reached by his masters is the point to which I advanced before my turning back;

(329) And the highest peak gained by those who thought themselves foremost is the lowest level that bears the mark of my tread;

(330) And the last pinnacle of that which is beyond indication, and where is no progress upwards (but only backwards)—*that* is where my first footstep fell!

(331) There is nothing existent but hath knowledge of my grace, nor aught in being but utters my praise.

(332) No wonder that I lord it over all who lived before me, since I have grasped the firmest stay (which is a verse) in (the chapter of the Koran entitled) *Ṭá-há*.

(333) My greeting to Her is metaphorical: in reality my salutation is from me to myself.

Here Ibnu 'l-Fáriḍ inserts in praise of his Beloved an ode of fifty-two verses (336–387) in the same metre and rhyme

dividuality). This stage is technically known as "the intoxication of union" (*sukru 'l-jam'*).

3. The "sobriety of union" (*ṣaḥwu 'l-jam'*), *i.e.* the stage in which the mystic returns from the pure oneness of the second stage to plurality in oneness and to separation in union and to the Law in the Truth, so that while continuing to be united with God he serves Him as a slave serves his lord and manifests the Divine Life in its perfection to mankind.

"Where is no 'to,'" *i.e.* the stage of "I am I," beyond which no advance is possible except by means of retrogression. In this stage the mystic is entirely absorbed in the undifferentiated oneness of God. Only after he has "returned," *i.e.* entered upon the third stage (plurality in oneness) can he communicate to his fellows some perfume (hint) of the experience through which he has passed. "An esoteric wisdom," *i.e.* the Divine providence manifested by means of the religious law. By returning to consciousness the "united" mystic is enabled to fulfil the law and to act as a spiritual director.

(328) "His masters," literally "his objects of desire" (*murádihi*), *i.e.* those eminent theosophists whom the disciple seeks to imitate, but who have not reached the highest degree of perfection.

(331) All created things glorify God with diverse tongues which are heard and understood by spiritual men. Cf. *The Mystics of Islam*, p. 64.

(332) *I.e.* "I have attained to perfection in *ittiḥád* through my faith in the verse (Kor. 20, 7): 'God, there is no god but He.'" This proves, according to the Ṣúfís, that nothing but God has a real existence.

as the rest of the *Tá'iyya*. Beautiful as this lyric interlude is and welcome for the relief which its warm colouring affords to imaginations fatigued by "the white radiance of eternity," it interrupts the course of the poem and may be omitted here.

After a short passage (*vv.* 388–393) concerning the "railer" and the "slanderer," whom the mystic when he regards them under the aspect of union (*jam'*) perceives to be really inspired by love, not by enmity, Ibnu 'l-Fáriḍ resumes his description of the unitive state at its supreme level, marked by the return from ecstasy to a new and enlarged consciousness of the One Reality which manifests itself in every form of thought and sense.

(394) And therein (in *ittiḥád*) are matters of which the veil was entirely raised for me by my recovery from intoxication, while they were screened from every one besides.

(395) A mystic can dispense with plain words and will understand me when I speak allusively on account of those who would trip me up.

(396) None may divulge them without making his lifeblood the forfeit, and in symbols there is a meaning that words cannot define.

(397) Now my exposition begins with the twain who sought to bring about my severance, albeit my union defies separation.

(398) Those twain are one with us (the Beloved and me) in inward union, though in outward separation we and they are counted as four.

(399) For truly I and She are one essence, while he who told tales of her and he who turned me away from her are attributes which appeared.

(396) The mysteries of Oneness cannot be revealed otherwise than symbolically: an open statement would not only cost the writer his life but would also fail to convey the meaning, which is too subtle to be expressed by direct explanation and definition.

(397) "The twain," *i.e.* the railer and the slanderer; cf. verse 51. "My union defies separation," because the mystic who has attained to permanent union (*ṣaḥwu 'l-jam'*) knows that all things in spite of their apparent plurality are really one.

(398-9) Under the aspect of union the Divine attributes are identical with the Essence: only in the realm of phenomena do they appear as particular modes of the Essence and distinct from it in respect of their particularisation.

(400) That one (the slanderer) helps the spirit, guiding it to its region for the sake of a contemplation which takes place in a spiritual mould;

(401) And this one (the railer) helps the soul, driving it to its companions for the sake of an existence which occurs in a material form.

(402) Whoever knows, as I do, (the real nature of) those figures, his doctrine in removing the perplexity of doubt (as to the Divine Unity) is unmixed with polytheism.

(403) My essence endowed with delights the whole sum of my worlds (of being) both in particular and in general, in order to replenish them with its all-embracing unity.

(404) And it bounteously poured forth its overflow when there was as yet no capacity for acquisition (of being), and it was capable (of overflow) before there was any preparation for receiving (the overflow).

(400) From the standpoint of "separation" (*farq*), the slanderer and the railer are types (cf. note on *v.* 51) of two influences which work upon the heart. The slanderer—literally, the spy whose affection for the Beloved impels him to prevent any rival from approaching her—is the spirit (*ruḥ*); the railer is the soul (*nafs*): in the language of theology the former is described as the Angel who inspires the heart with good thoughts; the latter as the Devil who tempts it with evil suggestions (see D. B. Macdonald, *The religious attitude and life in Islam*, p. 274 foll.). But in the sphere of union (*jam'*) there can be no duality: lover, beloved, railer and slanderer are so many aspects of the One Being. Here, then, the slanderer or the spirit (*rúḥ*) represents Universal Spirit, the first emanation from the Absolute; and the railer or the soul (*nafs*) stands for Universal Soul. [Cf. the introduction to K.'s commentary, p. 20 foll., where the First Intelligence, "the slanderer," is said to be the luminosity of Universal Spirit, and the Second Intelligence, "the railer," is said to be the luminosity of Universal Soul.] The human spirit is guided by Universal Spirit to its "region," *i.e.* the Divine Essence, while the human soul belongs to Universal Soul, which as the animating principle of the sensible world brings the soul into contact with its "companions," *i.e.* bodies.

(402) "Those figures," *i.e.* the Beloved, the lover, the railer, and the slanderer.

(403–4) In *v.* 403 I read *imdád*. The reading *amdád* gives the same sense, if taken (as it should be) as the plural, not of *madd*, but of *madad*. Cf. my *Selected Poems from the Díváni Shamsi Tabríz*, pp. 216 and 334. The process of emanation (*fayḍ*) by which Absolute Being diffuses itself does not depend on the existence of capacities for receiving that which is rayed forth. Plurality is the self-manifestation of the One, the irradiation whereby the One becomes visible to itself.

(405) The forms of existence were made happy by the Soul, and the spirits of (the plane of) contemplation were refreshed by the Spirit.

The inward oneness of the Essence with its attributes or emanations is now further illustrated by reference to what takes place in audition (*samá'*), when the mystic falling into ecstasy at the sound of music finds God, only to lose Him again as soon as the momentary transport has ebbed away.

(406) My twofold contemplation of a slanderer hastening to his region and a railer bestowing good advice on his companions

(407) Bears witness to my state in the *samá'*, a state caused by two things which draw me (to and fro), namely, the law of my abiding home and the law of the place where my sentence is passed.

(408) And my denial of being perplexed (with doubts touching *ittiḥád*) by the five external senses is established to be true by the agreement of the two images.

(409) Now, before (I come to) my purpose, let me tell thee the mystery of that which my soul received secretly from them (the external senses) and communicated (to the inward senses).

(410) Whenever the idea of beauty appears in any form, and

(405) "Made happy," *i.e.* endued with existence.

(406–7) "To his region"—cf. verse 400. The poet means to say that his contemplation of the Essence under the aspect of its two attributes symbolically described as the slanderer and the railer is analogous to his perception of oneness in the *samá'*: in each case the appearance of duality is illusory. His "state in the *samá'*," *i.e.* the state of agitation and suspense between "finding God" (*wujúd*) and "losing" Him (*faqd*), is the result of two diverse aspects which are inherent in the nature of the Essence itself. One of those aspects is "union" (*jam'*), *i.e.* the oneness in which plurality is non-existent or only potentially existent; the other aspect is "separation" (*tafriqa*) in which the Essence passes forth from its oneness in order that it may become conscious of itself. The former is the mystic's "abiding home." "The place where my sentence is passed," *i.e.* the phenomenal world, which the mystic, on coming forth from the state of "union" (*jam'*), judges to be the abode of "separation" (*tafriqa*).

(408) The unity of Being is affirmed by the correspondence existing between sense and spirit. The mystic finds God in every object perceived by the senses, so that the image of every object in his perception is identical with the image of God in his heart.

(409) "My purpose," *i.e.* to explain what is experienced in the *samá'*.

(410–12) These verses illustrate "the correspondence of the two images." Thought is inward sight and memory is inward hearing.

whenever one afflicted by sorrow raises a mournful cry in (reciting) the verses of a chapter of the Koran,

(411) My thought beholds Her with the eye of my phantasy, and my memory hears Her with the ear of my intelligence,

(412) And my mind brings Her in imagination before my soul, so that my understanding deems Her sensibly at my side,

(413) And I wonder at my drunkenness without wine, and am thrilled in the depths of my being by a joy that comes from myself,

(414) And my heart dances, and the trembling of my limbs doth clap its hands like a chanter, and my spirit is my musician.

(415) My soul never ceased to be fed with (spiritual) desires and to efface the (sensual) faculties by weakening them, until at last it waxed strong.

(416) Here I found all existing things allied to aid me—though the aid (really) came from myself—

(417) In order that every organ of sense might unite me with Her, and that my union might include every root of my hair,

(418) And that the veil of estrangement between us might be cast off, albeit I found it no other than friendship.

(419) Mark now—and do not hope to learn this by study—how the sense conveys to the soul by immediate revelation what She brings to light.

(420) When a north wind travelling by night from Her blows at dawn, its coolness recalls the thought of Her to my spirit,

(421) And mine ear is pleased when in the forenoon grey doves warbling and singing on the branches arouse it,

(422) And mine eye is gladdened if at eve flashes of lightning transmit and give it from Her to the pupil of mine eye,

(413–4) The ecstasy of vision and audition is not produced by an external cause, such as wine, dancing, and music, but is itself the mystic's dance and song.

(415 foll.) Perfect union with God depends on the strength of the soul, *i.e.* on its purification from sensuous impressions. But when the soul has been purified, it uses as a means of becoming united with God the same faculties which formerly hindered it from attaining its end. The poet says that this aid really comes from himself, because the senses cannot render it out of their own nature: the self must first be spiritualised, in order that through its organs all things may be perceived as essentially one, according to the doctrine of *ittiḥád*.

(418) "No other than friendship": cf. note on *v*. 82.

(420) There is only an allusion in this verse to the sense of smell, while the other four senses are mentioned explicitly in the verses which follow.

(421–4) "It" in these verses is "the thought of Her" (*dhikruhá*).

(423) And it is bestowed on my taste and touch by the wine-cups when they are passed round to me at night,

(424) And my heart conveys it as an inward thing to the mental faculties through the medium of the outward thing that was delivered by the bodily messengers (the senses).

(425) He that chants Her name in the assembly (of listeners) makes me present with Her, so that as I listen I behold Her with my whole being.

(426) My spirit soars towards the heaven whence it was breathed (into me), while my theatre of manifestation (my soul), which was fashioned by the spirit, stoops to its earthly peers.

(427) Part of me is pulled towards Her and part of me pulls towards itself, and in every pull there is a tug like giving up the ghost.

(428) The cause of this is my soul's recollecting its real nature from Her when She inspired it,

(429) So that it longed in the limbo of earth to hear the Divine call alone (uncontaminated by the call of the lower self), since both (the spiritual and the sensual natures) take hold of my bridle-reins.

(424) In Moslem psychology the heart (*qalb*) "suggests the inmost, most secret and genuine thoughts, the very basis of man's intellectual nature" (see D. B. Macdonald, *The religious attitude and life in Islam*, p. 221 foll.). It receives from the outer senses the outward idea of God, *viz.* the forms of sense-objects, and transmits the corresponding universal idea, *viz.* the essence and attributes of God, to the inner senses, *i.e.* to the cogitative, memorative, estimative, and apprehensive faculties. These two ideas are identical in so far as they are correlative aspects of Being. The mystic contemplates as pure reality that which he perceives objectively in the forms of phenomena. According to the commentator, the preposition which I have translated by "through the medium of" should have the meaning of "simultaneously with," *i.e.* the delivery of the sense-datum to the heart synchronises with its transmission by the heart to the intellectual faculties.

(425) Here the poet begins his promised explanation (which is based upon the foregoing theory) of his "state in the *samá'*." He says that, whilst listening to the music, he nevertheless contemplates God with his whole spiritual and sensuous self.

(426–9) These verses answer the question, Why does music agitate and transport those who hear it? Because, the poet replies, the higher and lower elements in man draw and are drawn in opposite directions. Man is led sometimes by the spirit (*rúḥ*), sometimes by the flesh (*nafs*); but music, in which God reveals Himself, brings back to him the recollection of what he was before he had a bodily existence: then he falls into ecstasy and his soul (*nafs*) struggles like a captive bird to escape from its cage.

(430) Concerning my state in audition a babe, even though he grow up to be dull, will inform thee by throwing it upon thy mind like (a flash of) inspiration or insight.

(431) When he moans because of the tight swaddling-clothes and restlessly yearns to be relieved from exceeding distress,

(432) He is soothed with lullabies, so that he lays aside all the weariness which came over him and listens to his soother like one attending silently,

(433) And the sweet words make him forget his bitter grief and remember the speech that passed in times of old,

(434) And by his state he explains the state of *samá'* (audition) and confirms the absence of imperfection from the mystic dance:

(435) When through the one that is hushing him he becomes distraught with longing and would fain fly to his first home,

(436) He is quieted by being rocked in his cradle as the hands of his nurse move it to and fro.

(437) I have felt, when She is called to mind by the beautiful tones of a reciter (of the Koran) or the piercing notes of a singer,

(438) As the sufferer feels in his agony when the angels of Death take to themselves his all.

(439) For one who feels pain in being driven to part (from his body) is like one who is pained by feeling (rapture) in his yearning after his (spiritual) companions:

(440) As the soul of the former had pity for that (body) in which it appeared, so my spirit soared to its high origins.

Having exhibited the phenomena of the *samá'* in their due relation to the doctrine of *ittiḥád*, Ibnu 'l-Fáriḍ returns to the region of the self-contained Unity which is sole actor on the universal stage.

(441) My spirit passed the gate which barred my going

(433) "The speech that passed in times (or 'covenants') of old"—see the notes on *vv.* 69 and 156.

(434–6) Many Ṣúfís looked with disfavour on the ecstatic dance, which is a well-known feature of the *samá'*. Cf. the saying, *al-raqṣ naqṣ*, "dancing is a fault." Ibnu 'l-Fáriḍ justifies it on the ground that it is an anodyne to the fever of the soul: its violent movements calm the agitating reminiscences awakened by music and rock the soul to rest.

(440) Cf. *vv.* 426–7. As death causes the lower soul (*nafs*) to grieve for the loss of its earthly home, so music causes the spirit (*rúḥ*) to grieve for the loss of its heavenly home.

(441) Elsewhere (*Díwán*, p. 217, l. 10) Ibnu 'l-Fáriḍ says: "If others are

beyond union (with the Beloved) and soared to where no barrier of union remained.

(442) He that like me makes it (this gate) his chosen quest, let him follow me and ride for it with firm resolution!

(443) Before entering it, I have plunged into how many a deep! wherefrom none that craved (spiritual) wealth was ever blest with a draught.

(444) I will show it to thee, if thou art resolved, in the mirror of my poesy, therefore turn the ear of insight to what I let fall.

(445) I cast aside from my speech the word "self-regard," and from my actions self-interest in any act;

(446) And my looking for fair recompense for my works, and my care to preserve my mystical states from the shame of suspicion,

(447) And my preaching—all these things I put away with firm resolution as one who is entirely disinterested; and my casting aside regard for my casting aside applies to each division.

(448) So my heart is a temple in which I dwell: in front of it (hindering approach) is the appearance from it of the attributes belonging to my veiledness.

(449) Amongst them my right hand is a pillar (corner-stone) that is kissed in myself, and because of the law in my mouth my

content with His image seen in dreams, I am not content even with being united to Him." In this verse (441) and also in the verse quoted he uses the word *wiṣál*, properly "conjunction." *Wiṣál*, *waṣl* and *ittiṣál* contain the idea of duality and are therefore inferior to *jam'* or complete union and *ittiḥád* or ἕνωσις. Cf. Nallino, *op. cit.* p. 60, note 1.

(443) The way to this gate is through the deeps of *faná*. Those who seek not God alone but spiritual wealth, *i.e.* good works and godly dispositions, desire the continuance of their phenomenal self-existence.

(445–7) These lines describe the poet's *ikhláṣ*, a term denoting freedom from every form of self-regard. Inasmuch as no one who is purely disinterested can attribute disinterestedness to himself, Ibnu 'l-Fáriḍ says that in every instance—words, deeds, works, and states—"he has cast aside regard for his casting aside," *i.e.* he is not disinterested (*mukhliṣ*) but unconscious of being disinterested (*mukhlaṣ*). See R. Hartmann, *Al-Ḳuschairîs Darstellung des Ṣûfîtums*, p. 17, and *Kitáb al-Luma'*, p. 218, l. 6 foll.

(448) The heart (*qalb*), in which the essence of man resides, is veiled by the attributes limiting that essence, just as the temple of a deity is shrouded by curtains.

(449) According to an Apostolic Tradition, God (the essence of man) is contained in the believer's heart, which is therefore likened to the Ka'ba, while by the same analogy ritual acts of worship performed in the pilgrimage are acts of the Essence, *i.e.* Divine acts. One of these rites is the

kiss (*qubla*) comes from my *qibla* (the object to which I turn in worship).

(450) My circumambulation in the spirit is really round myself, and my running from my Ṣafá to my Marwa is for the sake of my own face (reality).

(451) Within a sanctuary of my inward my outward is safe, while my neighbours around it are in danger of being snatched away.

(452) My soul was purified by my solitary fasting from other than myself, and gave as alms the overflow of my grace;

(453) And the doubling of my existence during my contemplation became single in my oneness (*ittiḥád*) when I awoke from my slumber;

(454) And my inmost self's night-journey to myself from the special privilege of the Truth is like my voyage in the general obligation of the Law;

(455) And my divinity did not make me neglectful of the

kissing of the Black Stone, "the right hand of God" (*yamín Allah*). Since the religious law is the Word of God, the kiss which it prescribes and which is included in it, comes, as it were, from the mouth of God, who as the essence of the creature (*al-khalq*) adores Himself as the Creator (*al-Ḥaqq*).

(450) Ṣafá and Marwa are two hills near Mecca. The commentator thinks that Ṣafá signifies the present life and Marwa the life hereafter.

(451) When the phenomenal self and its faculties are within the sanctuary of the heart, *i.e.* absorbed in God, they are safe from the assault of "otherness," to which they are exposed outside it (cf. Koran, 29, 67).

(452) The mystic's fast consists in abstaining from whatsoever is not real and Divine and in being alone with his essence; his alms-giving is the communication to others of the Divine grace which flows from his essence.

(453) The reference to prayers in this verse is indicated by the words *shaf'* (double) and *witr* (single), which may also be rendered "two genuflexions" and "a single genuflexion" in the canonical prayer (*ṣalát*). In *ittiḥád* the worshipper is made one with the object of worship and realises that his individual existence was a dream.

(454) The term "night-journey" is used in the Koran, 17, 1, of the ascension (*mi'ráj*) of the Prophet. Since an ascension from the Truth or the Essence implies that there is something higher than that, the poet answers this objection by pointing out that the journey of the Perfect Man from the Truth is like his journey in the Law, *i.e.* both journeys are really movements of his essence in and to and from itself. Here the "night-journey" denotes the third stage of Oneness (see note on *vv*. 326–7) in which the mystic returns from "the intoxication of union" to "the sobriety of union."

(455) Divinity (*láhút*) and humanity (*násút*) are correlative attributes or aspects of the One Reality. Man, created in the image of God, must nevertheless fulfil the law imposed on his corporeal nature, yet while recognising

requirement of my theatre of manifestation, nor did my humanity cause me to forget the theatre in which my wisdom is manifested.

(456) From me the covenants derived their binding power upon the soul, and by me the laws of religion were instituted to restrain the senses,

(457) Inasmuch as there had come to me from myself an Apostle to whom my sinning was grievous, one taking jealous care of me from compassion,

(458) And I executed my command (given) from my soul unto herself, and when she took charge of her own affair she did not turn back;

(459) And from the time of my covenant, before the era of my elements, before the (prophetic) warning was sent to (the world) where men shall be raised from the dead,

(460) I was an apostle sent from myself to myself, and my essence was led to me by the evidence of my own signs.

(461) And when I conveyed my soul, by purchase, from the possession of her own land to the kingdom of Paradise—

(462) For she had fought a good fight and had died a martyr in her cause and had gotten joy of her contract when she paid the price—

(463) She soared with me, in consequence of my union, beyond

and obeying it he must remember that as a spirit he is the oracle of Divine Wisdom.

(456) "The covenants," *i.e.* the acknowledgment by human souls in their state of pre-existence that they should love and worship God. Cf. note on verse 69.

(457–60) The Apostle is Universal Spirit, which emanates from the Essence regarded as Pure Oneness to the Essence regarded as Universal Soul. This emanation is, relatively at least, an eternal process. Mohammed (identified with Universal Spirit) said, "I was a prophet when Adam was water and clay," *i.e.* before the Creation. The "signs" or evidential miracles given to the Soul by the Apostle of Universal Spirit are the attributes of the Essence, which thereby reveals itself to itself.

(461–2) These lines are best explained by a passage in the Koran (9, 112): "Lo, Allah hath purchased of the true believers their souls and their substance, promising them Paradise in return, on condition that they shall fight in the cause of Allah and slay and be slain—a promise binding on Him in the Torah and the Gospel and the Koran; and who fulfilleth his pledge more faithfully than Allah? Rejoice therefore in the contract which ye have made."

(463) In the following verses (463–477) the poet describes himself in the state of union (*jam'*), *i.e.* on the plane of Absolute Being, emancipated from the relations to which he is subject in the phenomenal world. "The earth of

everlasting life in her heaven (Paradise), since I did not consent to incline towards the earth of my vicegerent;

(464) And how should I come under (the dominion of) that over which I am lord, like the friends of my kingdom and my followers and my party and my adherents?

(465) There is no celestial sphere but therein, from the light of my inward being, is an angel who gives guidance by my will,

(466) And there is no region but thereon, from the overflow of my outward being, falleth a drop that is the source of the clouds' downpouring.

(467) Beside my countenance the far-spreading light (of the sun) is like a gleam, and beside my watering-place the all-encompassing sea is like a drop.

(468) Therefore the whole of me is seeking the whole of me and is directing itself towards it, and part of me is drawing part of me with reins.

(469) Every direction tends to the all-guiding face of him who is above (the relation of) "below" and below whom is (the relation of) "above."

(470) Thus (in my experience) the "below-ness" of the earth is the "above-ness" of the aether, because of the closing of that

my vicegerent," *i.e.* the body. The human soul governs the body as the vicegerent (*khalífa*) of God.

(464) The "united" mystic (*ṣáḥibu 'l-jam'*) is lord over all relations, *i.e.* he transcends them and is not conditioned by any of them. "The friends of my kingdom, etc." *i.e.* those who follow me but have not attained to Oneness, so that they still belong to the realm of phenomenal existence.

(465–6) He means to say that, in respect of his mystical identification with the Absolute, he is the ultimate source of all that exists in the visible world as well as in the universe of the Unseen: the former is the external aspect of Reality, while the latter is its hidden ground.

(468) "Every part of me—spirit, heart, soul and body—is seeking my Essence, *i.e.* the Universal in which all particulars are comprised." When the spirit contemplates God alone, it draws to itself the heart, so that the heart desires God alone; and the heart then draws to itself the soul, so that the soul worships God alone and draws to itself the body, which God then causes to be employed entirely in good works.

(469) Absolute Being is the centre to which all particular objects converge.

(470) The phrase, "because of the closing, etc." is borrowed from Kor. 21, 31: "Did not the unbelievers discern that the heavens and the earth were closed until We clave them asunder and made every living thing of the water (that gushed forth)?" Whatever meaning the Prophet may have attached to these metaphors, Ibnu 'l-Fáriḍ evidently signifies by "the closing" that

which I clave asunder; and the cleavage of that which was closed is only the outward aspect of my way (*sunna*).

(471) And there is no doubt, since union is the essence of certainty, and no direction, since place is a (relation of) difference arising from my separation;

(472) And there is no number, since numeration cuts like the edge of a sword, and no time, since limitation is the dualism of one who fixes a definite term;

(473) And I have in the two worlds no rival who should doom to destruction what I built or whose command should cause the decree of my authority to be enforced;

(474) Nor have I in either world any opposite, for thou wilt not see amongst created beings any incongruity in their mode of creation, but all are alike (in perfection).

(475) And from me appeared that which I made a disguise to myself, and by means of me the phenomena were caused to return from me to myself;

(476) And in myself I beheld those who bowed in worship to my theatre of manifestation, and I knew for sure that I was the Adam to whom I bowed;

(477) And I discerned that the spiritual rulers of the earths

state which he elsewhere calls "union" (*jam'*), *i.e.* Being viewed synthetically as the inner unity in which all distinctions are reconciled, and by "the cleavage of that which was closed" the state of "separation" (*tafriqa*), *i.e.* Being viewed analytically in its external and phenomenal aspect.

(472) Number and Time involve division and limitation, which are inconsistent with real unity.

(473) "No rival," *i.e.* no partner in the attributes of deity; cf. Kor. 21, 22: "If there were any gods besides Allah in heaven or earth, verily both (heaven and earth) would be ruined."

(474) Kor. 67, 3: "Thou dost not see any incongruity (imperfection) in the creation of the Merciful (God)." Were there two opposed creators, like Ormuzd and Ahriman, their difference would manifest itself in the objects created by them.

(475) The illusion of phenomena does not impair the real unity which creates from itself, reveals to itself, and again withdraws from its manifested into its occult self.

(476) In reality the worshipper and the object of worship are one. The angels who worshipped Adam (Kor. 15, 28 foll.) symbolise the relation of a Divine attribute to its Essence.

(477) The Divine attributes as manifested in Man may be distinguished from each other, so that we speak of higher and lower natures, faculties, and powers, but they are fundamentally one and identical in respect of the Essence of which they are modes. For this symbolic use of "angels" cf. p. 115 foll.

amongst the angels of the highest sphere are equal in relation to my rank.

(478) Although my comrades craved right guidance from my horizon that is near (to them), the union of my unity was shown forth from my second separation,

(479) And in the swoon that crushed my senses my soul fell prostrate before me in order that she might recover ere repenting as Moses repented.

(480) For there is no "where" after (vision of) Reality, since I have recovered from intoxication, and the cloud that veiled the Essence has been cleared away by sobriety.

(481) The end of a self-effacement that preceded my (individual self's) conclusion is like the beginning of a sobriety (self-consciousness), because both are circumscribed by a period.

(482) I weighed in a scale him who is rapt by an obliterating effacement in death (to self) with him who is cut off by the sobriety of sense (self-consciousness) in separation (from God).

(478) The Essence appears from two horizons, *i.e.* in two aspects: (1) without attributes or actions; (2) qualified by the whole of its attributes and actions. "My horizon that is near" refers to the former epiphany, which produces in the mystic the state of union (*jam'*) without separation (*tafriqa*), a state necessarily accompanied by ecstatic unconsciousness. In the latter and more exalted epiphany, the Essence reveals itself together with its attributes as the unity of the One and the Many, the synthesis of union and separation. This aspect of reality is associated with "the second separation," *i.e.* the return from ecstasy to a higher plane of consciousness than any that was experienced before the ecstasy began (cf. notes on 233–5, 326–7).

(479) See note on *v.* 11 and *vv.* 288–9. "Ere repenting, etc." *i.e.* before coming back to the world of sense. Moses asked to see God with his phenomenal nature and was punished by being thrown into the state of "intoxication," in which it is not possible to have perfect clairvoyance; therefore his repentance and recovery involved a return to normal consciousness, whereas Ibnu 'l-Fáriḍ's recovery endowed him with the abnormal consciousness which is characteristic of the unitive life.

(480) "No 'where' (*ayn*) after Reality (*'ayn*)," which is free from all limitation. The meaning of the remainder of the verse has been sufficiently explained above.

(481–2) The higher mystical life, before it reaches the perfect oneness which is its goal, swings to and fro between states of ecstasy and consciousness: self-effacement (*maḥw*) and self-restoration (*ithbát*), intoxication (*sukr*) and sobriety (*ṣaḥw*), etc. This ever-changing succession (*talwín*) of complementary states only ceases with the conclusion of self-existence, *i.e.* when the mystic's individuality has entirely passed away, so that he is permanently one with the timeless and infinite being of God. Such permanent conscious oneness with God is described symbolically as "the second separation"

(483) Therefore the dot of the "*i*" of "film" was effaced from my sobriety, and the wakefulness of the eye of the Essence annulled my self-effacement.

(484) One who loses (God) in sobriety and finds (God) in self-effacement is incapable, owing to his alternation, of the fixity of nearness (to God).

(485) The drunken and the sober are alike inasmuch as they are qualified by the mark of "presence" or by the brand of "enclosure."

(486) No followers of mine are they in whom the attributes of "disguise" or the vestiges of any remnant (of these attributes) succeed each other.

(487) He that does not inherit perfection from me is faulty, a backslider into chastisement.

(488) In me is naught that would lead to the "disguise" resulting from a remnant (of self-existence), nor any shadow (of phenomenal being) that would condemn me to return (to an inferior degree).

(489) How little may a heart communicate in the form of thought or a tongue utter in the mould of speech!

(490) All sides (of Being) joined in me and the carpet of otherness was rolled up in virtue of the equality (of all),

(*al-farqu 'l-thání*) or "the second sobriety" (*aṣ-ṣaḥwu 'l-thání*). Viewed from that summit, negative or positive states, like *maḥw* and *ṣaḥw*, are equally imperfect; hence the poet says, "I weighed, etc," *i.e.* "I found both of them wanting." *Maḥq* (misinterpreted by K.) is nearly equivalent to *maḥw*. See *Kitáb al-Luma'*, 355, 17.

(483) "The dot of the '*i*' of 'film'": literally, "the dot of the (letter) *ghayn* of (the word) *ghayn* (film or cloud)," *i.e.* in the first place my individual existence was effaced from my consciousness; then self-effacement was superseded by "the wakefulness of the eye of the Essence," *i.e.* by the divine or cosmic consciousness, which is technically named "the second sobriety." *Ghayn* (film) becomes *'ayn* (eye or essence) when the dot of its initial letter is removed.

(484) Alternation (*talwín*), fixity (*tamkín*): cf. note on *vv.* 481–2 and *Kashf al-Maḥjúb*, p. 370 foll.

(485) Cf. verse 482. Perfect Oneness is the unity which combines two main aspects of Being as it is revealed to mystics (cf. note on *v.* 478). "Presence" (*ḥuḍúr*) is here equivalent to "union" (*jam'*), and "enclosure" (*ḥaẓíra*) to "separation" (*tafriqa*).

(486) Cf. note on *vv.* 481–2. "The attributes of 'disguise'" refer to the state of sobriety (*ṣaḥw*) and denote the normal consciousness which follows ecstasy and "veils" the mystic from God. "The vestiges of any remnant" refer to the state of self-effacement (*maḥw*) in which these attributes disappear.

(489) In this verse *waḥy* refers to the heart, *ṣígha* to the tongue.

(490) "All sides," *i.e.* contrary predications, such as eternity and time, above and below, first and last, etc.

(491) And my existence, in the passing-away of the duality of existence, became a contemplation in the abidingness of unity.

(492) That which is above the range of intellect—the First Emanation—is even as that which is below the Sinai of tradition—the last handful.

(493) Therefore the best of God's creatures forbade us to prefer him to the Man of the Fish, although he is worthy of preference.

(494) I have indicated (the truth concerning phenomenal relations) by the means which language yields, and that which is obscure I have made clear by a subtle allegory.

(495) The "Am not I" of yesterday is not other (than what shall be manifested) to him who enters on to-morrow, since my darkness hath become my dawn and my day my night.

(496) The secret of "Yea"—to God belongs the mirror of its revelation, and to affirm the reality of union (*jam'*) is to deny "beside-ness."

(497) No darkness covers me nor is there any harm to be feared, since the mercy of my light hath quenched the fire of my vengeance.

(498) And no time is, save where is no time that reckons the

(492) According to the monistic doctrine there is no real distinction in the universe of created things—from their metaphysical source in Universal Spirit to the Resurrection foretold by prophetic tradition, when "the whole earth shall be His handful and the heavens shall be rolled together in His right hand" (Kor. 39, 67).

(493) Mohammed is reported to have said, "Do not think I am better than Yúnus ibn Mattá (Jonah)."

(495–6) See note on *v.* 69. "Yesterday" means the Primal Covenant by which the souls, before their bodies were created, bound themselves to love God; "to-morrow" signifies the Resurrection. Time disappears in the oneness of the Essence: day is identical with night, and night with day. "The secret of 'Yea'" alludes to Kor. 7, 171: (When God said to the children of Adam) "Am not I your Lord?" and they answered, "Yea." Those who affirm the oneness of Being and deny "beside-ness," *i.e.* deny that anything exists beside God, know that "Yea" is the eternal Word of God, revealed and spoken by Himself to Himself.

(497) The commentator quotes two sayings ascribed to Mohammed: (*a*) that God said, "My mercy was before My wrath"; (*b*) that Hell will say to every true believer who approaches it, "Pass, O true believer, for lo, thy light hath quenched my fire."

(498) Time is not a reality except in the spiritual world where it is eternal and infinite.

existence of that existence of mine which is computed by the reckoning of the new moons;

(499) But one imprisoned in the bounds of Time does not see what lies beyond his dungeon, in the Paradise everlasting.

(500) Therefore 'tis upon me the heavens turn, and marvel thou at their *Quṭb* (Pole) which encompasses them, howbeit the Pole is a central point.

(501) And there was no *Quṭb* before me, whom I should succeed after having passed three grades (of sanctity), although the *Awtád* rise to the rank of *Quṭb* from the rank of *Badal*.

(502) Do not overstep my straight line, and seize the best opportunity, for in the angles there are hidden things.

The poet now describes some of his strange experiences in love. The first of these is a state which the commentator calls "the greatest absence from self" (*al-ghaybiyyatu 'l-kubrá*).

(506) Through Her I became oblivious of myself, so that I thought myself another and did not seek the path that leads to thinking myself existent.

(507) And my being oblivious (of myself) in Her, caused me to lose my reason, so that I did not return to myself or follow any desire of mine in consequence of my thinking (that I existed).

(508) And I became distraught for Her, engrossed with Her; and whomsoever She renders distraught through being taken up with Her, him She makes forgetful of himself.

(509) And I was so preoccupied with Her as to forget the preoccupation that made me forget myself: had I died for Her, I should not have been aware of my departure (from the world).

* * * * * *

(512) And I was seeking Her from myself, though She was ever beside me. I marvelled how She was hidden from me by myself.

(500) Real Being is the axis on which the phenomenal universe revolves as well as the circumference within which all particulars are contained.

(501) The explanation of this verse will be found on p. 194 *supra*.

(502) "My straight line," *i.e.* the mystical path by which I arrived at this supreme perfection. The poet adds that the doctrine taught in the *Tá'iyya* should be prized by Ṣúfís: in its obscure expressions they will discover the mysteries of the Truth.

(513) And I ceased not from going with Her to and fro in myself (in search of Her), because my senses were intoxicated by the wine of Her beauties,

(514) Travelling from the knowledge of certainty to the intuition thereof; then journeying to the fact thereof, where the Truth is.

* * * * * *

(521) (So was I seeking Her within me) until there rose from me to mine eye a gleam, and the splendour of my daybreak shone forth and my darkness vanished.

(522) Here I reached a point from which the intellect recoils before gaining it, where from myself I was being joined and united to myself.

(523) And when I attained unto myself, I beamed with joy because of a certainty that saved me from saddling for my journey;

(524) And since I was seeking myself from myself, I directed myself to myself, and my soul showed the way to me by means of me.

(525) And when I removed the curtains of the shroud of sense which the mysteries of mine own ordainment had let down,

(526) I lifted my soul's curtain by unveiling her, and 'twas she that granted my request (that the veil should be removed).

(527) And I was that which cleansed the mirror of my essence

(514) Certainty (*al-yaqín*) denotes real faith in the Unseen. The three stages or categories mentioned in this verse are variously defined by Ṣúfí writers. According to Káshání, a man who has the knowledge of certainty (*'ilmu 'l-yaqín*) knows that the object of his search is within him; in the second stage (*'aynu 'l-yaqín*) he sees this intuitively with the eye of mystical contemplation; in the last stage (*ḥaqqu 'l-yaqín*) the illusion of subject and object disappears and he reaches absolute unity (*ittiḥád*).

(522) Thought, which involves duality, cannot apprehend "the fact of certainty" (*ḥaqqu 'l-yaqín*), *i.e.* the pure Oneness allegorically depicted in the following passage.

(523) When the mystic realises the fact of *ittiḥád*, he has arrived at his journey's end.

(524) *I.e.* I was the seeker, the guide, and the object sought.

(525–6) The soul is "veiled" (ignorant of the truth) so long as she does not perceive that the bodily senses (sight, hearing, taste, etc.) are really attributes of the universal Soul with which she is essentially one.

(527) The attributes, which limit the essence and prevent it from being seen as it is absolutely, are compared to rust that darkens the surface of a steel mirror.

from the rust of my attributes, and the rays that surrounded it were from myself;

(528) And I caused myself to behold myself, inasmuch as in my beholding there existed none other than myself who might decree the intrusion (of duality).

(529) And when I uttered my name, that which uttered it caused me to hear it, though (in truth) 'twas my soul that listened and pronounced my name while sensation was banished.

(530) And I embraced myself, but not through contact of my limbs with my ribs: nay, I embraced my very essence.

(531) And I let myself smell my own perfume, while the perfume of my breath made fragrant the scents of bruised spices.

(532) And the whole of me was transcending the dualism of sensation, howbeit my transcendence was in myself, since I had unified my essence.

Human thought distinguishes the essence of God from His attributes, names, and actions, but in the mystic's vision of Oneness all is essentialised and every partial relation identified with the Whole.

(533) To praise my attributes because of me (my essence) enables my praiser to glorify me (for what I am essentially), but to praise me (my essence) because of my attributes is to blame me (my essence).

(534) Therefore he that beholds my attributes in my companion (my body) and beholds me (my essence) by means of them will never alight at my abode—for I veil myself (with my attributes).

(529) See *vv.* 539–540 and *vv.* 546–8 below.

(530) This verse refers to *v.* 519:

And I press my hand on my vitals that peradventure I may embrace Her when I lay it there in clasping.

The whole passage (*vv.* 521–531) is parallel to the verses immediately preceding it (510–520): the former describes mystical "intoxication" (*sukr*), the latter mystical "sobriety" (*saḥw*).

(531) *I.e.* I did not cry, like Mohammed, "O God, let me smell the perfume of Paradise!" for I myself was the perfumer, the perfume and everything that is perfumed.

(532) Cf. *v.* 529. The deified mystic is transcendent "in himself" because he is One and All.

(534) "Will never alight at my abode," *i.e.* will never attain to knowledge of my essence.

(535) And to call to mind my Names through me (my essence) is a waking vision (a revelation of the Truth), but to call me (my essence) to mind through them is the (false) dream of one that slumbers in the night.

(536) Likewise, he that knows me (my essence) through my actions knows me not, whereas he that knows them through me is a knower of the Truth.

(537) Receive, then, the knowledge of the principal attributes, which are attached to outward abodes (visible organs), from a soul well acquainted therewith,

(538) And (receive) the understanding of the Names of the Essence, which are made manifest through them (the attributes) but (themselves) reside in the inward (invisible) worlds, from a spirit that gives an indication thereof (by means of symbols).

(539) The manifestation metaphorically of my attributes (*e.g.* sight and hearing) from the names of my bodily organs (*e.g.* the visual and auditory faculties)—names by which my soul was named because of my judgment (that in reality they belong to the soul, not to the body)—

(540) Consists of a knowledge (latent in the soul)—marks traced on the veils of forms (bodily organs) and throwing light on what is beyond sense-perception in the soul.

(536) Knowledge derived by means of induction is inferior to knowledge revealed in contemplation. Perfect knowledge of God is truly a *re*-cognition of that which the soul contemplated before the existence of the body.

(537) "The principal attributes," such as sight, hearing, speech, and power, whose respective organs are the eye, the ear, the tongue, and the hand.

(538) The attributes, although their real nature is hidden in the Essence, manifest themselves in the bodily organs. The Names, having no such organs attached to them, cannot be manifested except through the attributes: thus, before we apply the name *al-Raḥmán* (the Merciful) to the Divine Essence, we must be assured that the quality of *raḥma* (mercy) is latent in the Essence.

(539–540) There is only a metaphorical (unreal) connexion between the attributes of the Essence and the physical faculties and organs with which they are associated. In reality these attributes belong entirely to the Essence, inasmuch as the faculties and organs through which they are manifested are themselves no more than objectified aspects of the Essence. When a man says "I saw" and "I heard," naming himself by the names of the attributes of sight and hearing, he does so because he judges that what really sees and hears is not his eye and his ear, but the spiritual essence underlying them.

(541) And the manifestation actually of the names of my essence from the attributes of my inward being, for the sake of mysteries whereby the spirit was gladdened,

(542) Consists of hints concerning treasures (of knowledge)—hints revealing the significations of a mystical doctrine and encompassed by the arcana of that which is hidden in the depths of the heart.

(543) And their effects in all that exists, together with the knowledge of them—and created things are not independent of the effects produced by them (the Names and Attributes)—

(544) Are (shown by) the existence of praise that is gained (by God) for strength of dominion, and by the beholding of thanks that are gathered in return for universal favours.

(545) They (the effects of the Names and Attributes) are theatres of manifestation for me: I appeared in them, although I was not hidden from myself before my epiphany (in them).

(546) For speech—and the whole of me is a tongue that tells of me—and sight—and the whole of me is an eye in me for regarding me—

(547) And hearing—and the whole of me is ears (*asmu'*) listening to the proclamation of (my) bounty—(and power)—and the whole of me is a hand strong to repel destruction,

(548) (All these faculties) are a means of manifestation for

(541–42) The inmost meaning of the Divine Names, which depend on the Divine Attributes (see *v.* 538), cannot be apprehended except mystically or conveyed otherwise than symbolically. Knowledge of the Names and Attributes gladdens the spirit by revealing the mysteries of Oneness (*ittiḥád*) and by exalting Man, as the microcosm, above all created beings.

(543–4) The whole world of phenomena exhibits the effects (*áthár*) of the Divine Names and Attributes, *i.e.* it is constituted, sustained, and replenished by a continuous series of illuminations (*tajalliyát*) proceeding from these Names and Attributes. All created beings praise God and render thanks to Him who endows them with existence, since they know—and this is the import of the words "together with the knowledge of them," *i.e.* the knowledge of the *áthár*—that His Names and Attributes are manifested in themselves.

(545) Before God actually revealed Himself in Man and Nature, He was potentially revealed to Himself in His eternal knowledge.

(546–8) All faculties which are separate and distinct in the body are united and indistinguishable in the soul. "The soul, having no parts, speaks with hearing and sight, and sees with hearing and speech, and hears with sight and speech, because all its attributes are involved in one another." The commentator assigns to *ma'ání* in *v.* 548 an unusual meaning, *viz.* "places

Attributes which established (the presence in the soul of) what transcends the (outward) vesture (the body) and for Essential Names which spread abroad that which sensation related (to the soul).

In language so figurative as to be almost untranslatable the poet describes (*vv.* 549–574) the Divine Names according to (1) their characteristic qualities; (2) the benefits which accrue from them to body and soul; and (3) their respective spheres of influence, *viz.*, the visible world (*'álamu 'l-shaháda*), the invisible world (*'álamu 'l-ghayb*), the world of dominion (*'álamu 'l-malakút*), and the world of almightiness (*'álamu 'l-jabarút*)[1]. Here again he rises to the plane of undifferentiated unity (*jam'*), where plurality (*tafriqa*) has disappeared. This phase, however, is momentary. As we have seen, in the highest mystical experience plurality returns under the form of unity: the One does not exclude the Many, but comprehends them in its own nature, so that every part is the essence of the whole.

(575) The whole of me performs that (devotion) which is required by the Path, while keeping the way of that (unity) which was required by my Truth.

(576) And when, no longer separating, I joined the rift, and the fissures caused by the difference of the attributes were closed,

(577) And nothing that leads to estrangement was left between me and a firm trust in the intimacy of my love,

(578) I knew for sure that we (lover and Beloved) are really One, and the sobriety of union restored the notion of separation,

of submission or will (to manifestation)"; but *ma'áni ṣifát*in may signify "realities (consisting) of attributes." "That which sensation related to the soul" is the multiformity of phenomenal existence, which corresponds to the variety of the Essential Names. From perception of sensible things the soul rises to knowledge of their spiritual realities.

(575) "Having realised the Truth (*ḥaqíqa*), namely, that subject and object are One, I continue to walk in the Path (*ṭaríqa*)," *i.e.* to observe the ascetic and ethical discipline which the Ṣúfí novice learns from his spiritual director.

(576) The phenomenon of "separation" arises from the diversity of the Divine Names and Attributes, not from any duality in the Essence itself.

(577–8) Lover and Beloved are two attributes of one essence (Love),

[1] The *'álamu 'l-malakút* and the *'álamu 'l-jabarút* denote the Attributes and the Essence.

(579) And my whole was a tongue to speak, an eye to see, an ear to hear, and a hand to seize.

All particular attributes being thus dissolved in the universality of the Essence, the "unified" mystic can say that his eye speaks, his tongue sees, his hand listens, etc., and that his sense of smell speaks, sees, hears, and takes, or conversely, that his tongue, eye, ear, and hand are endowed with the sense of smell; and can declare that all his faculties are exercised simultaneously by every atom of his body (*vv.* 580–88).

(589) Therefore I read all the knowledge of the wise in a single word, and show unto myself all created beings in a single look;

(590) And I hear the voices of them that pray and all their languages in a time less than the duration of a gleam;

(591) And ere mine eye winks, I bring before me what was hard to convey on account of its distance;

(592) And with one inhalation I smell the perfumes of all gardens and the fragrance of what (herbs) soever touch the skirts of the winds;

(593) And I survey all regions (of the earth) in a flash of thought and traverse the seven tiers of Heaven in one step.

The next passage indicates the origin and nature of these extraordinary powers which the poet claims not only for himself but for all prophets from Adam to Mohammed and for the Moslem saints in general. It is perhaps unnecessary to add that where he uses the words "I" and "my" he assumes the character of the universal Spirit.

(594) The bodies of those in whom remains no remnant (of self) because of my union (with them) are like the spirits: they are encompassed (with my union) and made light (subtle);

and their union *quâ* attributes is impossible, since the former is characterised by need, abasement and weakness, while power and pride are inherent in the latter. So long as they co-exist, they stand opposed to one another and in peril of "estrangement"; only by absorption in their essence, *i.e.* by ceasing to be attributes, do they become united. The mystic's real Beloved is the oneness of Love, which begins in a rapture obliterating all distinctions (*jam'*) but ends by "restoring the notion of separation" (*tafriqa*), *i.e.* perceiving clairvoyantly that Lover, Beloved and Love are one.

(595) And whosoever is sovereign or munificent or mighty in onset only finds his way (to these qualities) through my aiding him with a particle (of my union).

(596) He walked not on the water nor flew in the air nor plunged in the flames but in virtue of my volition,

(597) And I am the source whence he whom I aided with a particle (of my union) became changed in a moment from all his (normal) being,

(598) And whence he that with his whole being followed my union recited the Koran, from beginning to end, a thousand times in an hour or less.

(599) And had a breath of my grace been bestowed on a dead man, his soul would have been given back to him and caused to return.

(600) Such is the soul: if she cast off her desires, her faculties are multiplied and endow every atom with the (entire) activity of the soul.

(601) Union suffices thee (as an explanation of these miracles); they are not produced by a separation consisting in two extensions, namely, measurable space and finite time.

After enumerating some miracles of pre-Islamic prophets—Noah, Solomon, Abraham, Moses, Jacob and Jesus—the poet explains the unique position of Mohammed as the spiritual father of all prophets and saints and the real author of all miracles past, present and future.

(614) The inward notion that produced (miraculous) effects in outward things is that (oneness) which, by (Divine) permission, my moulded speech communicated to thine ear,

(615) And the notions underlying all (the effects) that

(595) Spiritual dominion, grace, and energy emanate from the Divine Essence with which the prophets and saints have been made one.

(596) "My volition" (*himma*), *i.e.* the concentration of my thought upon the particular Divine Names which are the causes of the (miraculous) effects that I desire to produce.

(600) Cf. notes on *vv.* 525–6, 539–40, and 546–8.

(601) Miracles are the effects of union (*jam'*) with the Essence, *i.e.* the unitive state. Time and Space belong to "separation" (*tafriqa*), *i.e.* the phenomenal world.

(615–6) The spirit of prophecy attained to complete and final manifestation in Mohammed, the Seal of the prophets; and since Universal Spirit, the

belonged to them (the former prophets) were brought (together) by him (Mohammed) who caused them to stream over us, thereby putting the seal upon a time when no prophets arise;

(616) And there was none of them (the former prophets) but had called his people to the Truth by grace of Mohammed and because he was Mohammed's follower.

(617) And a divine of ours is one of those prophets, while any one of us that calls (the people) to the Truth performs the office of apostle;

(618) And in our Mohammedan era our gnostic is (like) one of the old prophets, one who clave to the commandment and was firm (in obedience to the religious law).

(619) After him, the evidentiary miracles of the prophets became acts of Divine grace (*χαρίσματα*) towards his saints and vicegerents.

(620) His family and his Companions and the religious leaders of the next generation sufficed mankind instead of the apostles.

(621) Their miracles form part of what he conferred on them exclusively, in bequeathing to them a share of every excellence (of his).

* * * * * *

(627) And the saints who believe in him, though they never saw him, are elect in virtue of their affinity: they are near (to him) as brother to brother.

(628) And his being near them in spirit resembles his yearning towards them in form. Marvel, then, at a presence in absence!

The mystical union of the saints with the Logos expresses itself in language that might easily be mistaken for blasphemy.

first emanation from Absolute Being, is identified with Mohammed and was revealed by him in its whole essential nature, whereas the prophets before him manifested no more than particular aspects and attributes, his predecessors drew their inspiration from him and are logically his followers.

(617–8) Although prophecy ended with Mohammed, the Moslem divines and mystics may be described as the prophets and apostles of the Mohammedan era. Orthodox Ṣúfís take the strictest possible view of their religious duties (cf. *Kitáb al-Luma'*, p. 10, l. 11 foll.).

(619) For the distinction between *mu'jizát* (miracles of the prophets) and *karámát* (miracles of the saints) see *Kashf al-Maḥjúb*, p. 218 foll.

(628) Yearning (*ishtiyáq*) implies that the object of desire is present (to the mind), though absent (in the body).

(629) They (the prophets) who received the Spirit called (their peoples) to my way in my name and vanquished the miscreants by my argument;

(630) And in consequence of the priority of my essence they all revolve in my circle or descend from my watering-place,

(631) For albeit I am outwardly a son of Adam, yet in him is a spirit of mine that bears witness I am his father.

*   *   *   *   *   *

(637) Do not deem that this matter lies outside of me, for none gained lordship (as a prophet or a saint) except he entered my service,

(638) Since, but for me, no existence would have come into being, nor would there have been a contemplation (of God), nor would any secure covenants have been known.

(639) None lives but his life is from mine, and every willing soul is obedient to my will;

(640) And there is no speaker but tells his tale with my words, nor any seer but sees with the sight of mine eye;

(641) And no silent (listener) but hears with my hearing, nor any one that grasps but with my strength and might;

(642) And in the whole creation there is none save me that speaks or sees or hears.

(643) And in the world of composition (the sensible world) I

(629) "My way," *i.e.* the way of real oneness with God. "In virtue my name," *i.e.* the prophets manifested in their miracles the potency of the Divine Names, as Jesus, for example, called the dead to life by manifesting the Divine Name *al-Muḥyí*, the Quickener. "My argument," *i.e.* evidentiary miracles.

(630) Cf. note on *vv.* 615–6.

(631) Metaphysically, Mohammed is the father of Adam in the sense that the spirit or essence of Adam is Universal Spirit = the Logos = Mohammed.

(637) "This matter," *i.e.* prophecy and saintship.

(638) Cf. the Tradition in which it is related that God said to Mohammed, "But for thee I had not created the heavens." As the created universe is the form of the Logos, so is Divine contemplation an attribute of the same Supreme Spirit (*al-Rúḥu 'l-a'ẓam*), whence all human spirits derive their powers. The "covenants" have been explained above.

(643–5) These verses describe the self-manifestation of the Logos to the senses in the phenomenal world (*'álamu 'l-shahdda*), to the intellect in the intelligible world (*'álamu 'l-ghayb*), and to the spirit in the world of mystical contemplation, which the intellect is unable to reach (*'álamu 'l-malakút* and *'álamu 'l-jabarút*: cf. p. 251).

manifested in every (phenomenal) form a reality whereby that form was made fair;

(644) And in every reality that was not revealed by my phenomena I was imaged, but not in a corporeal shape;

(645) And in that which the spirit beholds by clairvoyance I was hidden from fatigued thought by my subtlety.

The clairvoyant spirit contemplates itself as the Whole that pervades every aspect of reality and as the Identical in which all contraries are united.

(646) In the mercy of "expansion" the whole of me is a wish whereby the hopes of all the world are expanded;

(647) And in the terror (wrath) of "contraction" the whole of me is an awe, and o'er whatsoever I let mine eye range, it reveres me;

(648) And in the union of both these attributes the whole of me is a nearness. Come, then, draw near to my beauteous qualities!

(649) In the place where "in" ends I ceased not to feel, through myself, the majesty of contemplating myself—an experience arising from the perfection of my nature;

(650) And where is no "in" I ceased not to contemplate in myself the beauty of my Being, not with the sight of mine eye.

Perception of reality is impossible so long as sense-impressions, which affirm that things exist by themselves, are allowed to stand in the way.

(651) So if thou art of me, seek union with me and efface the distinction of my separation and be not turned aside by the darkness of Nature,

(652) And receive the signs of my inspired wisdom which

(646–7) "Expansion" (*basṭ*) and "contraction" (*qabḍ*) are modes of feeling in the gnostic which correspond to "hope" (*rajá*) and "fear" (*khawf*) in the lower stages of the mystical life: cf. R. Hartmann, *Al-Ḳuschairîs Darstellung des Ṣûfîtums*, p. 84. *Basṭ* is the effect of Divine mercy, *qabḍ* of Divine wrath. Cf. Kor. 2, 246: وَٱللّٰهُ يَقْبِضُ وَيَبْسُطُ.

(648) "A nearness," *i.e.* a negation of farness (difference) in the ground of Pure Being. Distinction first appears when the Essence manifests itself through its Names and Attributes.

(649) In the sphere of the Essence there is no "in," *i.e* limitation of space and time. "The perfection of my nature" denotes the inherent self-identity (*jam'*) in virtue of which the Essence eternally contemplates itself in and by itself as the One in Many and the Many in the One.

(651) *I.e.* do not seek me in the phenomenal world, where my attributes appear to be separated from the underlying reality.

will remove from thee the false judgments of opinion formed through sensation.

Ibnu 'l-Fáriḍ naturally condemns metempsychosis, a special form of the already repudiated doctrine of incarnation (*ḥulúl*)[1].

(653) Have nothing to do with one that believes in ***naskh*** (the transmigration of souls into human bodies)—for his is a case of ***maskh*** (the transmigration of souls into the bodies of animals)—and hold aloof from his doctrine;

(654) And let him alone with his assertion of *faskh* (the transmigration of souls into plants)—for if *raskh* (the transmigration of souls into minerals) were true, he deserves to suffer it everlastingly in every cycle.

If we scorn the notion of a spirit doomed to perpetual confinement in matter, how shall we represent the true monistic relation between them? Our minds can never know that relation as it really is: like all mystical truth, it is unseizable by thought. But mystics have their own ways and means of communicating with each other, and the poet has just announced himself as a hierophant (*v.* 652), bidding his readers attend to "the *signs* of his inspired wisdom." The best commentary on this phrase is Ibnu 'l-'Arabí's remark that mystical "states" cannot be explained, but can only be *indicated symbolically* to those who have begun to experience the like[2].

(655) My coining parables for thee time after time concerning my state is a favour from me to thee.

(656) Consider the *Maqámát* of the Sarújite and draw a lesson from his variety (of disguise)—then wilt thou deem it good to have taken my advice,

(656–8) The following passage should be compared with *vv.* 239–85 and *vv.* 525–48 *supra.* The metaphor of "disguise" (*labs*: cf. note on *vv.* 284–5) shadows forth the oneness of reality and appearance. In Ḥarírí's *Maqámát* (see my *Literary History of the Arabs*, pp. 329–336) the hero, Abú Zayd, a native of Sarúj in Mesopotamia, assumes all sorts of disguises to get money from his dupes. "In whatever form and shape," *e.g.* in the eye or the ear and in sight or hearing. "For the soul labours not in earnest," *i.e.* "if any one objects that Ḥarírí's fiction does not correspond with the nature of Reality,

[1] See *v.* 277 foll.

[2] *Tarjumán al-ashwáq*, p. 68.

(657) And thou wilt perceive that the soul in whatever form and shape she appears, inwardly masks herself in sensation;

(658) And if his (Ḥarírí's) work is fiction, yet the Truth makes of it a parable, for the soul labours not in earnest.

(659) Therefore be understanding, and while doing justice to thy soul look upon thy phenomenal actions with thy (faculty of) sense;

(660) And wouldst thou have thy soul unveil herself, contemplate what thou seest without doubt in the burnished mirrors.

(661) Was it another that appeared in them? Or didst thou behold thyself by means of them when the rays were refracted?

(662) And listen how the sound of thy voice, when it dies away, is returned to thee by the walls of lofty buildings.

(663) He that talked with thee there, was he some one else? Or didst thou hear words uttered by thy voiceful echo?

(664) And tell me, when thy senses had been hushed in slumber, who imparted to thee his lore?

(665) Ere to-day thou didst not know what happened yesterday or what shall happen to-morrow,

(666) And now thou art acquainted with the histories of them that are past and with the secrets of them that shall come after—and the knowledge makes thee proud.

(667) Think'st thou it was another, not thyself, that conversed with thee in the drowsiness of sleep touching diverse sorts of noble knowledge?

(668) 'Twas none but thy soul, what time she was busied with her own world and disengaged from the theatre of humanity.

(669) She unveiled herself to herself in the invisible world in the form of a sage that led her to the apprehension of wondrous meanings;

(670) For already had the sciences been imprinted on her, and

I reply that my analogy is perfectly just, inasmuch as the soul creates and maintains the *illusion* of phenomenal existence." Cf. *v.* 677, where phenomena are described as the playthings of a soul in earnest, and also *v.* 709.

(659) "Doing justice to thy soul," *i.e.* recognising that all bodily activities are effects (*áthár*) of the soul.

(668) The body is the theatre in which humanity (human nature) is exhibited.

(669–71) In dreams the soul knows itself as it was in the state of pre-existence, *i.e.* as one with the Being which is the subject and object of all

she was anciently taught the names (realities) thereof through the inspiration of fatherhood,

(671) Not by knowledge derived from the "separation" of otherness was she blest; nay, she enjoyed that which she dictated to herself.

(672) Had she become naked (detached from the body) before thy dream, thou wouldst have beheld her, as I do, with an eye that sees true (in a waking vision).

(673) And her being normally detached (in sleep) in the first place confirms her being detached in the eternal world (of mystical contemplation) in the second place; therefore be steadfast,

(674) And be not one whom his studies made foolish, so that they enfeebled and unsettled his mind;

(675) For there, beyond tradition, lies a knowledge too subtle to be apprehended by the farthest reach of sound understandings.

(676) I received it from myself and derived it from myself: 'twas with mine own bounty my soul was replenishing me.

One of the most amazing things in Von Hammer's version of the *Tá'iyya* is his translation of *vv.* 677–8. Their language could scarcely be plainer, they introduce a passage in which the poet dwells on the relative *value* of sense-perception viewed as an illustration of the nature of reality—and this is how Von Hammer translates them:

> Du spiele nicht mit Scherz und fasle nicht im Leben,
> Du sei den Possen nicht, dem Ernste sei ergeben!
> O hüte dich und wend' dich ab von allen Bildern,
> Von allen Fantasei'n, die nur Geträumtes schildern.

In a different context Ibnu 'l-Fáriḍ might have said this or something like it; but here, as it happens, he says just the opposite.

knowledge, and which, *quâ* Universal Spirit (the father) eternally begets in itself, *quâ* Universal Soul (the mother), the ideal, *i.e.* non-externalised, essences of individual things. Cf. Kor. 2, 29: "And He (Allah) taught Adam the Names, all of them." See also p. 186, note 4, and *v.* 631 *supra*.

(672) "Become naked" (*tajarradat*): so Plato speaks of ἡ ψυχὴ γυμνὴ τοῦ σώματος.

(673) Cf. a passage of the *Masnaví* quoted and translated in *Selected Poems from the Díváni Shamsi Tabríz*, p. 298 fol.

(677) Be not wholly neglectful of the play (illusion), for the jest of the playthings (phenomena) is the earnestness of a soul in earnest,

(678) And beware of turning thy back on every tinselled form or unreal and fantastic case;

(679) For in the sleep of illusion the apparition of the shadow-phantom brings thee to that which is shown through the thin (semi-transparent) curtains.

Here Ibnu 'l-Fáriḍ refers to the shadow-lantern by means of which leathern figures, moved by wands against a muslin curtain, are illuminated and made visible to the spectators on the other side (see Nallino, *op. cit.*, p. 93). The verses immediately following (680–706) have been translated above (p. 189 foll.). They describe how the showman, standing behind the screen, displays his figures in every variety of action and causes the spectators to sympathise with the representation; yet when the screen is taken away, he alone is seen to be the real actor. This analogy guides us to the truth of things. The showman is the soul, the shadowy figures are the phenomena of sensation, the screen is the body: remove it and the soul is one with God.

(707) Even thus (like the showman) I was letting down between me and myself the curtain that obscures the soul in the light of darkness,

(708) That in producing my actions at intervals I might appear to my sensation gradually, thereby accustoming it (and preparing it for complete illumination).

(709) I joined the play (illusion) thereof to my work (reality),

(677–9) "The phenomenal is a bridge to the real" (*al-majáz qanṭaratu 'l-ḥaqíqa*). Cf. *Tarjumán al-ashwáq*, p. 100: "In the survival of the substance of phenomenal being the Divine Presence and its lovely Names are manifested, and this is the beauty of phenomenal being; if it perished, thou wouldst not know aught, since all kinds of knowledge are divulged by means of forms and bodies."

(707) The body is dark, inasmuch as it belongs to the world of appearance, but also light, in so far as knowledge of reality first comes to the soul through sense-perception. Regarded as faculties of the soul, the senses are capable of receiving gradual illumination.

in order to bring near to thy understanding the ends of my far-off purposes.

(710) Although his (the showman's) case is not (essentially) like mine, there is a resemblance between us in regard to the two forms of manifestation:

(711) His figures (puppets) were the forms in which, with the aid of a screen, he displayed his action: they became naught and withdrew when he revealed himself;

(712) And my soul resembles him in action, for my sensation is like the figures (puppets), and the (bodily) vesture is my screen.

(713) When I removed the screen from me, as he removed it (from him), so that my soul appeared to me without any veiling—

(714) And already the sun of contemplation had risen, and all existence was illumined, and through myself the knots of the tethering-rope (of sense-perception) were untied—

(715) I slew the youth, my soul, while on the one hand I was setting up the wall (of consciousness) to safeguard my laws and on the other staving in my (bodily) boat,

(716) And turned to shed my replenishing grace over every created being according to my actions at every time;

(717) And were I not veiled by my attributes, the objects in which I manifest myself would be consumed by the splendour of my glory.

(712) The soul acts on the senses through a corporeal medium in the same way as the showman uses a screen in order to act on his puppets.

(713–5) These lines describe the states of *faná* and *baqá*—the lifting of the bodily veil and the consequent union with reality—which are here indicated by means of metaphors strange to us but easy for any Moslem to understand, since they refer to a famous passage in the Koran (18, 64–81). "I slew the youth, my soul," *i.e.* I died to self (*faná*). "While...I was setting up the wall...to safeguard my laws," *i.e.* my living (*baqá*) in and through God was accompanied by the maintenance of the religious law. The perfect mystic, after having "staved in his boat," *i.e.* having destroyed his individual existence, nevertheless in his unitive state "makes the Law his upper garment and the Path his inner garment" : cf. *The Mystics of Islam*, p. 163.

(716) The unified soul is one with the eternal source of energy whence the existence of phenomena is diffused and perpetually renewed. *Imdád* in this verse has its usual meaning: see *vv* 403–4.

(717) A paraphrase of the celebrated Tradition concerning the 70,000 veils of light and darkness which hide the face of Allah.

Once the illusion of selfhood is destroyed, nothing remains but "the Master of the Show," the one real person in the drama

> Which, for the Pastime of Eternity,
> He doth Himself contrive, enact, behold.

(718) The tongues of all beings, wilt thou but hearken, bear eloquent witness to my unity.

(719) And touching my oneness (*ittiḥád*) there hath come down a sure Tradition, whose transmission by (oral) relation (from the Prophet) is not infirm,

(720) Declaring that God loves (His creatures) after they draw nigh unto Him by voluntary works of devotion or by the observance of that which is obligatory;

(721) And the point that the doctrine bids us mark is made as clear as the light of noon by the words "I am to him an ear."

(722) I used the (religious and devotional) means to reach unification until I found it (unification), and the agency of the means was one of my guides (thereto);

(723) And I unified in respect of the means until I lost them, and the link of (this) unification was the way of approach (to unity) that availed me best;

(724) And I stripped my soul of them both, and she became single (detached from the world of relations)—yet had she never at any time been other than single (in her real nature);

(725) And I dived into the seas of union, nay, I plunged into them in my aloneness and brought out many a peerless pearl,

(719) The poet refers to another and equally apocryphal Ḥadíth (see p. 5 *supra*), the gist of which lies in the statement that those whom God loves are one with Him, so that He is their organ of sight, hearing, and speech.

(722) Although the mystic at the beginning of his unification values devotional exercises as a means of attaining to union with God, he ultimately comes to know that the attainment of union does not depend on secondary causes, which are non-existent in reality, or on any act that he may ascribe to himself. Cf. *Kashf al-Maḥjúb*, p. 202 foll.; *The Mystics of Islam*, p. 74 foll.

(723) "I unified in respect of the means," *i.e.* I perceived that God is the real agent in every act.

(724) "I stripped my soul of them both," *i.e.* both of my regard for the means themselves (*v.* 722) and of my regard for my unification of them (*v.* 723). Even in the latter there is still a remnant of dualism, inasmuch as the unification is attributed to the individual self.

(726) That I might hear mine acts with a seeing ear and behold my words with a hearing eye.

(727) So if the nightingale lament in the grove, whilst the birds in every tree warble a response to her,

(728) And if the flute-player make music in accord with the strings touched by the hand of a singing-girl

(729) Who chants tender poetry, so that the souls (of the hearers) mount to their Paradisal lote-tree at each trill—

(730) I take delight in the effects of mine own art, and I ever declare my union and society to be free from partnership with others.

It follows from the doctrine of *ittiḥád* that all forms of worship are essentially divine. Even dualism and polytheism represent certain aspects in which God expresses Himself. This passage (*vv.* 731–49) should be compared with the views set forth by Ibnu 'l-'Arabí and Jílí (see pp. 130 foll. and 157 foll.).

(731) Through me the assembly of them that praise my name is (attentive like) the ear of one reading (a book), and for my sake the wine-seller's shop is (open like) the eye of a scout;

(732) And virtually no hand but mine tied the infidels' girdle; and if it be loosed in acknowledgement of me, 'twas my hand that loosed it.

(733) And if the niche of a mosque is illuminated by the Koran, yet is no altar of a church made vain by the Gospel;

(734) Nor vain are the books of the Torah revealed to Moses for his people, whereby the Rabbis converse with God every night.

(726) In union (*jam'*) each attribute is identical with every other attribute and with the Essence.

(729) The words "mount to their Paradisal lote-tree" depict the highest rapture of which the soul is capable, as the *sidratu 'l-muntahá* (Koran, 53, 14) marks the boundary of the seventh heaven, and neither prophet nor angel may pass beyond it.

(731) "The assembly of them that praise my name" alludes to Ṣúfís who meet together for the purpose of *dhikr* (see *The Mystics of Islam*, p. 45 foll.). Every student of Persian mystical poetry knows what is meant by "the wine-seller's shop": others may consult the *Gulshani Ráz* of Maḥmúd Shabistarí, ed. by E. H. Whinfield, p. 78 foll. of the English translation.

(732) Christians, Jews and Zoroastrians under Mohammedan rule wore a girdle round the waist to distinguish them from the Faithful; hence their "loosing" it would be a sign of their conversion to Islam.

(735) And if a devotee fall down before the stones in an idol-temple, there is no reason for religious zeal to take offence;

(736) For many a one who is clear of the shame of associating others with God by means of idolatry is in spirit a worshipper of money.

(737) The warning from me hath reached those whom it sought, and I am the cause of the excuses put forward in every faith.

(738) Not in any religion have men's eyes been awry, not in any sect have their thoughts been perverse.

(739) They that heedlessly fell in love with the sun lost not the way, forasmuch as its brightness is from the light of my unveiled splendour;

(740) And if the Magians adored the Fire—which, as history tells, was not quenched for a thousand years—

(741) They intended none but me, although they took another direction and did not declare the purpose they had formed.

(742) They had once seen the radiance of my light and deemed it a fire, so that they were led away from the true light by the rays.

(743) And but for the screen of existence, I should have said it out: only my observance of the laws imposed on phenomena doth keep me silent.

(744) So this is no aimless sport, nor were the creatures created to stray at random, albeit their actions are not right.

(737) Those who disobeyed the Divine message delivered by the prophets are to be excused on the ground that God did not create in them the spiritual capacity which would have enabled them to understand and obey.

(738) God in one aspect or another is the real object of every religious belief.

(740) The extinction of the sacred Fire of the Persians, after it had burned unceasingly for a thousand years, is recorded amongst the portents that occurred on the night of the Prophet's birth (A.D. 572–3).

(743) "Were it not that I appear under the form of externality, as a creature dependent on the Divine will and subject to the Divine law, I should have said plainly that nothing exists in reality except One Being, who manifests Himself in every thought and action."

(744) The language of this verse is borrowed from Kor. 23, 117: "Did ye think that We created you in idle sport?" and 75, 36: "Doth man think he shall be left uncontrolled?" The existence of evil, *i.e.* relative imperfection, follows by necessity from the self-manifestation of the Absolute. See pp. 85 93, 131.

(745) Their affairs take a course according to the brand of the Names; and the wisdom which endowed the Essence with (diverse) attributes caused them to take that course in consequence of the Divine decree,

(746) Disposing them in two handfuls—"and I care not...and I care not"—one destined for happiness and one for misery.

(747) Oh, let the soul know that the case stands thus, or else let her not (seek to) know (at all), for according to this the Koran is recited every morning.

(748) And her knowledge arises from herself: 'twas she that dictated to my senses what I hoped (of mystic knowledge).

(749) Had I singled, I should have swerved (from the truth) and been stripped of the signs of my union (*jam'*) through associating my handiwork (as an equal partner) with myself.

Protesting that he is not to be blamed for having divulged the sublime mysteries with which the grace of God illuminated him, the poet bids his disciple farewell. Let him follow in his master's footsteps and be one with the Essence, even as he is one.

(759) In the world of reminiscence the soul hath her ancient knowledge—my disciples beg it of me as a boon.

(745) Good and evil, salvation and perdition, are effects determined by the Divine Names, *e.g. al-Hádí* (He that guides aright), *al-Muḍill* (He that leads astray), and by the Divine Attributes, *e.g. i'záz* (exaltare humiles) and *idhlál* (deponere potentes).

(746) Ibnu 'l-Fáriḍ refers to the Tradition that when God created Adam, He drew forth his posterity from his loins in two handfuls, one white as silver and one black as coal, and said, "These are in Paradise and I care not; and these are in Hell-fire and I care not."

(747) "For according to this," *e.g.* in Kor. 16, 95: "Allah misguides whomso He pleaseth and leads aright whomso He pleaseth."

(748) Cf. *v.* 671 and *vv.* 675–6.

(749) "Had I singled," *i.e.* if I had limited the action of the soul by singling out and assigning to her the attributes of beauty (which are the source of good), while I deprived her of the attributes of majesty and awe (which are the source of evil), then I should have set up beside her a rival Being in whom these latter attributes and the effects proceeding from them must, *ex hypothesi*, subsist.

(759) This is the Platonic doctrine of ἀνάμνησις. In dreams and in moments of ecstasy the soul recovers the knowledge of true being which is hidden from her during her bodily existence. Cf. *vv.* 428–9 and 664 foll.

(760) Do thou, therefore, make haste to enjoy my eternal union, in virtue of which I found the full-grown men of the tribe (of Ṣúfís no wiser than) little babes.

(761) For my contemporaries drink only the dregs of what I left; and as for those before me, their (vaunted) merits are my superfluity.

INDEX I

NAMES AND TITLES

Arabic names to which the definite article al- is prefixed will be found under their initial letter. Titles of books and poems are printed in italics.

INDEX II

SUBJECTS

ascent of the soul, 138; the true doctrine of, 140

Ḥadíth. *See* Traditions of the Prophet
Hearing, the Divine attribute of, 101, 129
Heart, the, 113–115, 159, 236, 239; comprehends God, 115, 238; is reflected by the universe, 115; compared to the Ka'ba, 238. See *qalb*
Heavens, the seven, 122–123
Hell, 125, 135, 206, 245, 265; defined as selfhood, 64; the mirror of Divine Majesty, 100, 136; created from the Form of Mohammed, 135; will not exist actually until after the Resurrection, 135; a temporary state, 136; the seven limbos of, 136; dislike of Koranic texts describing the torments of Hell, 56; the pleasures of Hell, 132, 137, 160

Iblís. *See* Index I
Idolaters, 131, 132, 198
Illumination, mystical, 24, 25, 164, 174, 200; three (or four) phases of, 85, 125 foll. See *tajallí*
Incarnation, the Mohammedan doctrine of, 79. See *ḥulúl*
Indians, the, distinguished by a monistic tendency, 163
Intelligence, the First, 112, 113, 116, 123, 184, 233; the Second, 233
Intoxication, mystical term, 184, 195, 197, 199, 200, 218, 220, 221, 224, 228, 243, 248

Jealousy, a sign of duality, 213
Jews, the, 132, 133, 138, 141, 263. *See* Pentateuch
Jinn, the, 101, 124, 190, 220
Judgment, the Day of, 120

Knowledge, defined as a relation depending on the object known, 151, 157
Knowledge of God, is self-knowledge, 50, 215; unattainable by the intellect, 50, 116; an illumination, 152; a recognition, 249. See *ma'rifa*
Knowledge, the Divine attribute of, 101, 102, 103, 128, 151
Knowledge, three kinds of, imparted to Mohammed, 139
Koran, recitation of the, 13, 15, 16, 75, 79; immutable, 159; not the final and absolute standard of truth, 59–60; interpreted allegorically, 82, 149; typifies the third and last stage in the mystical ascent of the soul, 138

Law, the Mohammedan religious, 16, 20, 33, 34, 54, 57, 60, 184, 196, 261
Letters of the Arabic alphabet, used symbolically, 209
Life, definition of, 134
Life, the Divine attribute of, 85, 101
Life, the future, 134 foll.
Life, the mystic, three stages of, 221
Logic, the use of, by Jílí, 82, 88, 94 foll., 127
Logos doctrine, the, in Jílí and Ibnu 'l-'Arabí, 87, 104 foll., 154 foll.; in Ghazálí, 111; in Philo, 138, 142. *See* Mohammed; Man, the Perfect; Spirit, the created
Logos, union of the saints with the, 254
Lordship, the Divine attribute of, 98, 99, 119, 120, 137, 139
Love, disinterested, 4, 5, 18, 208, 212, 215, 238
Love, Divine, 3, 4, 5, 18, 52, 80, 103, 168, 174, 184, 185, 186, 199, 208, 212, 214, 224, 251, 252, 262
Love, the essence of God's essence, 80, 102; the highest form in which God is worshipped, 161
Love, the monistic doctrine of, 80, 251, 252
Love-poetry, Arabian, 163, 178

Macrocosm, the, 121–125
Magians, the, 132, 133, 264
Magic, high, 139
Mahdí, the, 135
Majesty, the Divine attributes of, 85, 100, 120, 131, 265. See *jalál*
Man, the earthly, 82; the heavenly, 82, 103 foll.
Man, the Great, 155. *See* Macrocosm
Man, the nature and function of, 154 foll.
Man, the Perfect, 77 foll., 184; unites the One and the Many, 78, 84; created in the image of God, 79, 80, 86, 106, 107; the microcosm, 82, 84, 106; the Quṭb and preserver of the universe, 86, 105, 130; the vicegerent of God, 113, 130, 156; his threefold nature, 86 103, 104; identified with Adam, 154 foll.; identified with Mo-

INDEX III

TECHNICAL TERMS, ETC.